THE WORLD OF **LUCHA LIBRE**

AMERICAN ENCOUNTERS/GLOBAL INTERACTIONS

A series edited by Gilbert M. Joseph and Emily S. Rosenberg

This series aims to stimulate critical perspectives and fresh interpretive frameworks for scholarship on the history of the imposing global presence of the United States. Its primary concerns include the deployment and contestation of power, the construction and deconstruction of cultural and political borders, the fluid meanings of intercultural encounters, and the complex interplay between the global and the local. American Encounters seeks to strengthen dialogue and collaboration between historians of U.S. international relations and area studies specialists.

The series encourages scholarship based on multiarchival historical research. At the same time, it supports a recognition of the representational character of all stories about the past and promotes critical inquiry into issues of subjectivity and narrative. In the process, American Encounters strives to understand the context in which meanings related to nations, cultures, and political economy are continually produced, challenged, and reshaped.

HEATHER LEVI

THE WORLD OF **LUCHA LIBRE**

Secrets,

Revelations,

and Mexican

National

Identity

DUKE UNIVERSITY PRESS   DURHAM AND LONDON   2008

© 2008 Duke University Press

All rights reserved.

Printed in the United States of America on acid-free paper ∞

Designed by Heather Hensley

Typeset in Warnock Pro by Keystone Typesetting, Inc.

Library of Congress Cataloging-in-Publication Data appear
on the last printed page of this book.

CONTENTS

ILLUSTRATIONS

PREFACE

Mexico's 1988 presidential election was the first time the ruling Partido de la Revolución Institucional (Party of the Institutional Revolution, PRI) had faced a serious electoral challenge since 1940. The party candidate, Carlos Salinas de Gortari, handpicked by the outgoing president, faced the usual ineffectual challenge from the right-wing Partido de Accion Nacional (Party of National Action) and their candidate Manuel J. Cloutier. More unusual, and more problematic for the party candidate's legitimation, was a challenge from the left. A major recession in 1982 followed by a devastating earthquake in 1985 had seriously weakened the party's formerly undisputed hegemony in Mexican politics. The earthquake, in which thousands died and tens of thousands more were left homeless in Mexico City alone, revealed the cracks and fissures in the political as well as geological terrain. Some of the worst damage occurred in hospitals and housing projects, government buildings that had been constructed with federal funds. In the aftermath of the earthquake critics blamed the government for failure to enforce building codes before the earthquake and for a slow and ineffective response in the days that followed. The government's response to the earthquake itself was slow and ineffective. In the face of apparent bureaucratic indifference, city residents formed improvised brigades to dig through the rubble in search of survivors and shelter those who had lost their homes.

In the year following the earthquake, the political landscape of Mexico shifted. In Mexico City, a number of grassroots organizations emerged to demand housing for those left homeless by the disaster. By the end of 1986, these groups united with a number of tenant's rights organizations to form a coalition called the Asemblea de Barrios. Meanwhile, a left-wing coalition that included a group of dissident members of the PRI put forth its own candidate for president, Cuauhtémoc Cárdenas, son of the populist former president Lázaro Cárdenas. With the recruitment of Cárdenas, the new party, calling itself the Partido de la Revolucion Democrática (Party of the *Democratic* Revolution), appropriated the legitimating symbols of the PRI, positioning itself as the real heir of the Mexican Revolution.

Although the Asemblea de Barrios later endorsed Cárdenas, its members were initially unwilling to compromise their independence by endorsing *any* party. Instead, on November 17, 1987, they unveiled their own candidate in front of the Juarez Monument in the Alameda Park: Superbarrio. Resplendent in his red and yellow tights, boots and cape, the letter s printed on his chest, his face covered by his mask, the candidate promised to perform "superpolitics of Superbarrio for housing, employment, schools and land" (quoted in Cuéllar Vasquez 1993: 128). Soon after, Superbarrio withdrew his candidacy and threw his weight behind Cárdenas and the PRD. Salinas de Gortari won the presidency in an election marked by widespread accusations of fraud and spent the next six years implementing the neoliberal economic programs that were to lead to NAFTA and the Zapatista rebellion. Superbarrio, meanwhile, became a fixture of the left-wing opposition in Mexico City, acting as official spokesman for the Asemblea de Barrios.

Superbarrio's political career draws on a performance genre that can be seen live at least four nights a week in the Mexico City metropolitan area alone, and on television at least weekly: *lucha libre* (literally, free wrestling or free struggle), the Mexican version of professional wrestling. The history of professional wrestling in Mexico goes back to 1933, when a promoter named Salvador Luttheroth decided to bring a group of wrestlers from

Texas to Mexico City. Soon afterward, lucha libre came to be among the most popular and culturally resonant entertainments in Mexico. From the mid-1930s on, it was a fixture in working- and lower-class neighborhoods of the capital and many other cities in the center and north of the country. In addition to regular performance in permanent arenas, wrestlers toured small and medium-sized towns throughout Mexico. While lucha libre shares many features with professional wrestling as it is practiced in the United States and elsewhere, it developed in ways specific to its Mexican incarnation.

Lucha libre is popular in Mexico. It's colorful, dramatic, acrobatic—a lot of fun to watch. But why did it make sense for grassroots activists in the mid-1980s to choose a professional wrestler (or, at any rate, someone dressed as a professional wrestler) as their representative? Why, in particular, did it make sense for members of the left-wing opposition to see professional wrestling as a source of symbolic legitimation? The success of figures like Superbarrio lay in the capacity of lucha libre to invoke a series of connections between sometimes contradictory domains: rural and urban, tradition and modernity, ritual and parody, machismo and feminism, politics and spectacle. Lucha libre's capacity to signify has been shaped, in large part, by the particular configuration of media through which it has circulated in Mexico since the 1950s.

In the chapters that follow, I will relate lucha libre to different discursive fields: gender, electoral politics, nationalism, cultural authenticity, corruption, and mass mediation. My argument is that lucha libre (and related phenomena like Superbarrio) makes sense because it is a performance genre that draws on and reproduces a series of contradictions that are broadly intelligible in the context of the shared historical and cultural background of its Mexican fans. Lucha libre is a practice of staging contradictions.[1]

METHODOLOGY

My goal has been to analyze lucha libre as a signifying practice whose meaning is to be found in the interaction between different domains of experience. Lucha libre's capacity to signify is not reducible to or exhausted by the intentions of the performers or the reception strategies of the audience. Its meaning is constructed in the public performance as such, but it is also created and communicated in the daily lives of wrestlers, in the performance of the wrestling audience, in the circulation of wrestling performances in various forms of mass media, in the circulation of lucha libre imagery outside of the context of the ring, and the overall cultural and political context within which the performance takes place. This work is not, therefore, a community study of wrestlers or of wrestling fans, but a study of lucha libre as a social phenomenon and as a signifying practice. It is the product of fifteen months of multisited fieldwork in Mexico City between 1996 and 1998, with follow-up visits in 1999, 2000, and 2001.

I approached the project with the assumption that in order to understand the use of lucha libre in Mexican political discourse it would be necessary to understand the genre itself, and vice versa. To that end, I used a variety of research strategies. During the fieldwork period, I observed over fifty live wrestling events (as well as a number of televised events), attending to both the performance and (in the former case) the audience reaction. I interviewed a variety of people directly involved in the occupational subculture of lucha libre: wrestlers at different stages of their careers (and affiliated with different leagues), referees, officials, promoters, and reporters. I attended events—dances, retreats, Christmas parties, and so on—sponsored by different institutions in the lucha libre community and observed training sessions in a number of different locations. In addition to these more traditional strategies, I took classes in lucha libre with a retired wrestler, Luis Jaramillo Martinez. Training in lucha libre enabled me to understand both the rules of performance and the process of training and socialization of wrestlers in ways that I would otherwise have missed. In addition to participant observation with wrestlers, I used written materials —magazines, newspapers, archival documents—to examine the representation of lucha libre in the mass media, to keep track of the profession's internal politics (as they circulated in the wrestling magazines), and to reconstruct a history of lucha libre in Mexico City.

This project also seeks to be a history of the circulation of lucha libre, both the performance itself, and the related images and tropes, across different media. I have used archival sources and oral histories to analyze the controversial relationship between lucha libre and mass media. I have, as well, followed the circulation of lucha libre in avant-garde artistic movements and its appropriation in left-wing political discourse, primarily through interviews with artists and political organizers who have used lucha libre imagery in their work.

Most of the Spanish terms used in lucha libre can be easily translated into English. There are some, however, that I have chosen not to translate. North American and Mexican styles of professional wrestling are formally very similar, yet those forms, as I will argue, have undergone subtle yet extensive resignification in the Mexican context. In order to underline the specificity of the Mexican versions of those forms, then, I will keep some terms in Spanish.

In Mexico as elsewhere, professional wrestlers include both women and men. In Spanish, a wrestler is called a *luchador* if male, and a *luchadora* if female. I will use wrestler and luchador interchangeably in situations where distinguishing the gender of the wrestler is unnecessary or undesirable. However, in those sections where I need to distinguish male from female wrestlers, or I need to distinguish Mexican (and other Latin) wrestlers from other wrestlers, I will use the Spanish terms. I will also use the Spanish terms that mark the good guy/bad guy roles in Mexico: *técnico* and *rudo*. *Técnico* corresponds to the "baby face" role in North American wrestling. *Rudo* corresponds to the North American "heel." Yet for reasons that I will make clear in chapter 3, the ways in which the two roles are conceived, enacted, and evaluated, as well as their connotations, differ in important ways from their U.S. equivalents.

Like many anthropologists, I find myself faced with a dilemma regarding the identification of the men and women whose life histories I recorded, whose parties I attended, who shared their time and opinions. In my case, the problem has a particular twist. As I will show in the chapters to follow, secrecy is an essential element of lucha libre performance. It is difficult to write about lucha libre without revealing at least of few of its secrets. In general, I have chosen to "reveal" those secrets that seem to me to be common knowledge (for the probable readership of this book). In addition, I have decided to use "real" names to identify some of my informants and pseudonyms to identify others. Wrestlers are public figures, many of whom keep their "real" identities hidden. Many who spoke with me did so with the explicit desire that their wrestling names appear in print. In cases where I understood our conversation to be "for the record," I have identified wrestlers and other public figures by their real names, or their wrestling names. In other cases, when wrestlers or others made remarks or expressed opinions that they may not have intended to appear identified with them in print, I have protected their anonymity, separating the comment from the wrestler who made it. I have also edited some details that might, in print, compromise the ability of masked wrestlers to remain anonymous to their public. I have identified my *profe*[2] by his real name, as I know he would wish.

THE CHAPTERS

This study looks at lucha libre on three levels: as a performance, as a subculture, and as a symbol that circulates in cultural politics and political culture in Mexico. Chapter 1 will introduce lucha libre as an object of study. Professional wrestling is a liminal performance that sits on the border of sport, theater, and ritual. Much of its power as a cultural performance derives, in fact, from its parodic and potentially destabilizing relationship to the category of sport. This chapter will situate lucha libre within two literatures—that of the relationship between sport, modernization, and the formation of the nation-state in Mexico, and that of the semiotics of professional wrestling in the United States and other non-Mexican contexts.

Chapter 2 focuses on the role of secrecy in the production of lucha libre. Lucha libre is constructed around the secret that everyone probably knows: The matches are "fixed." Yet, as I will make clear, the secret of the fixed ending is only one of a number of secrets that animate the genre. Through an account of training in lucha libre, this chapter explores the power of secrecy (and talk about secrets) to organize the socialization of wrestlers and the performance of lucha libre.

Chapters 3, 4, and 5 will focus on different aspects of lucha libre performance. Chapter 3 will examine the relationship between wrestlers and the characters they incarnate. One of the features that distinguish professional wrestling from amateur wrestling is that professional wrestlers enter the ring as morally coded characters. Professional wrestling is thus a ritual drama in which good and evil (or at least bad) struggle for domination. Analysts of professional wrestling in anglophone contexts have further observed that wrestling characters represent the social world. Thus, to ask what kinds of characters circulate in lucha libre is to ask what kinds of social actors are possible, who can have agency in the Mexican context. Attention to the moral and social marking of wrestlers thus provides a window onto and commentary on the social and moral cosmos, on the culturally specific relationship between morality and social action in mid- and late-twentieth-century Mexico.

But wrestling is performed by flesh-and-blood people who, out of a range of motivations, and through the concrete practices of professional wrestling insert themselves into webs of social and institutional relationships. Lucha libre performance thus consists of three levels—the lifeworld of the wrestlers, the complex set of oppositions and alliances between socially marked characters, and the Manichean opposition between the good guys and the bad guys. This chapter will address each of these levels in turn. Section 1, "Real Life," examines the recruitment, socialization, and organization of wrestlers. The second section explores the range of lucha libre characters. Section three explores the discourse of morality in the ring through an analysis of the contrast between the roles of rudo and técnico.

Chapter 4 draws upon the juncture between character and secrecy in lucha libre as it takes up the multiple functions of the lucha libre masks. Masks, masking, and unmasking are themes that pervade not only lucha libre, but also Mexican culture as a whole. This chapter will explain how the mask matters in lucha libre, both by its capacity to shift the rules of performance and by its capacity to align wrestling performances with other discourses about culture and nation, and with Mexico's political culture. The chapter will examine the mask as a means of connecting lucha libre with the discourse of *indigenismo*, which identifies Mexican national culture with that of Mexico's pre-Hispanic past and (with far more ambivalence) its contemporary, subordinated, indigenous ethnic groups. The chapter will also explore the mask as a metaphor in the arena of public politics. It will show how the trope of unmasking in lucha libre, where it functions as a metaphor for risk or loss of status, inverts the trope of unmasking as it appeared in late-twentieth-century Mexican political culture (where it functioned as a metaphor for empowerment). It will then examine the phenomenon of "social wrestlers," the adoption of masked wrestler personae by representatives of social movements in the late 1980s.

Chapter 5 will look at representations of gender in lucha libre. Scholarly treatments of gender in Mexico tend to emphasize the importance of *machismo* (roughly defined as a system of male domination that equates masculine self-worth with the oppression of women and humiliation of other men) as the central organizing principle of the Mexican sex/gender system.

The picture that emerges in the works of writers from Samuel Ramos to Maarit Melhuus is of a coherent, consistent Mexican gender system, in which real men are recognized by their capacity to dominate and penetrate women and less masculine men, women are categorized either as self-sacrificing virgins/mothers or as whores, and effeminate men, in their inevitable failure to defend their boundaries, prop up the masculinity of the machos. In this chapter, I will use an examination of lucha libre as a gendered performance to problematize this account.

The chapter will examine several different gendered identities that are displayed in lucha libre performances: male wrestlers who perform a masculine role, male wrestlers who cross-dress and perform a feminine role (and wrestle against the former), female wrestlers who wrestle each other, and female spectators and fans. Lucha libre is a performance that is open to multiple readings on the axis of representations of gender, even when it is performed by two men. In its most conventional version, lucha libre is a struggle for physical and psychological domination between two machos. But, as I will show, lucha libre performance also functions as a laboratory of gender experimentation that even its most conventional version parodies and problematizes the standard analyses of a Mexican sex/gender system.

Chapter 6 addresses the circulation of lucha libre in Mexico in two senses: as the dissemination of lucha libre performance through the mass media, and as the circulation of lucha libre imagery as an icon of class identity and cultural authenticity. As regards mass media, the chapter will focus on the relationship of lucha libre to film and television. Although lucha libre was televised briefly in the early 1950s, it was not televised between 1955 and 1991. In the interim, it developed as two parallel genres: as a live performance directed to a physically present audience, and as a genre of action movie. I will argue that the lucha libre's exile from television had important consequences for the range of meanings that the genre could communicate. Its return to television in the early 1990s was an important locus of conflict in the world of lucha libre. Hence, I will focus on the history of lucha libre's engagement with television.

This chapter will also return to the theme of the appropriation of lucha libre by political organizers and avant-garde artists that is first addressed in chapter 4. In postrevolutionary Mexico, as in settler states like Australia or Brazil, the discourse of national cultural autonomy has been constructed largely through identification with (indigenous or African descended) minorities who are, in practice, excluded from the hegemonic culture. In the dominant discourse of postrevolutionary Mexico, the Indian has been considered both the repository of the authentic national culture and the site of backwardness. But if, in the dominant discourse of Mexican nationalism, the sphere of the rural and Indian stood for the realm of the authentic and popular (as well as figuring as a site for state intervention), the urban poor were portrayed as lacking any culture. The remainder of this chapter will focus on a group of artists and intellectuals, sometimes referred to as the neo-pop group, who engaged in a cultural project in opposition to both the official nationalism of the Mexican state and the elitism of the arts community by celebrating urban popular cultural forms as loci of authentic identity. It will explore how and why this group came to define lucha libre, in particular, as a counterhegemonic practice ("popular" rather than "mass" culture), and how their celebration of lucha libre allowed the genre to enter into the new spheres of circulation: "high" art and politics. Finally, I will show how a group of wrestlers and promoters, threatened by the televising of lucha libre, appropriated the discourse of the neo-pop movement to assert the existence of an authentic, traditional form of lucha libre, and to argue that lucha libre, a practice that many believe to be intrinsically vulgar, intrinsically corrupt, was instead a popular tradition, part of the national patrimony, and worthy of the state's protection from corruption and vulgarization.

ACKNOWLEDGMENTS

This book would not be possible without the help and support of many people. I would like to begin by thanking Isabel Pinedo, Anne Rubenstein, and Kelly Kuwabara, whose warm friendship and ongoing support—emotional, intellectual, editorial, and material—has been essential to me at every step. I particulary thank Anne, whose description of *lucha libre* matches led me to the topic, and whose collegiality has been invaluable. I consider this project to be entirely her fault.

Thanks to the following people for their careful reading of earlier versions of this work: David Valentine, Henry Goldschmidt, Ben Chesluk, Angela Torresan, Laura Kunreuther, Amy Paugh, Randy Martin, Toby Miller, and Marc Moskowitz. Thanks to Claudio Lomnitz of Columbia University, and Fred Myers, Thomas O. Beidleman, Thomas Abercrombie, and Diana Taylor of New York University. Thanks as well to Andy Coe for assistance early in the project, to Janina Moebius for her generous help in Mexico, and to Valerie Millholland and the editorial staff of Duke University Press.

I would also like to thank my martial arts teachers who

prepared me to study lucha libre: Annie Ellman and Brooklyn Women's Martial Arts, and Tom Bisio, Jan Vanderlinden and the North American Tang Shou Dao Association. Thanks as well to my mother, Edith E. Levi, my brother, Michael Levi, and my sister, Carolyn Levi for everything.

This project would not have come to fruition without the openness and hospitality of the *luchadores*. I would like to thank Sandra Granados and the Empresa Mexicana de Lucha Libre for opening the Empresa's doors to me; I would also like to thank the Asociacion de Luchadores, Referís y Retirados and, especially, the veterans of the Agrupacion de Luchadores Retirados. I wish to thank and honor the memory of Hara Kiri. Finally, I would like to thank Luis Jaramillo Maritnez, who welcomed me into his school and *almost* turned me into a luchadora.

PROLOGUE

FIELD NOTES: THURSDAY, MAY 22, 1997, 8:00 P.M.

At the Pista Arena Revolucion, in the *colonia* Mixcoac, the crowd is still pretty thin. The first few rows are full, and there are a few groups of spectators scattered among the upper rows. In the front, small groups of older men sit together and joke with the concessionaires. Groups of four or five teenagers—some male, some mixed, one female—talk among themselves or buy drinks and snacks from the vendors. In the southeast corner, a stern couple in their sixties or seventies sit perfectly straight in their usual seats. She wears a black housedress, her hair tightly coiffed. Her husband wears short sleeves and tan work pants, and a gimme cap that reads PRI. The second and third rows are filled with families as well as more groups of adults. Toddlers are passed from lap to lap, and fathers buy child-sized wrestling masks for their sons from a vendor who wanders from aisle to aisle, a dozen glimmering examples dangling from a stick, a few more perched on his head.

At 8:05 the lights dim in the arena and focus on the ring in the center of the room. A muscular young man dressed in a Powerhouse gym T-shirt, black and white striped tights, and black boots enters the arena, saunters up to the ring, and hoists himself over the ropes. He is followed by another, dressed in black tights and silver boots, his face covered by a black mask. These, the audience knows, are the *rudos* (roughly, "bad guys"). They stand in the southwest corner of the ring and wait as two more wrestlers leave the dressing rooms and stride into the arena. The first is wearing a red and white lycra bodysuit and a matching mask with an insignia on the cheek. The second is dressed in a black bodysuit with silver horseshoes along the legs and black mask. These, all know, are the *técnicos* (roughly, "good guys"). There are a few scattered cheers to mark their entrance, but most people are still socializing, buying snacks, playing with their children. A mustachioed man at ringside trades barbs with one of the rudos. The announcer, who looks like an accountant in his brown suit, tie, and respectable spectacles, begins to announce the match, as the referee pats down the wrestlers. "In the corner of the *rudoooos*, Albazan and Predador." The first wrestlers to enter raise their fists and exhort the crowd, which pays them little attention. It's the first match of the night, and the audience is not warmed up yet. "In the corner of the *técnicoooos*, Stelaris and Justiciero!" The second pair turn to receive a few cheers. Predador and Stelaris cross to the outside of the ropes, leaving Albazan and Justiciero in the ring. The announcer steps down from the canvas, blows his whistle, and the lucha begins amid the murmurs and laughter of the inattentive audience.

The two men circle each other, then face each other in beginning position. They grapple together, exchanging locks until both fall to the ground. They separate and stand. Albazan sweeps Justiciero's leg. The latter escapes with a backspring, grabs his opponent by the back of the neck, and drops to the ground, throwing Albazan across the ring. The latter finds his feet, turns, and the two go back to grappling, keeping a controlled rhythm. At the referee's signal, they leave, and their partners enter.

As Predador enters the ring, he catches Stelaris off guard with a takedown, then he grabs his leg and twists it. The técnico rolls out of the lock and reverses it, so that the rudo is caught with his arm twisted. Predador escapes the arm lock, but Stelaris hooks him by the elbow and throws him to the ground, this time locking the arm behind his back. Predador twists his body and escapes again. As the lucha continues, the wrestlers increase their speed as they attempt more attacks, more defenses. As the thumps of bodies striking canvas come in quicker succession, the spectators start to pay closer attention. Predador throws Stelaris across the ring, into Justiciero. He bounces off the ropes into Predador, whom he slaps across the chest with the back of his hand. Predador slaps back. Albazan shouts from behind the ropes, "Hit him, you idiot!" He slips between the ropes to enter the ring. Justiciero, seeing him enter, vaults over the ropes to join the fight. Justiciero and Stelaris glance at one another, separate, and run to opposite corners. They climb onto the third rope, turn, and jump onto Albazan and Predador, pinning them to win the first fall.

The wrestlers return to their sides, waiting for the second round to start. All four enter the ring. The rudos attack the técnicos, swinging at them wildly, but the técnicos duck and the rudos hit each other instead. The técnicos seize the moment and throw the rudos out of the ring. The two rudos stalk the aisles while the referee counts—they have twenty seconds to return to the ring or be disqualified. At the count of seven, Predador enters to face Justiciero. Predador throws him into Albazan, who kicks him from behind the ropes. He crosses the ropes, and the two rudos continue to kick Justiciero. Justiciero drives both from the ring. He leaves and Stelaris enters, with a cry of "yapayapayapa!" The rudos gang up on Stelaris until the referee makes Albazan leave the ring. Justiciero tries to enter the ring, but Albazan runs over and back-kicks him out. Stelaris climbs the ropes to jump onto Predador, but misses, hitting the canvas with a loud whap. Then Justiciero does enter the ring, just in time for Predador to climb the ropes, jump on top of him, and put him into a submission hold. Justiciero wiggles his hands to show that he submits, and the referee pulls the rudo off. The rudos win the second fall.

At the beginning of the third fall, the rudos enter the ring before the técnicos. The crowd is finally warmed up, shouting insults at the rudos. A woman in the third row holds a three-year-old on her lap. She says to the child, "Say 'chinga tu madre'" (fuck your mother), and the child's delighted voice repeats, "Chinga tu madre!" The woman laughs and jostles him on her knee. The técnicos enter together, and the rudos flee. The referee begins the count, and they reenter at seventeen seconds. Albazan squares off against Justiciero. They slap each other. Meanwhile, Predador and Stelaris enter. Predador runs up to Justiciero and, while the referee's back is turned, kicks him in the groin. While Justiciero is bent over, clutching himself, Predador throws him to the ground. He picks him up, brings him to the ropes, and calls Albazan. Stelaris pulls Predador off of Justiciero, who is recovering from the foul blow. They attempt to put both rudos in an *estrella* lock, but it doesn't work. Justiciero jumps onto Albazan's shoulders, then dives between his legs to put him into a *rana* lock, but, again, fails. Stelaris tries to put Predador in a swastika, but Albazan kicks him from behind, and he releases too soon. Suddenly, Predador grabs Stelaris and falls backward, trapping him with his back in an arc. Meanwhile, Albazan gets behind Justiciero, grabs his wrists, and plants his foot in his back, locking his shoulders. The técnicos wave their hands in submission, and the referee pulls the rudos away, declaring them the winners.

It's a disappointing result for the fans. The older woman in the southeast corner stands up to scold the rudos as they return to the dressing room, but nobody is too upset. After all, it's only the first match of the night, and a short one. These wrestlers are not stars, and there are four more matches to go. And there's always next week, or even the weekend, if you can't wait that long.

1

STAGING CONTRADICTION

In the months leading up to my doctoral fieldwork, when I told people that I intended to study Mexican professional wrestling, their most common response would be to ask: "Is it totally corrupt there, like it is here?" This raised a fairly obvious question: Why did they consider professional wrestling to be corrupt? In fact, professional wrestling is often derided as simplistic, contrived, and full of gratuitous violence. Such criticism, however, is seldom extended to equally simplistic and dangerous practices like hockey, football, or rugby. Those performances are conventionally considered "real" contests of skill. While they may not be classified as high culture, they are not disparaged as "corrupt" or "false," like professional wrestling. Yet the goal of most sports—to score points—is as contrived and artificial as anything that happens in professional wrestling. Why, then, should professional wrestling be the object of more disdain than these other practices?

Perhaps it is because professional wrestling is a liminal genre, one that is closely connected with the category of "sport," but cannot be contained by it. Lucha libre, I have suggested, is a practice of staging contradictions. It is an embodied performance that communicates apparently conflicting state-ments about the social world. During its seventy-five-year history in Mex-ico, it has stood for modernity and tradition, urbanism and indigenismo, honesty and corruption, machismo and feminism. Why should lucha libre be the vehicle of such a complex and contradictory set of associations? I would suggest that its capacity to signify comes from the very fact that it occupies a space somewhere between sport, ritual, and theater and is thus capable of drawing its power from all of those genres.

PROFESSIONAL WRESTLING

Professional wrestling is a transnational performance genre that has been the object of the sporadic attention of academics since Roland Barthes's groundbreaking 1957 article "The World of Wrestling." It is a performance genre based on (but also parodying) the conventions of so-called amateur wrestling. Wrestling, in one form or another, is among the oldest and most widespread sports or games in the world. Like other sports and games, wrestling underwent a process of modernization in the nineteenth and early twentieth centuries, during which time its rules were codified and its practice organized within particular institutional contexts (such as the university or the club). At the amateur level, wrestling is divided into three main styles: Greco-Roman, Olympic, and Freestyle (or Intercollegiate). In the first two styles, a match ends when one wrestler pins the other's shoul-ders to the mat. Olympic rules allow leg holds, whereas Greco-Roman rules prohibit contact below the waist. In Freestyle wrestling, a match can end with a pin but can also end if the winner places the loser in an immo-bilizing hold.

These three forms of amateur wrestling are often called "real" wrestling and distinguished from another type of wrestling that was promoted as a popular entertainment, during the same period, in the United States and parts of Europe. Charles Wilson traces professional wrestling to a style called "collar and elbow" that was developed in Vermont in the early nine-teenth century. (The name refers to the starting position, in which each wrestler grasps the other by the elbow with one hand, and the collar with the other.) Vermont soldiers brought collar and elbow wrestling to the barracks of the Civil War, where it became a favorite recreation among Union soldiers. After the army was demobilized, collar and elbow wrestling moved from the barracks to saloons in New York City where saloon owners promoted matches to draw customers.

By the end of the century, P. T. Barnum instituted wrestling as a circus "spectacular." With wrestling's transition from the barroom to the circus came an important change. In the beginning, Barnum's wrestlers would fight challenge matches against untrained marks from the audience. By the late 1890s, however, they began to fight fixed contests against shills planted in the audience instead. With this innovation, the performance changed from a contest to a representation of a contest. During the first decade of the twentieth century, this type of exhibition wrestling grew in popularity both in cities, and on the county fair circuit. The county fair circuit in turn spawned a system of intercity wrestling circuits by 1908 (Wilson 1959).

Exhibition wrestling, by then known as "professional" wrestling, grew in popularity during the first decades of the twentieth century in both the United States and Europe, reaching a peak in the 1920s. Greco-Roman wrestling was already a popular bar entertainment in late-nineteenth-century Europe, but in the early 1920s European wrestlers adopted the North American collar and elbow style (Oakley 1971). Promoters organized international tours for wrestlers from both continents. During this period individual wrestlers began to add theatrical gimmicks to their wrestling performance to mark themselves as memorable characters. In the United States, it became common for immigrants or children of immigrants (like the Italian Joe Savoldi, Jimmy "The Greek" Thepos, Polish Stanislaus "The Boxcar" Zbyszko, or Turkish Ali Baba) to stress their national origin as a gimmick in performance.

The conventions that govern professional wrestling today were fairly well established by the beginning of the 1920s. In common with amateur wrestling, the basic unit of performance in professional wrestling is the match. In contrast to amateur wrestling matches, the professional match normally takes place inside a boxing ring. A fall is defined the same way that it is in freestyle wrestling: the winner either pins the loser's shoulders to the ground for three seconds (as counted by the referee) or puts the loser in an immobilizing (and pain inducing) hold (either a joint lock, or a hold that hyperextends or compresses the losing wrestler's torso). In the United States a match usually ends with a fall, and in Mexico it usually ends when one side wins two out of three falls. In Mexico, a lucha libre event is called a *función* (show) or *programa* (program—in the United States this unit is called a "card") and usually consists of five matches played out over the course of about two hours.

Professional wrestling is distinguished from freestyle wrestling by three things. First, the wrestlers fight as morally coded characters. On one side is the "clean wrestler, in that he follows what are supposed to be, and what are perceived by the audience, as the rules." On the other side is "the wrestler who breaks these supposed rules in order to gain what the audience should consider an unfair advantage" (Birrell and Turowetz 1984: 263). Second, techniques that are forbidden in amateur wrestling are considered both legal and conventional in the professional version. These include some holds, but also hitting (as long as it's not with a closed fist), running away, bouncing or jumping off the ropes surrounding the ring, and so on. Finally (and decisively), in professional wrestling, the outcome of the match is decided in advance.

LUCHA LIBRE AND THE PROBLEM OF GENRE

The fixed ending in professional wrestling produces a category crisis similar to the one that J. Lowell Lewis has described in his study of capoeira. Capoeira is a Brazilian movement form that defies conventional genre boundaries. Even capoeira participants, he reports, disagree over whether it is a martial art, in which music, ritual, and other expressive aspects of performance serve to hide its applications from the uninitiated; or a form of "expressive, dancelike play;" or "something like a sacred path to righteous living" (Lewis 1995: 222). Professional wrestling, likewise, sits on the border between the normally separable categories of sport, theater, and ritual.

In general (as I will develop below), professional wrestling has been deemed worthy of scholarly attention because and insofar as it can be defined as a ritual confrontation between social categories and/or between representations of good and evil. In other words, academics have found it interesting insofar as it could be analyzed as a form of theater. But, while Mexican wrestlers are aware of this aspect of lucha libre, it is not one to which they themselves draw attention. Nearly all of the wrestlers I knew insisted that lucha libre had to be understood as a sport. Whenever I asked them to define it or describe it, they would emphasize the rigor of their training regimen, the years of physical preparation, and the hours spent in the gym. The wrestler Máscara Año 2000 explained away other interpretations of professional wrestling (at least in its Mexican incarnation)[1] as instances of misunderstanding. The public may misrecognize lucha libre as something other than sport, he told me, because they don't understand the rules. The rules of the sport, he implied, are mistaken for a script.

Many outside of the lucha libre world view professional wrestling as a corruption of amateur wrestling and thus dismiss it as a kind of fraud. In Mexico, commentators usually expressed that view by describing lucha libre (*profesional*) as "circus, tumbling, and theater," and dismissing professional luchadores as mere "tumblers" (*maromeros*). Yet my teacher, who always insisted that lucha libre was a sport, would nevertheless embrace the "circus, tumbling, and theater" definition by resignifying its terms. It was circus, he would tell us, because the first professional wrestlers performed in the ancient Roman circus. It was tumbling because wrestlers use acrobatic rolls to escape from locks and pins. Finally, it was theater because people watched wrestling for the same reason they watched theater—to be entertained. Like most wrestlers, he saw no contradiction between lucha libre's spectacular and theatrical aspects and its categorization as sport.

It would be easy to attribute wrestlers' aversion to describing their activities as anything other than sport to their need to continue to fool the public (or at least not to force their public to acknowledge the fact of the fix). Like a magician, a wrestler's ability to entertain an audience depends on the maintenance of an illusion, on not showing the audience how the trick is done. But in Mexico, at least, the issue is more complex. The question of whether professional wrestling is a sport is complicated by the fact that the definitions and connotations of the term *sport* are not as clear-cut as they may seem. The placement (or nonplacement) of a given activity into the category of sport has historically been tied to discourses of modernity and, in the Mexican context, national progress.

MODERN SPORT

> I beseech you in the most attentive manner to interpose your valuable aid so that I
> might be given a new boxing license, which was taken from me by the mayor of
> this city who because he is antisport and backward-spirited is not bringing any
> [boxing] programs. You promote sports, and the Oaxacan constitution doesn't
> prohibit [boxing], just cockfights, bullfights and gambling.
>
> LETTER FROM JOSÉ JUAN CANECO TO ABELARDO RODRIGUEZ, PRESIDENT
> OF MEXICO, FEBRUARY 23, 1933

In 1933, a boxer in Oaxaca wrote to the president of Mexico, hoping for assistance in his dispute with the local mayor.[2] His petition is one of many to be found in the files of the Archivo General de la Nación, in which citizens appealed to the president himself for all kinds of (usually economic and legal) assistance, and also for donations of balls, bats, uniforms, and other sporting equipment. I do not know if the president assisted him or not, but it is clear that the boxer felt entitled to press his case to the highest level. His was neither a defense of traditional rights, nor, strictly speaking, an assertion of his right as an individual to have a boxing license. He made his case, instead, by appealing to the president as a forward-looking promoter of sports.

The promotion of sport in postrevolutionary Mexico, as in many countries, was closely connected to the goals of the modernizing, paternalist state. Sport itself is a modern phenomenon, distinct from superficially sportlike practices such as games or ritual combats. In Bourdieu's terms, it is a field: a semiautonomous site "of quite specific social practices, which have defined themselves in the course of a specific history and can only be understood in terms of that history" (Bourdieu 1991: 358–59). Bourdieu traces the origins of sport per se to the nineteenth century English public school system as part of a pedagogy of bourgeois political philosophy exemplified in the ideology of "fair play." In the course of nineteenth and early twentieth centuries, political elites in Latin America and elsewhere viewed sport as both an index of modernity and a tool for its advancement.

The most popular sports in contemporary Latin America, such as soccer, baseball, and boxing, were developed in England or the United States during the nineteenth century and were introduced to Latin American elites by administrative personnel of European- and North American–owned corporations operating in the region (Beezley 1987; Stein, Carvallo, and Stokes 1987). For Mexican elites in particular, participation in and promulgation of sporting practices became a key index of commitment to the economic and cultural projects of the modernizing dictator Porfirio Díaz, who ruled Mexico from 1876 to 1910, a period known as the "Porfiriato." Díaz and his supporters (who referred to themselves as the *científicos*—scientists) promoted a broad economic program of state investment in infrastructure and encouragement of foreign investment. This economic program was coupled with a cultural program committed to the emulation of European and North American models, and with systematic and violent repression of dissent. Those of the "Porfirian persuasion" valorized leisure practices associated with European positivism, while traditional, popular pastimes (for example, cockfights) were discouraged and at times suppressed. For example, the bullfight, ambivalent symbol of Mexico's Iberian heritage, was banned in Mexico City and the port city of Veracruz from 1879 to 1886. Participation in sport, as opposed to participation in more traditional leisure activities served as a sign of distinction (in Bourdieu's sense), and marked identification with the Porfirian project (Beezley 1987).

The revolution that began in 1910 swept Díaz from power within a year, but fighting between different revolutionary factions continued until 1917 and beyond. Eventually, a political system was established under President Plutarco Elias Calles, who, with his allies, founded a single party that would integrate (albeit unevenly) the range of factions and interests that had achieved armed expression (as it were) during the revolution. That party, eventually known as the PRI (Party of the Institutional Revolution), remained in power from 1928 until the presidential election of 2000.

There is an ongoing debate in twentieth century Mexico historiography over whether (or to what extent) the postrevolutionary Mexican state was a radical departure from Porfirianismo or its continuation (in a disguised or modified form). I will not summarize the arguments here, except to note that the postrevolutionary state shared the Díaz regime's commitment to a program of modernization for the country and centralization of the national power structure, and that sport continued to figure as a tool and signifier of cosmopolitan modernity. During the Porfiriato, sports, although primarily a pastime of elites, were introduced to workers through paternalist programs in British- and U.S.-owned factories, mining camps, or plantations (Arbena 1991 and 1992). After the revolution, the state took over that role in a variety of ways. First, the national government instituted physical education as part of the obligatory (and, in some areas violently resisted) system of secular primary education. Along with literacy, it became a key ground of struggle between the (relatively) leftist government and the conservative Catholic opposition both before and after the Cristero War in the late 1920s.[3] Second, the state (at national and regional levels) promoted recreational sport through the selective donation of sporting equipment as a form of patronage (Knight 1994, Joseph and Wells 1987) and as an integral part of local level civic rituals (Vaughn 1994).

As before, sports were contrasted with other sportlike forms of entertainment that were, to a greater or lesser degree, discouraged. In general, pastimes that fit into the category of sport became, like literacy and industrialization, identified with the modernizing, nationalist project of the postrevolutionary state and were supported through legal and material interventions. The status of some activities within this discourse was unclear. For example, since the seventeenth century, the bullfight has been associated with a kind of reactionary Iberianism that fit poorly with the goals of the modernizing state (Viquiera-Albán 1987, Beezley 1987). Moreover, in the 1920s, some in the new state viewed it as representing or encouraging bloodlust and violence, which was inimical to the project of stabilizing the postrevolutionary nation-state (Anne Rubenstein, personal communication).[4] But despite the ambiguity surrounding its status in the early part of the century, the bullfight was eventually assimilated to the category of sport. At present, the bullfight news is found in the sports section of the newspapers and the sports segment of broadcast news.[5] And while postrevolutionary regional governments may have distinguished between ball sports like basketball and soccer, and "bloodsports" like bullfights and cockfights, the status of some activities, like boxing, may have been open to dispute as the complaint cited above suggests.[6]

It has been argued that the association of sports with projects of modernization and cultural modernity is far from coincidental. Roberto González-Echeverría (personal communication, 1999) has suggested a link between the rise of team sports and that of nineteenth-century nationalisms, arguing that sports teams (with their uniforms, banners, and connections to geographical territories) function as a metaphor for national armies. Perhaps of greater significance, however, is that the features that mark sport off from other sportlike practices are features that connect it to a trajectory of rationalism. Allen Guttmann (1978) identified the following characteristics of sport that distinguish it from games, rituals, or other related practices: secularism, equality of opportunity to compete and in the conditions of competition, specialization of roles, rationalization, bureaucratic organization, quantification, and the quest for records. These characteristics align sport with ideologies of modernity.

Although Guttmann's model is useful, it is incomplete. For one thing, it assumes that all real sport is competitive, yet there are many activities that count as sport even if they are practiced not for competition but for "recreation," or for a specific kind of cultivation of the body (Bourdieu 1991). For example, people may swim or cross-country ski without ever racing or even intending to race, yet both activities are classified as sport. In these cases, however, participation implies a commitment to certain ideas about cultivation of the body and, therefore, the self. Cultivation of the body is not a specifically modern ideal, but certain practices and beliefs about the reasons for bodily cultivation (for example, eugenics or the disciplined body) and class-inflected ideas about the appropriate kind of body to display through exercise have been central both to the modern project and to the definition of sport (Foucault 1978, Bourdieu 1990, Brownell 1995).

There is, moreover, another element that is important to the categorization of some activities as sport: the relationship between amateur and professional levels of participation. Historically, as participation in sport moved down the social ladder, the organization of sport became increasingly hierarchical and bureaucratic. As the separation between spectators and participants intensified (at least in some sports), players themselves were divided between amateurs and professionals. At present, in most sports, there is typically a continuum from casual practitioners through serious amateurs to professionals. For example, most people (or at least most men) who watch professional baseball have played the game themselves at some time in their lives. There thus exists the expectation that any spectator (although conventionally gendered and perhaps raced) can identify with the professional competitor.

Sport, then, is a relatively complicated category, closely associated both chronologically and ideologically with discourses of modernity and rationality. The assertion that wrestling is not a real sport, then, is not only about the fixed ending. The fixed ending is merely the last and most defining of a list of violations. Read against Guttmann's model, professional wrestling is not a sport: it has no fixed specialization of roles, except for the distinction between good guys and bad guys. Opportunities are not supposed to be equal, since bad guys are supposed to cheat. There are records (for example, the number of masks and championships won by the wrestler El Santo), but they are not made in order to be broken, and there is rela-

tively little interest in quantification. Finally, there is little continuity between amateur and professional levels. Children may play at being wrestlers, but that is not the same as wrestling. Moreover, whereas in most
sports, the move from amateur to professional entails an increase in status
for a player, wrestling is an exception. As Sharon Mazer points out, it's "the
one sport where participants lose legitimacy when they move from 'amateur' to 'professional'" (1998: 19).[7] Most amateur wrestlers prefer to distance themselves from the professional ring, and an amateur career is not a
prerequisite to going professional. To summarize, wrestling does not fit the
model that posits sport as a ritual of liberalism and modernity. In this
sense, Roland Barthes (1972) was correct: professional wrestling refuses to
do the ideological work of sport.

Lucha libre is not, however, unconnected with the discourse of sport.
When wrestling was first promoted in Mexico, it was explicitly advertised
as a modern and modernizing practice. It was aligned with the politically
salient category of sport and institutionally organized in such a way as to
distance it from cockfights, bullfights, and the like. Moreover, when wrestlers reject other definitions of what they do, it is often to assert their
identities as disciplined athletes. To be a professional wrestler means training diligently in the gym as well as performing in the ring. Most of all, it
means cultivating and displaying a wrestler's body, living as the embodiment of a particular kind of physical power.

When outsiders insist that professional wrestling is not sport, they place
it into another category. At worst, they categorize it as a fraud; at best, they
treat it as a folk theatrical form or a ritual. One function of ritual is to
establish or dramatize the existence of categories of social personhood. As
Roberto Da Matta has noted, "the distinctive feature of ritual is dramatiza-
tion, i.e. condensation of some aspect, element of relationship which is
spotlighted and set in relief" (1991: 20). In this sense, conventional sport is
also a ritual, one that displays and celebrates a particular model of personhood. In team sports, uniforms make the players appear interchangeable
with one another (except for players in certain specialized roles, like the
goalie or the catcher). Beneath the uniform, the players are individuated
both in terms of specialized function (position) and in terms of having a
unique personality. This feature of team sports produces a visible difference
between the public (abstract, interchangeable) and private (inner, with

innate abilities leading to achieved position) individual. The team, as a team, may be identified with a place, but the players themselves are not; players are loyal to the team for which they play that season, not their hometown. It could be argued, then, that team sports ritually present the ideal social person as an abstract individual whose loyalties are based on contractual agreement. Within those premises, players play according to rules, which determine who is considered to win, and who to lose the game. In lucha libre, the relationship between rules, performance, and personhood is radically different—it is a different kind of ritual. Although there are regulations in lucha libre, they do make sense not as a set of rules to determine losers and winners in a given event, but as performance conventions.

Lucha libre is regulated by two kinds of rules: rules that the audience is explicitly supposed to know, and rules that are not supposed to be recognized as such. Spectators should know what counts as a fall, what techniques are permitted, and which are forbidden. They know who is allowed to enter the ring, and when. They recognize and know the names (and sometimes histories) of the holds used to finish an opponent, especially those associated with a particular wrestler. All know that eye gouges, punches, and blows to the groin (among other techniques) are prohibited. They know that removing an opponent's mask during the match is forbidden as well. Lucha libre spectators take an active role in identifying violations of the rules, calling the referee's attention or shouting or gesturing interpretations for the referee. But the event itself is also arranged in ways of which spectators may not be conscious. The structure of the three falls is not random; each has its own etiquette. The match proceeds according to a set sequence that displays the full range of performance possibilities of lucha libre. It moves in a progression of increasing speed, violence, and complexity until the final pin.

A typical match, if it is early in the program, starts with two wrestlers facing each other and starting to wrestle. They exchange locks, throws, and near pins for several minutes. Then, if they have teammates, one might tag in a partner, or the referee may tell them to stop. They exit the ring, strutting and posturing, and the next pair enters. If there are teams, the referee will signal for more wrestlers to enter until all the wrestlers are in the ring. Eventually, someone will win the first fall, and the wrestlers will have a brief rest before the start of the next round.

In most matches, the first round moves more slowly than the others. The action is primarily a display of wrestling as such, an exchange of holds between pairs of wrestlers. Even when the match is between two teams, the wrestlers usually start fighting one-on-one. Although the rudos may enter or threaten to enter out of turn, their interference only punctuates the action, which mostly takes place on the canvas in the center of the ring. Little "narrative" work gets done: enmities are seldom recalled or initiated. No betrayals or intense rivalries are expressed. Despite the initial phase of posturing, the action usually proceeds in a relatively orderly manner (at least in the preliminary matches).

The second round usually displays mastery of the acrobatic component of lucha libre. The luchadores move more within the ring, out of the center, along horizontal or diagonal axes. They run back and forth, jumping over each other, somersaulting, exchanging positions, and setting traps. They make more use of the ropes and turnbuckles to jump from, bounce off of, or trap their opponent against. The rudo can start to play up his or her role with blows, bites, and bullying. The técnico shows off his or her leaps, flips, flights, and jumps. In the third fall, which Rafael Barradas described to me as the *bonita* (the "beaut"), everything (apparently) goes. This is the most narratively rich segment of the match, where the betrayals, humiliations, and grand gestures of injustice or vengeance are supposed to happen. It is also the one fall that always must follow the script.

As the event as a whole continues and bigger stars take the canvas, the matches appear less structured. The last or second to last match may begin with the wrestlers attacking each other before the announcer has a chance to introduce them. Props used as weapons (chairs, belts, guitars, whatever) might be employed right away, rather than saved for the last fall. The action of an event is neither pure choreography nor pure chance. There is an order that determines what can happen when, what is displayed when. These are not rules of play in a conventional sense, but aesthetic considerations.

Like the bullfight, lucha libre has long been assimilated to the category of sport. Many (though by no means all) newspapers in Mexico report the outcomes of important lucha libre matches in the sports section. Viewed as a ritual, however, lucha libre problematizes the model of a universal trajectory toward modernity that other sports could be said to endorse. Unlike the "player"—both interchangeable with others and thoroughly individual

—the wrestler dramatizes a nonarbitrary relationship between the role and the individual. Wrestling characters are not interchangeable with each other, and (as I explore in later chapters) the relationship between the character and the human being behind the mask is quite complicated. Furthermore, the (apparent) loyalties of the wrestlers are personal and nonarbitrary as well. Unlike "players," they are not on the side of their team, but on the side of good or evil.

The fixed ending (which some fans are aware of and others are not) calls attention to the importance of the actions themselves: as Roland Barthes noted, every moment is intelligible. But not every moment is equally intelligible to everyone. A "beautiful" exchange of locks might be read as boring; a gesture may be read as accident or betrayal. But in the final instance, the last fall has a qualitative meaning rather than a quantitative one. One doesn't arrive at a championship by winning preliminary matches, but by answering challenges. Victory doesn't tip a numerical balance but might realign relationships between wrestlers. Unlike most sports, what matters to the fans is not only (or even primarily) ability, but affinities, connections, loyalties, and enmities. Lucha libre thus posits a different moral universe than do conventional team sports. From within the modernizing category of sport, it mocks the very terms of the discourse of modernization in the Mexican context (which I will address in subsequent chapters).

PROFESSIONAL WRESTLING AS OBJECT OF STUDY

It is the theatrical aspects of professional wrestling that have drawn the most attention from professional scholars. It is primarily from these aspects, and from the genre's status as a modern morality play, that questions of authorship, agency, and political valence emerge. The earliest and most influential such analysis was the opening essay in Roland Barthes's *Mythologies* (1972). In the introduction to *Mythologies*, Barthes identified his agenda as "that [of] treating 'collective representations' as sign systems [by which] one might hope to go further than the pious show of unmasking them and account in detail for the mystification which transforms petit-bourgeois culture into a universal nature" (9). Yet in "The World of Wrestling" (15–25, originally published in 1957) he portrayed professional wrestling as a relatively demystified cultural form. He argued that appreciation or understanding of the genre required recognizing its contrived nature. In contrast to Olympic or Greco-Roman wrestling, which he characterized as "a false wrestling, in which participants go to extraordinary lengths to make a show of a fair fight" (15), he celebrated "all-in" wrestling as the "true" form (thus inverting the conventional equation of amateur wrestling as real and professional as fake). The (assumed) fact of its staging, he argued, was irrelevant to its reception by the public and necessary to its value as a system of gesture signification: "The public is uninterested in whether or not it is rigged because it abandons itself to the primary virtue of the spectacle—what matters is not what one thinks, but what one sees" (15). The difference between wrestling and boxing is not that the latter is real and the former fake, but that a boxing match constitutes a narrative that moves toward an intelligible outcome. In wrestling, in contrast, each moment is intelligible, and this intelligibility is predicated on the excessive clarity of every gesture. The roles of the wrestlers are written in their physiques; holds and pins are used not to elicit conventional signs of defeat, but to dramatize suffering and abasement of the vanquished. Rules exist to be exploited. To Barthes, wrestling portrayed "an ideal understanding of things." The use of fakery, rather than debasing wrestling as a sport, elevated it as theater. Stripped of the conceits of fairness and order, he suggested, it revealed rather than concealed the nature of capitalist social relations.

Barthes's piece influenced almost all subsequent treatments of professional wrestling in North America and the anglophone South Pacific in one form or another. In general, academics who raise questions about professional wrestling have done so along two axes. First, there is the question of the process of signification: who is responsible for the production of meaning in wrestling? Is it a collaboration between the wrestlers and the spectators, or is its meaning located in the narrative text of the matches themselves? The second question, closely related to the first, is about the content of wrestling's message: what political ends does professional wrestling serve? Is it a counterhegemonic critique of social relations under capitalism, an exercise in the representation and demarcation of ethnic boundaries, or a celebration of militaristic patriotism? With one exception (see below), all have started from the assumption that the matches are fixed.

Jim Freedman (1983), for example, observing that small-town Canadian spectators acknowledge that wrestling is "all phony" but still enjoy it, proposed that the sport's appeal lies in the ability of the audience to read it as a critique of the ideology of the capitalist work ethic. The inefficacy and corruption of authority and the futility and irrelevance of fair play that are central features of the genre dramatize the disjuncture between the ideology of liberal capitalism and its practice as experienced by small farmers. Irene Webley (1983), writing about Australia and New Zealand, agrees with Freedman about the importance of the spectator's interpretation of the event but claims a different meaning for the wrestling "text." According to Webley, the meaning of wrestling is constructed through the relationship between the wrestlers and the "crowd." That relationship constitutes the spectacle itself; the wrestling match per se is only its motor. The central dramatic tension of the match, however, is found in the intersection of moral and ethnic coding of the wrestlers.[8] For these two critics, as for Barthes, the contrivance of wrestling is intelligible as a process of sign production in which both the wrestlers and their audience participate.

Other analysts instead read wrestling as a text produced, with a greater or lesser degree of conscious intent, by the authors of the wrestling scripts. Bruce Lincoln (1989), applying a structuralist analytical framework to professional wrestling in the United States, argues that it should be understood as an inversion ritual at the level of the card (the set of matches at a given event).[9] In a set of successive matches, individual wrestlers are placed within a classificatory system, which in turn determines the outcome of each individual match, and of the event as a whole. In line with Webley, he highlights the significance of the ethnic marking of the wrestlers: wrestlers are marked not only as "heel" and "baby face" (as the bad-guy and good-guy roles are known in the United States), but as more or less "mainstream" American (that is, white, Anglo-Saxon Protestant, neither markedly rural nor markedly urban). In each set of matches, he argued, the intersecting codes of virtue/wickedness and more American/less American constitute a dialectic, leading from an initial match which the less-American baby face wins, through a series of matches won by American heels, to a resolution in which the American baby face triumphs. Like Freedman, Lincoln reads the middle set of matches as a critique of the Protestant work ethic, but he sees it as a liminal phase, leading to the final match, which vindicates the ideology that the earlier matches critique. The text of wrestling, carefully constructed by wrestling promoters, thus works to legitimate the

dominant order. Thus, while Lincoln agrees with Webley about the importance of the ethnic as well as the moral coding of the wrestlers, he sees very
little room for the interpretive agency of the wrestling audience in determining the meaning of the matches.

All of these analyses share one premise: the meaning of wrestling is
found in the fact of its falsehood. Its staging may be understood to take
place at any number of levels—as intentionally produced, ongoing narrative strategies or as dramatic spectacles of ideal types and grand gestures—
but in each instance these scholars take theatrical contrivance as a starting
point of analysis. That the fighting is faked, that there is no "reality" to the
contest, is treated as a given. But in fact, how much of what one sees is
choreographed and how much is "real" may not be so obvious. Is it not
possible that while the characters are "fake," the matches are not, or not
always? In contrast to all the rest of wrestling's analysts, Donald Nonini and
Arlene Teraoka (1992) make the claim that wrestling is not rigged, and that
the assumption of fakery is merely an instance of bourgeois misrecogni-
tion. Echoing the discourse of wrestling fanzines, they cite the list of injuries wrestlers suffer in the ring (too severe and sustained too frequently,
in their view, to be reasonably attributable to accident) as evidence that the
fighting is real. They propose an alternative interpretation of the excessive,
theatrical gestures (that Barthes and the rest read as dramatic conventions), seeing them as tactics used to fake out an opponent and actual
responses to physical pain. Likewise, they explain the graduated character
of violence in a match (in which harmless but loud slaps may follow or be
followed by apparently more damaging blows), and disregard for or manipulation of the rules, as a range of tactics available to the wrestler in order to
pin the opponent. Like other workers, they argued, wrestlers sell their labor
power, put their bodies at risk, and try to do the minimum necessary to "get
the job done" (in this case pinning the opponent). Wrestling thus recapitu-
lates the labor process under capitalism, and that is its appeal for the
working-class audience. Other academics and journalists, as representatives of the bourgeoisie, cannot recognize wrestling for what it is for the
same reason they cannot afford to recognize the brutality of the labor
process. The class habitus of the bourgeois analyst precludes not only the
taste for but understanding of the sport.

Writers who attend to long-range narratives tend, like Lincoln, to emphasize the conservative messages embedded in wrestling. By analyzing the

ongoing fortunes of one wrestler, Sergeant Slaughter, during the winter of 1991, Sam Migliore (1993) showed that the sequence of Slaughter's actions (taking on an Iraqi manager, making anti-American statements in and out of the ring, and reverting to his original role as "heel") produced a metaphoric association between opposition to the Gulf War and betrayal of the country. Slaughter's subsequent moral reclamation following the war, he argues, functioned as a symbolic repatriation of the war's opponents. His analysis is similar to that of Michael Ball (1995), who interprets professional wrestling as a scripted performance that ritually affirms and promotes jingoism, sexism, and a generally conservative political agenda, and also that of Jeffrey Mondak (1989). Mondak, looking, at the long-term pattern of popularity of the sport in the United States, concluded that professional wrestling has always peaked in popularity during periods when isolationism and xenophobia are most intense and widespread.

In general, there is an important difference between those who see wrestling as a hegemonic form and those see it as counterhegemonic. Their analysis of the meaning of the performance (and the process through which meaning is produced) depends on whether they attended live matches or watched televised events. Migliore acknowledges as much, conceding that the anticapitalist subtext that Freedman observed may exist at live events in small arenas, although it is absent from the televised, mass-mediated phenomenon seen by most spectators. He attributes the tendency to see professional wrestling per se as a counterhegemonic performance as a failure to distinguish between "participatory and media constructed rituals" (1993: 68). As a media constructed ritual, wrestling loses the subversive edge it might have in other contexts, while its longer-term narratives serve as Barthes's mythic signs.

What is missing from all of the foregoing analyses is an engagement with the production of professional wrestling. Two exceptions to this are the work of Sharon Mazer (1998) and Alan Turowetz (Birrell and Turowetz 1984). Their work shows that attention to the production of professional wrestling reveals its essential ambiguity as a signifying practice. Mazer, who observed wrestling classes in Brooklyn, and Turowetz, who spent four years as a journalist for a wrestling magazine in Montreal, show wrestling to be constructed through contradictory expectations and values. The violence of wrestling (to paraphrase Eve Sedgwick [1993])[10] is kind of choreographed, kind of not. Wrestlers, promoters, and trainers value different sets of skills and are motivated by different goals. The finishing moves of matches are indeed predetermined, but much of the rest of the activity that constitutes professional wrestling as a genre is left to choice and skill. Their portrait of the performance genre comes much closer to what I found in Mexico. There are certainly patterns to lucha libre performances, but they are not nearly so neatly constructed as Lincoln portrays them to be. The conservative politics that Lincoln, Migliore, Ball, and others read into it are present, but so is the kind of counterhegemonic critique seen by Freedman and Barthes. Mazer contends that professional wrestling is primarily about the display of alternative models of masculinity, and she's probably right, too. In other words, professional wrestling is a polysemic performance, capable of carrying contradictory meanings.

A BRIEF HISTORY OF LUCHA LIBRE

Any interpretation of lucha libre, as a practice, a signifying system or both, must take into account a paradox central to the genre. In contrast with Europe and North America, where professional wrestling seems to have developed from local traditions, lucha libre began as an import from the United States. Except for a few exhibition matches in the first years of the century, professional wrestling wasn't practiced in Mexico before 1933. Yet fans, wrestlers, and others understand lucha libre as a specifically Mexican performance genre. It was brought to Mexico by a promoter named Salvador Lutteroth after he saw a match performed in Eagle Pass, Texas. On September 21, 1933, Lutteroth and his partner Francisco Ahumado sponsored their first wrestling event in Arena Nacional, just south of the Alameda Park. When the owners of the Arena declined to continue to make the arena available the following year, the two bought and renovated an arena a few blocks away, renamed it Arena Mexico, and incorporated themselves as the Empresa Mexicana de Lucha Libre (EMLL).

In the next years, lucha libre developed roots in Mexico. Local talent emerged and local fan bases grew. Innovations in costuming, character, and technique further Mexicanized the genre. At first, it was promoted as modern and urban. Armando Bartra (1994) has argued that this period marked a cultural shift in Mexico, as a number of practices of mass cultural consumption—reading comic books, attending sporting events, going to movies—opened new spaces of identification. Lucha libre was one of these practices. While lucha libre audiences are assumed to have come from the popular classes, the evidence for the class status of the early audience is unclear. The writer Salvador Novo confessed to being an aficionado, even exchanging his Friday night season tickets to the ballet for Tuesday night tickets so that he could be free to attend the luchas (although, in all fairness, Novo was a notorious enthusiast of slumming; see Novo 1965: 324).[11] In his writing, he celebrated the participatory nature of lucha libre spectatorship and the relative blurring of the roles of performer and spectator that took place in the arena. He described the typical lucha libre fan of 1940: "Each rheumatic and bald owner of a two peso ticket at ringside loses the kilos and years necessary to transform himself, during a quarter of an hour, into Jimmy el Apolo, and with equal ease, find in El Hombre Montaña or in Alberto Corral his enemies scattered about the world—the landlord, the section chief, his own father-in-law—and contributes from his seat to exterminate them, to kick them, to throw them out of the ring" (Novo 1994: 600).

In the 1940s, lucha libre spectatorship was not an activity of the Mexican elites as such, but it was a practice associated with urbanism and modernity. By the time I arrived, however, lucha libre had acquired another set of connotations. In Mexico City it had, for decades, been considered a pastime of the urban poor. Despite its U.S. origin, it was seen as a specifically (for some embarrassingly) Mexican institution. It changed from an imported novelty that attracted different classes, to a local tradition that members of the middle and upper classes avoided. Televised broadcast of lucha libre in the early 1950s attracted a middle class audience, but it was taken off the air after a few years. Although it subsequently provided subject matter for hundreds of films, it remained primarily a live performance. But at the time of my research, that had changed. To the dismay of many in the wrestling community, lucha libre broadcasts began anew in 1991 (see chapter 6).

INSTITUTIONAL ORGANIZATION OF LUCHA LIBRE: SOME DEFINITIONS

Empresas

Lucha libre is organized by *empresas*, private enterprises minimally consisting of a promoter and a stable of wrestlers. An empresa might or might not own its own arena(s). A "promoter" may be the owner of an empresa, or an agent for individual wrestlers, or the owner of an arena. The stability of any of these entities depends on their overlap. An empresa without an arena is in an inherently unstable position, as is an arena owner without wrestlers. The only empresa in Mexico City to succeed in maintaining both elements over a long period is the EMLL. The first and oldest empresa in Mexico, the EMLL owns both of the main arenas in the Federal District: Arena Mexico (which was renovated and expanded to seat 18,000 in 1957), and the smaller Arena Coliseo, built in 1943 in a neighborhood just northwest of the Zócalo, at the southern edge of Tepito.[3] Both arenas are still open. In the early 1960s, the empresa opened a third arena, the Pista Arena Revolucion in the neighborhood of Mixcoac, but it was closed in 1997. In addition to their Mexico City arenas, the EMLL owns arenas in Puebla, Cuernavaca, Acapulco, Guadalajara, and other cities around the country.

In addition to the EMLL, many smaller empresas have operated in and around the capital. At the time of research, at least five more operated in or near the Federal District. These smaller organizations survived in part by developing a kind of patron-client relationship with the EMLL, promoting events that might feature independent wrestlers in the opening matches and EMLL stars in the last match. The second largest empresa to operate near the Federal District, Lucha Libre Internacional (LLI), started promoting events in the Toreo Cuatro Caminos, a bullring just over the border in an area technically within the state of Mexico (rather than the Federal District). Between the 1970s and 1990s, the LLI competed with the EMLL for some of lucha libre's biggest star performers. At the time of my research, the EMLL's main competition came from two large-scale empresas that operated without permanent access to any particular arena. The first, called the AAA, was owned by the media conglomerate Televisa. The second, PromoAzteca, was owned by the rival TV station Azteca. At present, lucha libre can be seen live in most states of the republic, at least from time to time. In Mexico City and its environs, live matches take place at least five nights a week in venues ranging from arenas dedicated primarily to lucha libre, to gymnasiums, dance halls, bullrings, *palenques* (dedicated to cockfights), and outdoor plazas. It can be seen on television at least once a week.

Unions

Empresas are not, however, the only institutional structures of relevance to lucha libre. Wrestlers were organized into unions early in the history of the sport. The Sindicato Nacional de Luchadores (National Wrestlers Union,

SNL) was founded sometime before 1940, and organized a strike at Arena Libertad in 1941. The SNL is affiliated with the powerful Confederacion de Trabajadores Mexicanos (Confederation of Mexican Workers, CTM). In the late 1990s, there were several additional wrestling unions or unionlike organizations active in Mexico City. One, the Asociacion de Luchadores, Referís y Retirados (Association of Luchadores, Referees, and Retirees—hereafter the Association), was founded in the early 1980s by retired wrestler and waiter Juan Alanís. It was affiliated with the Consejo Regional de Obreros y Campesinos (Regional Council of Workers and Peasants, CROC) and shared offices and personnel with the CROC affiliated waiter's union (also headed by Alanis). The Association was conceived as a reform project: in Alanís's words, it "was born as a consequence of the doubts of a gastronomic worker, that is, myself," and represented a number of freelancers and novices as yet unaffiliated with an empresa.[4] In the late 1990s, the interests of wrestlers affiliated with the EMLL and the AAA were represented by in-house organizations.

Comision de Lucha Libre

Lucha libre is overseen by an office of the Federal District called the Comision de Lucha Libre (originally Comision de Box y Lucha Libre). The commission was founded in the late 1930s as a branch of the Oficina de Espectaculos Publicos (Office of Public Spectacles), itself a division of the Departamento del Distrito Federal (DDF, the government of the Federal District), which oversaw all manner of public entertainments, from opera and theater to cinema and sports. Each state should, in theory, have its own commission, but the wrestlers, promoters, and even commissioners held different opinions about the degree of authority the Federal District Commission had over other commissions. Since the government of Mexico City was, in effect, a branch of the federal government until 1996, appointments to the Federal District Commission were, essentially, low-level presidential appointments.

Rafael Barradas Osorio served as secretary of lucha libre from 1953 to 1986. He came to have enormous influence over the organization of lucha libre during his long tenure. At the time of his appointment Barradas Osorio (an acquaintance of the recently elected president, Adolfo Ruiz Cortines) hoped to parlay his experience in the Veracruz film industry and his relationship with the president into a position in the Office of Public

Spectacles, where he hoped to continue working in film. The president sent him to see the head of the office, Adolfo Fernandez Bustamante. Much to his surprise, Bustamante put him in charge of lucha libre (interview with author; also see Barradas Osorio 1992). Under Barradas Osorio, the commission took charge of regulating all aspects of the spectacle. These included setting the basic rules, determining what activities would be permitted in performance, licensing wrestlers and referees, and registration of characters.

CONCLUSION

Lucha libre is apparently simple. Two or more wrestlers enter a boxing ring and put on a show of fighting until one of them is pinned or surrenders. Yet it is also a complex performance that integrates a range of ideas about agency, power, modernity, gender, and national culture. It does so because it is a fundamentally contradictory form. It both is and is not a sport. As such, it both is and is not associated with a set of ideas about modernity and the Mexican nation-state. It arrived in Mexico as a cosmopolitan practice, but (as I will show in chapters 4 and 6) it came to signify the continuity of the pre-Hispanic past in the urban present. It both endorses and challenges an ideology of gender that equates dominance and penetration with masculinity, and passivity with feminine virtue. Its generic ambiguity makes it an ideal format for the staging of contradictions.

> For a secret to be realized, someone must not only conceal something, but someone else must know or suspect this concealment (Bellman 1981). Consequently, while the import of a secret may remain hidden, the act of concealment must be revealed if the secret is to have an audience and hence a social existence.
>
> BEIDELMAN 1993: 6

2

TRADE SECRETS AND REVELATIONS

I would like to begin this chapter with a confession. Everything I have written or published about lucha libre has felt like an act of betrayal. In order to write about lucha libre, I must reveal a secret. It is a secret, however, that every likely reader probably already knows: professional wrestling matches are fixed. Even though "everybody knows," even though no one ever asked me to keep it a secret or even said that it *was* a secret, it still doesn't feel right to say it in print. My personal relationship to this (public) secret is complicated, as I trained in lucha libre for a year and a half. Often, during that time, I idly contemplated "going native," maybe staying long enough to get my wrestling license and then . . . but being an anthropologist seemed more practical and (sadly) more lucrative. At no time in the course of that training did any wrestler, trainer, or fellow trainee ever explicitly communicate to me the fact that lucha libre was fixed. Even though I "knew" (I had been told as much by two wrestling reporters, a retired official of the commission of lucha libre, and a wrestler's ex-girlfriend—besides, everybody knows that professional wrestling is fixed), I always wondered if everybody might not be wrong.

The sensation of doubt came to me in particular moments. The first, I suppose came at a match I attended in Puebla in 1994. In one of the most interesting matches I've ever seen (to which I will return in chapter 5), I watched El Loco Valentino (captain of the rudos) throw the técnico Seminarista out of the ring and begin smashing his head against the front-row seats. When blood began to flow from behind Seminarista's mask, I assumed that he was using blood capsules—everyone knows that professional wrestling is "fake." But then, as the match wore on, I realized that I didn't just see blood, I smelled it, metallic and unmistakable. The smell of blood seemed to bear witness against my belief that it was all just an act. If it was real blood, how could the match not be equally "real?" In all my time studying lucha libre—training as a luchadora, watching classes, matches, interactions, I was always troubled by the doubt that it might not be fixed. At the same time, I never understood why I doubted what everybody knows to be true.

That understanding finally came very late in my research when I returned for a visit in 1998. The summer after I completed fieldwork, I returned twice to visit my wrestling teacher and my old classmates. Between the two visits, my classmates and some of the other wrestlers who hung around the gym were scheduled to go to give what, for most of them, would be their first public display of lucha libre. As with many aspiring wrestlers, their debut would take place in the plaza of a rural village as part of the festivities celebrating the local patron saint's day. An employee of the gym had asked my teacher, Luis Jaramillo, if he would put together an event for the annual festival in his hometown in Oaxaca in exchange for transportation, housing, food, and drink. He organized a group of nine participants to go. In my absence, my classmates chose their personae, designed and bought their costumes, and began to train more intensively in preparation for the event. A month before they were to go, I came back for a visit.

Class started that night with the usual warmups, then those of us who were not going to Oaxaca were asked to clear the ring. As my friends stood around the Profe, he explained that they would start with a *batalla campal* (a battle of each against all) and that they should eliminate each other in the following order: starting with Pedro, then Santiago, and ending with Arturo and Garibaldi. Before they started, he paired them up, Santiago with Pedro, Garibaldi with Manuel, Jorge with Rafa and, for the last match,

Gabi and Garibaldi against Arturo and Pedro. Profe warned them to look out for each other, reminded them that he would be playing the referee, and gave them the signal to start.

From my perspective on the sidelines, all hell broke loose. Manuel kicked Rafa in the stomach and, as he doubled over in pain, grabbed him by the head and threw him across the ring. Others threw forearms, leg tackles, and arm twists, seemingly at random. When Gabi pinned Pedro, all the others jumped on top of him to make sure he stayed pinned. He left the ring, and soon the same thing happened to Santiago, then Garibaldi, and so on, until only Arturo and Gabi were left. Since the order of defeat determined the order of the subsequent matches, Santiago returned to wrestle with Pedro (as Jaramillo had instructed at the beginning).

The two ran into problems right away. Pedro threw Santiago, grabbed him by the arm, pulled him to his feet, and tried to fling him by one arm into the ropes so he could clothesline him on the rebound. Pedro jerked Santiago's arm, but Santi didn't move toward the ropes. He tried it again, but Santiago just stumbled forward. Finally Jaramillo, rather than scold Santiago, admonished the more experienced Pedro: "He isn't catching your drift because you're pulling him by the wrist," instead of grabbing him near the armpit. Without the proper hold, Santiago couldn't feel how he was supposed to react. Pedro adjusted his grip, and Santiago flew to the ropes, rebounded straight into Pedro's forearm, and fell to the ground. Pedro pinned him to win the first fall.

The two returned to their corners until the Profe signaled them to enter the ring again. Pedro circled behind Santiago, and put him in a compression hold from the back. Santiago, gasping for breath, tried to give up. He waved his hands, wiggling his fingers in the gesture of "I surrender," but Jaramillo wouldn't allow it. Finally, after great effort, he escaped the hold, threw Pedro and pinned him to win the second fall. As the two stood in their corners waiting for the signal to start the last round, Jaramillo walked up to each in turn and said something too quietly for the rest of us to hear. The third round started and ended quickly, Pedro pinning Santiago to the mat.

Then Jorge and Rafa replaced them in the ring. More agile than the first pair, they worked faster, using more throws, but still relying on the fling-to-the-ropes-and-clothesline-on-the-rebound sequence. After a particularly hard throw, Jorge, dizzy, tried to leave the ring, but Jaramillo made him get back in. Rafa, playing against his usual type, was transformed into a smirking, violent rudo, as Jorge fell into the role of abject técnico. Again and again he suffered through Rafa's joint locks, throws, and blows. He landed hard on the mat and writhed in pain but somehow won the first fall. Rafa won the second. Then, once again, I saw Jaramillo go up to Jorge and, this time, heard him (in his official capacity as referee) give explicit instructions for how he should end the last fall. Immediately afterward, he went up to Rafa and let him know how he was supposed to lose.

The rest fought their matches in turn. I could see that the wrestlers were working incredibly hard. They were not so much performing a choreography as they were mounting an improvised display of exquisite sensitivity. In the middle of the last match, Pedro and Garibaldi (two of the most experienced students) threw in a short choreographed sequence that I had seen them practice together before class. Here it was: the link between training and performance, a link that had never been made explicit before (at least for me). For the first time in nearly two years of training, I finally got to watch how the techniques and sequences we had practiced together could be realized in front of an audience. I could see where the match was improvised, where it was choreographed, where it was free-form, and where there were restrictions. After class I wished everyone luck and went back to New York.

Two months later I came back for another visit. The first person I saw as I entered the gym was Arturo. In June he had worn his hair long, well below shoulder length, but now he sported a crew cut. Jaramillo and Gabi came out of the locker room, and I asked them how the Oaxaca trip had gone. "Great," they said. "They loved us. They asked for our autographs! We even did a *lucha de apuesta* (betting match) of Gabi's mask against Arturo's hair."[1] (That explained Arturo's haircut.) "Gabi won, of course," said Jaramillo. And then, as if I hadn't seen them practice, as if I had no idea how it was done, he added: "Because Gabi, as you know, is much bigger than Arturo."

In the world of lucha libre, the story is always under construction. Even if "everybody knows" that the matches are fixed, that does not excuse wrestlers from presenting an alibi, from constantly recreating a story of what is really going on. And the question of what is "really" going on is complicated. Some fans and commentators (for example, Nonini and Teraoka 1992) point to the list of injuries suffered by wrestlers as evidence that it is not fixed. The real damage to real bodies is represented as an indication of the reality of the contest. That was my assumption when I smelled Seminarista's blood in Puebla. Yet, in that instance, as in others, the status of "realness" was complicated. Wrestlers are sometimes paid extra to bleed. Before the wrestler is supposed to bleed, someone (the wrestler, or sometimes the referee) makes small incisions on the wrestler's forehead. At the proper moment, the opposing wrestler hits the cuts to reopen them, and the victim appears to bleed from the blow.[2] A trick? Sure, but it is their real blood. Perhaps that is the *real* secret—that there is no blood capsule, no ketchup, no chicken blood: just the real human blood of the wrestler.

Lucha libre is thus constructed around the public secret of the fixed ending. Yet the secret of the fixed ending is only one of a number of back secrets, of stories told and stories hidden, of secrets revealed to conceal still others. The secrecy of the fix stands for a series of dissimulations, for the mystery that animates the genre.

The socialization of the wrestler and the revelation of secrets are *embodied* processes. Professional wrestling is inscribed in the body. It is the result of corporeal training, of gradual changes in habitus.[3] It is an experience had by few of the academics or journalists who write about wrestling.[4] It was in the context of training that the theme of the secret repeatedly emerged during my fieldwork. Indeed, my teacher and others often described our interactions as that of teaching me the secrets of lucha libre. One might thus expect the training process to be one of revelation of secrets, of getting "let in on the game" (Mazer 1998: 53). Yet, as I've said, there was no moment in which I was explicitly let in on the secret. Knowing the secret aspects of lucha libre did not come as moments of revelation of the hidden, but as a gradual decoding of the discreet.

LEARNING THE SECRETS

The gym I trained in was not well known as a center of lucha libre training. Like most spaces where aspiring luchadores learn the ropes, it was used for a variety of activities: weight training, handball, tae kwon do. It was located less than a block from Metro Hidalgo, probably the busiest metro stop in the city center. Busy during the day, with a reputation of being dangerous at night, it is located at a crossroads of the city: the transfer point between the two longest lines that cross the greatest spatial and (arguably) social distances of the metro system. The station is known as a cruising ground for gay men, especially cross-dressers, and was the site in 1997 of an apparition of the Virgin of Guadalupe in a floor tile, discovered by a worker during a renovation (the floor tile was subsequently placed in a small shrine outside of the entrance where it was found). The gym itself was located above a convenience store, announced by a plastic figure, about three feet tall, of a half-naked man with bulging muscles, flexing both biceps. Below him a sign read GIMNASIO METROPOLITANO: BODY BUILDING, WEIGHTS, JUDO, KARATE, LUCHA LIBRE.[5] The entrance to the gym itself was on the second floor. Two or three middle-aged men would play endless card games between handing out locks and collecting monthly dues in a tiny glassed-in office at the entrance. The glass wall of the office was covered with memos—various jokes, reminders about fees, and the grim warning: ANYONE CAUGHT URINATING IN THE STEAMROOM WILL HAVE HIS MEMBERSHIP CANCELED..

Most of the space in the gym was dedicated to free weights and rudimentary weight machines. At one end, a ten- by twenty-foot space was walled off on three sides and used as a handball court. At the other end there was a large glassed-in area for tae kwon do classes. The tiny women's locker room was located in the center of the gym, and the men's locker room was near the tae kwon do room. The men's locker room, a large area, had a space in the back with a cast-iron spiral staircase. The lucha libre ring was at the top of the staircase, only a little smaller than the room that held it. In that ring, two-thirds of the size regulated by the Commission of Lucha Libre (for performance), Luis Jaramillo Martinez gave classes three days a week.

A gray-haired, stocky, muscular man in his early sixties, Jaramillo was deeply committed to teaching the classical Mexican style of professional wrestling. In his prime, he had wrestled as Jefe Aguila Blanca (Chief White Eagle), a character based on the Apaches and other Indians from Hollywood westerns. He started his career in the 1950s, and had been retired (or at least semiretired) for at least a decade. When I first met the profe and explained my project, he shook my hand, sat me down, and told me that if I wanted to learn the *real* lucha libre, he was willing to teach me. But, he warned, he would not teach me the "clownshow you see on television," but the real, Mexican item. Then he looked at my sneakers and sweatpants, advised me to get a pair of lycra shorts, and, to my surprise, told me that we would start that night. That night turned out to be the monthly endurance class, given downstairs in the handball court. It started with light jogging, then lap after lap of leapfrog and of jumping over a row of students as they waited on all fours. Then we ran some more, vaulted more, and finally did a series of rolls on the bare floor. I woke up the next day my back one big bruise, and so became his student.

The classes in which the "secrets" of lucha libre are imparted to students follow a set structure. At the beginning of class, students line up outside of the ring in the order of their length of time training. The most experienced student stands at the front of the line, the newest at the back. The class begins with a series of rolls and break falls, collectively referred to as *maromas* (tumbling), that serve as a warm-up. Once the warm-up ends and class begins, the students line up to one side of the ring while the teacher calls the first student into the center of the canvas. He or she then teaches the class a short routine, one move at a time. The teacher shows the first student the first two moves of the routine, and then calls in the second student to perform the moves with the first. Student one goes to the end of the line, the third student steps in, and student two takes over the first student's role. The students continue to work in round-robin fashion. Every time the first student begins a new cycle, she or he is taught the next move of the routine and incorporates it into whatever came before. Eventually an entire set of moves leading to a finishing hold is built up and practiced by all the students. In Jaramillo's classes, once the class performed a set, it was never repeated. The goal was not to learn choreographed sequences, but to train the body to respond to physical cues.

Hence, the essence of lucha libre training was found in the maromas practiced at the very beginning of class. These initial exercises teach the student how to fall without injury and condition his or her body to perform with a partner. For this reason, *they* are sometimes referred to (by luchadores, but also by fans and journalists) as the *secrets* of lucha libre. The basic falling skills that a luchador(a) must master are the *maroma de frente* (forward roll), the *tres cuatros* (three-quarters roll), the *maromas pa'tras* (backward roll), the *caida* (rear break fall), a front break fall called a *plancha* (iron), and the *salto mortal* (death leap).

Although these techniques are related to the rolls and break falls used in Asian martial arts, the body mechanics are quite different. For example, in the jujitsu or aikido forward roll, the player contacts the ground with the arm and shoulder, which are held in a relaxed curve. The idea is to make the body resemble a wheel, with the arm, the shoulder, and a diagonal line across the back forming its rim, the center of the body its axis. In lucha libre front rolls, the wrestler contacts the ground with the hands. The maroma de frente is done like a somersault, starting with the feet parallel. The tres cuatros roll resembles the aikido forward roll, but it begins with the left foot and hand slightly forward. The wrestler then places both hands on the ground, and pushes off with the back leg to begin the roll, while keeping the right leg bent behind the left. In the tres cuatros *larga* (long three-quarters), the hands don't actually touch the ground, and the left hand slaps out as one completes the roll. In contrast to related rolls in Asian martial arts, the wrestler looks straight ahead and keeps the body extended until the last moment.

The roll that my teacher emphasized as the key technique of lucha libre was a flip with a rear break fall, called a salto mortal (death leap). In the salto mortal, the wrestler jumps, does a flip in midair, and lands on his or her back, weight distributed between the soles of the feet, the upper back and the arms (which slap out with the landing). At the beginning of class, wrestlers do repetition after repetition of each roll. Sometimes they combine them into sequences and add short excursions onto the ropes, or vault over other students into the roll. In our classes, Jaramillo would tell new students to do just the warm-up for the first night or nights, and then watch the rest of class, paying close attention to everything the other students did.

Like most trainers and wrestlers I interviewed, Jaramillo insisted that a professional wrestler must have a solid base in Greco-Roman, Olympic, and Freestyle wrestling. Accordingly, we had irregular lessons in Olympic or Freestyle wrestling. On those nights, Jaramillo would sometimes teach techniques that he identified as Olympic, but usually we were just given a partner, informed of the rules, and told to start wrestling. He and others often cited grounding in amateur wrestling as a key difference between real professional wrestlers and "the clowns on television," but despite its ideo-

FIGURE 1
Working the
routine

logical importance, we seldom practiced it. There may have been several possible reasons for our relative neglect of amateur wrestling techniques. Perhaps it was because we were there to learn professional wrestling, and that was Jaramillo's area of expertise. But in addition, the mechanics of amateur wrestling, which seemed to depend on extremely close body contact and raw power, appeared to have little in common with the mechanics of professional wrestling.

Also, my presence in the class may have inhibited Jaramillo from scheduling Olympic wrestling sessions. Our amateur wrestling classes were one of the few situations in which attention was called to my gender, since I was generally not expected to wrestle Freestyle or Olympic with the men (who ranged in size from about 121 to 242 pounds). During the professional classes, I worked with whoever stood next to me in the line, but Profe preferred that I practiced amateur wrestling with another woman. His few other female students attended classes only occasionally, however. The three times that I did wrestle (Olympic style) against men, I was paired against not the smallest, but the most mature opponents: once against Pedro, one of the more experienced students (who outweighed me by at least 50 pounds), and twice against Jaramillo himself. It seemed that we were more likely to do an Olympic class if there was another woman present for me to wrestle, and it may be that he would have scheduled them more often if it hadn't been for me.

In the beginning, because I came to lucha libre after training in Asian martial arts, I had a hard time making sense of the maromas. Placing my hands on the floor in order to roll disrupted harmonious circularity I had learned in my sporadic encounters with aikido or jujitsu. Eventually, though, I came to understand that the mechanics were entirely different. In aikido rolls, contact with the mat stands for contact with the ground. In lucha libre rolls, however, the contact of the wrestler's hands with the floor stands for contact with the other wrestler's body. Thus every throw, every lock is a technique of mutuality. For a throw to work correctly, the arms of both partners form a frame, like spokes of a wheel with the attacker at the hub. The first thing one has to learn of the basic mechanics is where to put one's hands on the partner's body in order to maintain a framelike contact. Most throws start from joint locks or head locks, and there is always a configuration within the lock where the defender can release pressure on the locked joint by using his or her free arm to form a triangle between him- or herself and his or her opponent. The frame allows the wrestler to anticipate the next move and his or her part in it. A painless and beautiful fall is the outcome of both familiarity with the "basic steps" of lucha libre and exquisite sensitivity to the opponent's body. Like following in tango, one has to feel one's partner's intentions and respond instantly. The process of learning to fight is one of learning to cooperate.

The next thing that a wrestler has to learn is physical courage, especially on the ropes. During the first year of training, wrestlers learn to jump onto the ropes and throw themselves off of them into somersaults, planchas, and saltos mortales.[6] They learn to leave instinct behind, to jump from four feet off the ground to land face down on the mat. Technique is important, but faith, the belief that they can and will do it, is even more so. Courage is also important when a wrestler learns to catch a partner leaping or somersaulting off of the ropes. As students progress, they learn other skills: special finishing holds, how to enter and exit the ring, orientation in the physical space of the ring, and so on. All of these and other skills are taught within the same format—in the context of sets learned from week to week, but then forgotten. There was always a level of ambiguity, then, in the relationship between the routines we learned and professional performance (to which we aspired). Were we supposed to think of them as examples of the kind of choreography we were supposed to perform, or were they just skill-building sequences, to teach us techniques? In short, the structure of the training process allowed one to suspend disbelief (in the "reality" of wrestling) even as one learned to be a professional wrestler.

INITIATION AND SOCIALIZATION

There is a saying among professional wrestlers: *Un luchador no se hace, se nace* (wrestlers are born, not made). Nevertheless, one enters into the profession through a process of training and socialization. One enters a wrestling school, stands at the back of the line, works routines with the second newest student and then with the most experienced as the line cycles around. If a student stays a few months, his or her place in the line moves up as new students come and old students drop out. Those who stick with it eventually take the licensing exam, pass it (or don't), and (if they are lucky, connected and/or talented) become professional wrestlers.

One becomes a wrestler through a change in bodily awareness. There is, however, one mechanism of socialization that some wrestlers told me about, an induction ritual that they call *bautizo* (baptism). I learned about baptism not in the course of training but in an interview with a working professional, whose first teacher had been Luis Jaramillo Martinez. When I asked him if there was anything else that he thought I should know about lucha libre but had not thought to ask, he responded that I should know "how difficult it is to be a beginner."

> It's very hard at first, because there's a kind of code of honor among luchadores that they don't teach you right away. They push you a bit. They mistreat you very badly, and if you come back, they treat you badly again. And if you come back, they treat you badly again. Then if a week passes and you were able to stand it,

then you're in and they start to treat you better[, saying]: "Don't do it like that, you have to protect yourself." You say, "Oh, you shoulda told me!" But no, they let you fall down with all your inexperience, and if you come back, they see that yes, you like it. (Guerrero del Futuro 1997)

That experience, he said, was called a baptism.

As he described it, baptism sounded like the ritual that Sharon Mazer (1998: 12) encountered in Gleason's gym in Brooklyn: that of "getting your face pushed to the mat." She writes: "Getting your face pushed to the mat is the rite of passage any newcomer to wrestling faces in the early weeks. Typically, he unintentionally provokes the wrath of a more experienced wrestler, who then verbally and physically abuses him as others stand back and watch. If the newcomer sticks it out and returns subsequently, he has passed a crucial test and is deemed worthy of a higher degree of respect than before, and is assimilated into the group." Yet there seemed to be some significant differences between the two practices. For although baptism sounds like a fairly straightforward rite of passage (religious overtones and all), I found it to be quite ambiguous. First, it did not seem to be something that every wrestler had to go through. Although the opponent in a wrestler's first professional match is thereafter called his "padrino" or her "madrina" (godmother/godfather), that experience is never called a baptism, just a debut. Furthermore, Guerrero del Futuro was the only wrestler who talked about his own baptism. Some would talk about other, very public baptisms of wrestlers who went on to become stars, but not about baptisms that they suffered, witnessed, or carried out. Furthermore, I never witnessed or experienced a baptism, at least not as a discrete ritual that all must undergo. First, Jaramillo always kept raw novices (as opposed . to new students who had trained elsewhere) from doing anything except warm-ups the first day. Then he would show them how to do a break fall, and send them over to the other side of the ropes. Furthermore, some students, it seemed, could bypass baptism completely while others, the clumsier, the weaker, suffered something more like ongoing harassment by the head of the line.

Like Mazer (who suspects that some of her verbal interactions with the wrestlers at Gleason's may have been an oral version of "pushing her face to the mat"), I do not know if I was baptized or not. During my training, there were some allowances made for my sex—I was sometimes allowed to give up on the finishing holds that require lifting a partner up and over one's shoulder. Jaramillo periodically would declare that he went easy on me so that I (being a woman) wouldn't get hurt, but as far as I could tell (other than fewer threats of being hit with a weight belt—which he actually carried out only with one of the most advanced students), he didn't treat me differently from anyone else. He may have been slightly more tolerant if I tried to bow out of something than he was with the men, but only slightly. I too was told to get back in the fray, threatened with the belt, and made—or allowed—to catch a two-hundred-pound man as he jumped off the top rope. My male classmates, in turn, may have treated me more gently than they treated each other, but not always. If I had to locate a moment of baptism, it might have been on that very first night when, without instruction, I was told to roll across a bare floor. I could certainly construct it in retrospect as a baptism. If I hadn't already had some rolling and falling skills, it would have been excruciatingly painful. As it was, I woke up stiff and aching with lurid bruises, but returned two days later and was taught lucha libre's more effective techniques. But it didn't seem to conform to any regular, universal induction ritual.

There was one other incident that I could read in retrospect as a baptism. When I began training, the head of the line on most nights was a talented wrestler I knew as "Julio." When I started classes, he had already passed the licensing exam and was freelancing as a wrestler. I never saw him perform, but I always assumed that he worked as a rudo.[7] His movements, his expressions—corporeal more than facial—communicated sadistic glee, fury at loss, contempt for his fallen foes, and frustration at his own defeats.

During the first month or so, I stood in the last place in line, so I worked with him as the line cycled. He never played his part of the set too fast or too rough for me to keep up. Until, that is, one night after I had trained for several months. By then I was no longer the newest student, but the less advanced students were absent or late, so I worked with Julio. We were working a set that included a plancha. In the plancha, the defender lies on his back, and the attacker belly flops on top of him, landing so that their torsos are perpendicular. Just before the moment of impact, the defender has to raise her shoulders off the floor and lift her arms slightly, in order to catch her opponent and minimize the impact of the technique. As with many techniques in lucha libre, the defender can protect herself as long as she has a structurally sound frame.

As it turns out, there are two different ways for the attacker to execute the plancha. The attacker can land in a position that distributes his weight between his or her forearms and thighs (the legs are bent), which prevents his full weight from landing directly on his or her opponent. Or, as I learned that night, by putting just a little more curve in his or her back, he or she can land his or her full weight on his or her partner's ribcage. For the first several months, my partners always landed the first way. That night, however, Julio used the second technique, and I discovered that my frame was not sound, and that my defensive technique was not effective. When he landed, I felt the distinctly unnerving sensation of my ribcage bending inward, pausing, and springing back into place, the wind nearly knocked out of me. Was that a baptism?

Most nights, however, I worked with students near my level. Julio, in the lead position, usually worked with Gabi, a tall, husky twenty-nine-year-old (another student told me he weighed over 220 pounds) who had trained with Jaramillo for several years. When the circle came around to the back of the line, Julio worked with "Marcos."

Marcos started about a month after I did. He was a short, chubby thirteen-year-old, neither strong nor graceful. He trained with the group for at least nine months before he stopped coming. The first night he showed up, Jaramillo showed him the basic rolls, then told him to watch the rest of class. He got bored easily—periodically, I would notice him kicking a medicine ball around or studying his feet instead of watching the ring. Over the months he trained, he improved very, very gradually, but never enough to look comfortable in his body, let alone in the ring. It looked to me like Julio decided to keep it that way. I never saw him hesitate in setting up a technique long enough to let Marcos find where to place his hands or how to anticipate the fall. Marcos, in turn, suffered awkwardly through each attack. One night Julio pulled the same trick on Marcos that he had pulled on me, landing his plancha with his full, considerable weight. Marcos, utterly surprised, couldn't get his breath and began crying, unable to stand up. Jaramillo ordered him to get up. He finally crawled out of the ring and went back to his place in the line to wait for the next round of torture. Jaramillo told Julio to take it easier next time.

Eventually, Julio's career picked up and he stopped coming to classes. Gabi became the usual head of the line. Behind him was Pedro, then Rafa or sometimes Garibaldi. Then some combination of three or four others stretched to the back. When he was the usual second-in-line, Gabi had seemed to act like a técnico. I thought of him as the flying cow, because whenever he did a tres cuatros larga, he reminded me of an illustration from "Hey-Diddle-Diddle," of the cow jumping over the moon. He would look straight ahead and arch his back to extend the time in the air, in seeming defiance of gravity.

When Gabi became the head of the line, though, he changed his style. He sped up his attacks, making it harder for his partners to set up for the fall—especially if his partner was a novice. With Marcos, he took up where Julio left off, entering suddenly, never giving him time to think about what was happening, let alone where to put his hands. Nobody ever made fun of Marcos in my presence (except to call him *licenciado*, the formal title used to address university graduates, and name of a character from the television show *El Chavo del Ocho*). Outside of the ring they treated him with benign indifference, so far as I could tell. But the ring was a constant baptism for him. It never ended until he stopped coming to classes.[8]

A few other students were treated the same way. Gabi, in front position, would begin his techniques abruptly, making it very hard for the new student to remember what Jaramillo had just shown him, let alone to do it. But for the most part, anyone who stuck out more than a few lessons would move up the line as new students came, sometimes staying for no more than a few sessions. The process looked less like baptism than weeding. Those who stayed on were made into luchadores, not through a rite of initiation, but through a gradual change in bodily habitus.

In Mazer's analysis of student interactions in Brooklyn, the closest equivalent to baptism (the rite of "getting your face pushed to the mat") was understood as the prerequisite to the revelation of secrets, of "getting let in on the game" (1998: 53). "Getting let in on the game" consisted of explicit instruction in the theatrical aspects of performance. In my experience of lucha libre, however, the theatrical aspects of performance constituted another instance of ambiguity. Although Jaramillo often told me that I was learning the "secrets" of lucha libre, the actual relationship between the choreography of training and the practice of performance was kept vague.

According to one of my fellow students, luchadores really did compete in the arenas, but their competition was governed by an "ethic" or "etiquette" (*etica*) that made it appear fixed. For example, if one wrestler is about to jump onto his or her opponent from the top rope, the wrestling ethic forbids the second wrestler to step aside. Even though we always learned lucha libre as a set of choreographed sets, this student understood the theatrical aspects of performance as the observation of professional courtesy.

When we received explicit instruction in the theatrical aspects of lucha libre, they were usually presented as pragmatic techniques. For example, the tres cuatros larga should end with a loud slap-out. In lucha libre, the slap-out is called a *registro*, because the sound "registers" the fall. Jaramillo presented the registro as a strictly technical matter designed (like the slap-out in Asian martial arts) to protect the body by dispersing the energy of the impact along the arm and out the fingers. In my experience, the sound of the slap-out was irrelevant to its effectiveness. Jaramillo, however, judged the quality of our rolls by the volume of the registro. As I later learned, a loud slap-out served two functions. First, it did give Jaramillo a means of making sure that we were, in fact, slapping out (and thus protecting ourselves from injury). In addition, he was giving us an implicit lesson about how to entertain the audience. As another retired wrestler explained as we watched a match together, the registro was a way to incorporate sound and rhythm in the performance, intensifying the audience's engagement with the match by gradually speeding up the tempos of thumps on the mat. The registro brings the spectators' experience of the match to an auditory and visceral (in addition to visual and cognitive) level. He presented this information, incidentally, as another of the secrets of lucha libre.

Another set of theatrical elements was presented to us as part of the development of an appropriate habitus. For example, the instruction to "run" around an opponent or around the ring meant running in a specific way: with large, loose steps, arms swinging at the sides, bent at a ninety degree angle, torso tilted forward. This particular way of running, we were told, showed that we were really luchadores, and would signal to an audience that we "knew what we were doing." Likewise, we were taught that certain ways to enter the ring—by stepping between the ropes, somersaulting or vaulting over them, crawling under them—were identified as specifically appropriate for rudos or for técnicos.

On a very few occasions, Jaramillo would explicitly remind us that we were learning to perform for an audience. Some routines had a moment built into them when we were told to turn to the audience for congratulations or curses, in order to give our opponent the chance to attack from behind. Another example was a fine point in a technique called a *japones* (Japanese throw). In the japones, one wrestler stands with his back to his opponent. The other wrestler runs at him from behind. As the second wrestler reaches him, the first wrestler turns his waist, hooks his arm under the attacker's armpit across his back, and turns his waist forward to throw wrestler number two into a salto mortal. One night, after months of practicing the technique, our teacher suddenly asked us why the thrower would turn to see the attacker (and thus be able to execute the technique). We stood silently a moment, before he answered: "Because the public yelled 'Aguas'!" (Watch out!). Likewise, if we were about to receive a plancha from the ropes, he admonished us not to anticipate the technique by raising our arms for the catch before the partner began the jump.

Jaramillo seldom gave us instruction on how to act as a técnico or rudo. A few times, we worked routines where one wrestler was supposed to pull hair or refuse to release a hold when the other wrestler touched the ropes, and so play the rudo. In general, though, learning to display oneself as a técnico or a rudo was picked up by watching more advanced students, and by watching professionals in the arenas. As advanced students became comfortable with the technical aspects of wrestling, they would add spontaneous displays of emotion. Role preference would develop over time based on a combination of body type and temperament. Jarmillo discouraged beginning students from adding theatrical elements to their practice; a beginner (or even an advanced student) who added too much mugging might be accused of playing and threatened with the weight belt. While he expected advanced students to be expressive, expressiveness was not formally taught. Instead, we were taught a set of techniques and their possible outcomes, a sense of spatial orientation (moving along diagonal axes or horizontal axes, awareness of location of the center of the ring and of the surrounding public), and sensitivity to each other's movement.

On the one hand, our training practices showed us that wrestling was choreographed. Yet part of the training process was listening to Jaramillo's preclass stories of his days as a performer, and these sometimes contra-

FIGURE 2 Luchadoras practicing an exit

dicted what we learned in the ring. He never bragged about victories—he made it quite clear that victory wasn't the point. His favorite stories were about arduous struggles: the match that he and his opponent took an hour and a half to finish, or the match in which one wrestler put his opponent in such a powerful headlock that he burst a vein in his ear and blood shot up to the ceiling. He never talked about things that would mark lucha libre as definitely choreographed (at least not in my presence). For example, he complained bitterly about the politics of promoters in general, but never about the politics of deciding who would win and who would "go down." The theatricality of wrestling was not kept secret from the trainees, but it was also seldom made explicit. It was kept *as if* secret from them.

In addition to training at the Metropolitano, I observed classes in a number of other, better-known gyms, including the Nuevo Jordan, Ham Lee, Charles Bronson, and the EMLL gym in Arena Mexico. Except for the EMLL gym, the class format diverged little from the classes at the Metropolitano. Some teachers used shorter routines than he did, and some didn't end them with a definite finishing hold. Training sessions at the EMLL gym were somewhat different. At the time of my research, the EMLL held classes for students five days a week, and trainings for their professionals twice a week or so. The official trainer, a retired wrestler called El Faisán, taught both the amateur and the professional sessions. The classes for nonprofessionals were carefully organized on the model of Diablo Velasco's school in Guadalajara. Three classes a week were devoted to conditioning, one class to amateur wrestling, and one to professional wrestling techniques. The training sessions for the professionals followed a different sequence. The first two segments were similar to any other lucha libre class—they would begin with maromas, and then work short sets together in a round robin. After working short professional routines, they would work Freestyle wrestling matches (still in round robin fashion). After the training section, pairs or trios of wrestlers would stay behind, and El Faisan would coach them on specific sets. This was the only time I saw wrestlers systematically coached on timing and expression.[9]

THE POWER OF SECRECY AND THE SECRECY OF POWER

> The secrets that we encounter in African artistic expressions . . . are not secrets in the common sense that Europeans and Americans today speak of defense secrets, of business secrets or scandalous private information . . . Instead, the secrets expressed in African arts are of two very different orders. Sometimes they are simply social conventions, *acknowledging the areas of silence and absence that create and maintain social differences and relations* . . . Sometimes they imply something nearer to mystery, to the dense, opaque, polysemous complexities of the universe which reverent people should fear and respect.
>
> BEIDELMAN 1993, EMPHASIS ADDED

The performance of professional wrestling depends on a conspiracy of secrecy. To many observers of wrestling in the United States, the secret of professional wrestling is that it is a lie: what appears to happen in the ring (a fight) is not what really happens in the ring. The difference between wrestlers, who know, spectators who don't know (or suspend disbelief), and spectators who derive pleasure from considering themselves "in on the game" (Mazer 1998: 53) seems to be of central importance to the pleasure that fans take from the sport. Now that the secret has become so open that it has ceased to be any kind of secret, the relative importance of these categories may have shifted, and the secret may no longer be important to U.S. professional wrestling at all.

The phenomenon of the secret, in Mexican lucha libre, is considerably more complex, since knowing and not knowing are never treated as absolute. The difference between those who "know" and those who do not "know" in Mexico seemed to me to be one of degree, not kind, for there are different kinds of secrets. Different people (or categories of people) are denied different degrees or types of knowledge. For example, the few times that I asked a wrestler or promoter to explain why a particular action took place in a match, I wanted to hear how it would further the long-term narrative or the immediate goals of the promoter or wrestlers. Instead, the wrestler or promoter would explain the sequence of events as they had happened in the ring, as if they had been unplanned. I was present in the EMLL offices one day when a reporter for *Box y Lucha* walked in and asked the secretary in charge of public relations if a certain wrestler would lose his mask that night. She hastily changed the subject, seemingly unwilling to talk about it in my presence (or, perhaps with the reporter). In general, wrestlers, promoters, and trainers would not mention the obvious—that the matches were prearranged—in my presence, even though, as a trainee, I had to know. Journalists who cover lucha libre, however, were happy to talk with me, and with EMLL staff, about the fixed ending. But neither the journalists nor many employees of the EMLL were allowed into the gym. The gym, they told me, was sacrosanct—no one who was not a wrestler or trainer would think of asking to enter. Yet, for some reason (possibly because I was in training myself), I was invited to enter, to watch, even to photograph practice sessions. Reporters and staff were allowed to know how the matches were programmed, who would win and who would lose, but they were not the secrets of the gym. Having been allowed into the EMLL gym and having trained at the Metropolitano, I still have a gnawing feeling that I never really learned the secrets of lucha libre, that I still don't know lucha libre. When my teacher or other wrestlers told me that they were teaching me the secrets of lucha libre, it only made me wonder: which were the *secrets*, and how would I know that I knew them? The basic techniques were called secrets, as were the tricks for engaging the audience, and the basic organization of the matches; I was explicitly let in on many of those. Yet, just because I trained as a luchadora and saw my classmates rehearsing for their matches in Oaxaca did not excuse Profe or my classmates from acting as if I didn't know that the matches were fixed. Just because I knew, and they knew that I knew, did not excuse me from acting as if I didn't. The secrets I did learn—the techniques, and the feeling —are still locked in my body. I feel no compunction about revealing them in this chapter (as I have tried to do) because I know that these secrets cannot really be communicated through text.

I would argue, however, that the importance of talk about secrets that I encountered over and over suggests that secrecy itself is a structuring feature of lucha libre. In other words, the discretion practiced around certain elements of lucha libre shows that the discourse of secrecy is not only about hiding the backstage from the audience. It is, instead central to the genre. Secrets are kept secret to generate the energy of secrecy. It is a process that reaches its apogee in the discourse of the mask (see chapter 4). The point is not to keep people ignorant, but to produce an indefinite deferral of revelation, a floating sense of indeterminacy. Lucha libre, ultimately, dramatizes the complex relationship between secrecy and power in twentieth-century Mexico.

3

OF *CHARROS* AND JAGUARS

The Moral and Social Cosmos of Lucha Libre

This chapter looks at lucha libre as a cultural performance. Wrestlers consider themselves athletes, and their activity a sport. However, they also recognize that lucha libre is also a "spectacle" and that their job is not to win or lose, but to put on a satisfying show. Professional wrestling is a ritual drama in which good and evil (or at least bad) struggle for domination—a conflict between moral actors. Yet wrestlers' identification as good or evil is complicated by two things. First, in addition to their ethical identification, wrestlers also enter the ring as fictional characters. As other observers have pointed out regarding U.S. and other Anglophone contexts, wrestling characters represent the social world. Thus, to ask what kinds of characters circulate in lucha libre is to ask what kinds of social actors are thought possible, who can have agency in the Mexican context. Second, the display of morality is itself problematic, and the moral discourse of lucha libre is surprisingly complex. Attention to the moral and social marking of wrestlers thus provides a window onto and commentary on the social and moral cosmos, on the culturally specific relationship between morality and social action in mid- and late-twentieth-century Mexico. To paraphrase Clifford Geertz (1973), lucha libre is a story that Mexicans tell themselves about themselves.

Yet, as John Emigh reminds us: "Cultures do not create performances, individuals living in complex and contested cultural circumstances do" (Emigh 1996: xix). Behind the wrestlers' masks, behind their *nombres de batalla* (noms de guerre), are flesh and blood people who, out of a range of motivations and through the concrete practices of professional wrestling, insert themselves into webs of social and institutional relationships. Lucha libre performance thus consists of three levels—the lifeworld of the wrestlers, the complex set of oppositions and alliances between socially marked characters, and the Manichean opposition between rudos and técnicos.[1]

I will address each of these levels in turn. The first section of this chapter, "Real Life," examines the recruitment and socialization of wrestlers. It looks at what kinds of people go into professional wrestling and their reasons for doing so, paying particular attention to the importance of kinship as both a trope and an organizing principle in the occupational subculture of professional wrestlers. The second section explores the range of lucha libre characters. Insofar as professional wrestling is a performance about conflict and power, the range of characters in professional wrestling says something about social agency. The range of characters in lucha libre makes a somewhat different set of statements about agency and power than are made in the U.S. version of the genre. The third section explores the discourse of morality in the ring. All wrestlers must take on a moral role when they become professionals and must communicate that role to their audience, primarily through nonverbal means. The conventional definition of good guys and bad guys, in Mexico as in the United States, is that bad guys cheat. Yet cheating or not cheating is only one indicator, and an unreliable one at that, of rudo and técnico performance. This third section looks at the performance of morality—how the relationship of rudo and técnico is mediated through movement, through the audience, through the referee, and through the structure of the genre. The three levels are analytically separable but come together in performance. Yet they are analyzable only as long as they are separated. As I will suggest in the conclusion, while each level can be analyzed, the relationship between the three levels is inherently mysterious.

Several months into my fieldwork, after I had done a number of interviews with wrestlers about their life histories, their careers, and their feelings about lucha libre, I had a conversation with a freelance reporter for *Box y Lucha*. Most wrestling reporters specialize, either in covering matches or in doing human interest interviews with the wrestlers and referees. This particular reporter specialized in the latter. As we were chatting about his work, he launched into a complaint: you could never trust wrestlers, he grumbled, especially masked wrestlers. They would lie about the most basic things. For example, he had interviewed one wrestler the month before he was scheduled to lose his mask and to have his identity made public.[2] In the interview, the wrestler said that he was from Guadalajara, and so that's what the reporter published. When he was unmasked a month later, and his true identity was announced in the wrestling press, he turned out to be from somewhere else entirely: one of the northern states like Chihuahua or Sonora.

The "truth" about professional wrestlers is not really unknowable. Wrestlers are just ordinary human beings in an unusual profession. But claiming to know the "truth" about wrestlers in "real life" can be problematic. I always assumed that wrestlers were telling me the truth about their life histories, and I still believe that they were. Still, several months after my conversation with the reporter, I had to wonder when I saw an interview by him with a wrestler who wasn't masked and who told him that she was from Chihuahua. I had interviewed the same wrestler a few months earlier, and she had told me that she was from Mexico City. I suppose she might have been born in Chihuahua and raised in Mexico City and had simply neglected to mention the Chihuahua connection to me. Maybe she meant that her family was originally from Chihuahua. Or perhaps she felt like being from Chihuahua when she spoke to him, or from the capital when she spoke to me. In short, information about the "real lives" of wrestlers (as with anyone) may say more about practices of self-representation than it does about "real life." Nevertheless, there are ways in which luchadores and luchadoras represent their profession, their career histories, their motivations, and their identities. In the section that follows, I will explore some of the recurrent themes in the discursive contruction of the wrestling life.

Bodies

One of the recurring themes in my interviews was the importance of bodies. The body is the main vehicle through which wrestlers signify. Lucha libre is inscribed in the body of the wrestler, and many wrestlers mentioned having "the body of a wrestler" as one of the key indicators of real professionalism. One may not be born with a wrestler's body, but it can be developed through training. Unlike professional wrestlers in the United States, luchadores are not expected to be physically enormous. Size, however, does matter in Mexico, albeit in more subtle ways.

Although there is a great deal of variation in body type among Mexican professional wrestlers, I was told by many in the business that it was the body *itself* that marks a wrestler as a wrestler. The ideal body, the body that I was told would make people say, "Ah, there goes a luchador," need not be tall, but should be thick and well muscled, a *cuerpo corpulente*. Wrestlers work to achieve such a body through weight training and weight gain (indeed, I noticed over the course of fieldwork that new professionals had a tendency to thicken over time, especially about the midsection). The preference for a thick physique is compromised, however, by lucha libre's distinctive acrobatic movement vocabulary, which favors quick, compact bodies. In short, there is an expectation that wrestlers display an impressive physique, but there is no expectation that their bodies seem larger than life. In the gyms and arenas, I saw many luchadores who were big for Mexican men; some luchadores are over six feet tall, and some weigh over 200 pounds. Most wrestlers, however, looked just a little taller and somewhat broader than the average man in Mexico City. Indeed, wrestlers of both sexes tend to be a little bit taller than the average member of the Mexico City wrestling audience. There is, however, a wide range of body types among luchadores, from the enormously obese Gran Markus to "mini" wrestlers, a category that includes both *enanos* (dwarves or midgets), and men who are just relatively small (around five feet tall). These wrestlers usually enter the ring as mini versions of "full-size" stars. Normally, minis only fight other minis, but full-size wrestlers of all sizes and shapes (but not all genders) wrestle each other.

The difference between the body size of most luchadoras and that of the average Mexico City woman is even less marked than it is for their male colleagues. Most luchadoras that I met were about my height (5'3")—some shorter, a few taller. Some are fat, some are thin, and most weigh between 110 and 140 pounds. The average Mexico City woman is smaller than the average luchadora, but not exceptionally so. Most of the successful luchadoras are unremarkable in appearance, with none of the improbable proportions of female professional wrestlers on U.S. television.

However, the fact that luchadores and luchadoras are, on average, slightly larger than most members of their public has particular implications in Mexico, since height is considered one important index of regional origin and racial (and class) status. Wrestling masks tend to obscure other racially linked features like hair and skin tone, but wrestlers' size, relative to most members of their audience, tends to mark them as mestizo rather than indigenous, northern or western rather than southern. Indeed, most wrestlers I interviewed said that they came from Mexico City or from greater Guadalajara.[3] Most of the rest came from states in the north— relatively few come from states with large indigenous populations like Oaxaca, Guerrero (except Acapulco), or the Yucatan Peninsula, despite heavy immigration to the capital from those regions. The few wrestlers and trainees that I met who were from Oaxaca were working or planning to work as minis.

La Familia Luchística

In the world of lucha libre, kinship is important both as a metaphor and as an organizing principle. Whenever the group of wrestlers, promoters, arena owners and employees, commissioners, and reporters are invoked as a collective, they never refer to themselves as a community but instead refer to themselves as the wrestling family: *la familia luchística*. The idea that members of the occupational subculture belong to a family (and belong to it for life) is reiterated in rituals throughout the year. Every December, the magazine *Box y Lucha* organizes the annual wrestler's ball, where they give out awards and crown a luchadora or a daughter or sister of a wrestler that year's Queen of *Box y Lucha*. For many years, every spring the Agrupacion Nacional de Luchadores Retirados, an association of retired wrestlers, would organize an excursion to a city such as Acapulco or Veracruz, where they would meet with the local retirees. The trip featured a benefit wrestling event, fought by local talent and stars from Mexico City.

The day after the 1997 event, which I attended, the veterans attended a mass and a soccer game in their honor. Afterward, they went to a lunch where the novices who had wrestled the night before declared their solidarity with the veterans and their faith that younger wrestlers would offer them the same support when they took their place. When a wrestler makes his or her professional debut, his or her opponent is known thereafter as his or her padrino or madrina (godfather/godmother). Wrestlers have also participated in religious and civic ritual processions as a corporate group. Like many other professional groups in Mexico, wrestlers have organized pilgrimages to the Basilica of Guadalupe, dressed in full wrestling regalia.[4] In the civic sphere, the EMLL used to organize its wrestlers to march in the May Day parade.[5]

The idea that wrestlers, as a corporate group, form a family resonates with the other uses of the family metaphor in Mexico. Notably, as Ilene O'Malley (1986) has argued, the rhetoric of the PRI and its precursors used the model of the patriarchal family to unite the surviving factions of the revolution into a single party, whose members were referred to as the "familia revolucionaria." In popular discourse, the power of the family is often contrasted with weakness of civil society. In a variety of situations, people remind each other that in Mexico "the only institution that works is the family." In the case of lucha libre, however, the metaphoric reference to the family intersects with the fact that many in the profession do come from families with one or more wrestlers. Many luchadores have family in the business. Some are sons, daughters, nieces, nephews, or godchildren of other wrestlers; others entered the business with a sibling or cousin.[6] I was told that most married luchadoras are married to a luchador (and my observations bore this out). There is thus a real sense in which becoming a wrestler means inserting oneself into a kin network, whether real or fictive.

Becoming a Wrestler

Most luchadores I met, however, did not come from wrestling families. Their parents might have been factory workers, peasants, construction workers, proprietors of taco stands, or in the repair trades. Their level of formal education ranged from a few years of elementary school to some postsecondary education. Most went as far as the (theoretically) mandatory eighth grade (which happens to be the average for the Federal District) or finished high school. They came from what would be characterized in Mexico as the *clase popular*, and most of them were drawn to lucha libre as a means of upward mobility or, for luchadoras, as a way of escaping family constraints.

Many wrestlers whose careers started before the 1960s discovered lucha libre by accident and pursued it because of the economic opportunity it offered them. For example, my teacher, who worked in construction in his teens to help support his natal family, was recruited in his hometown of Queretaro by an acquaintance who suggested that he try wrestling. The friend introduced him to a promoter, who found him a match. When he discovered that he could make more money in one match than he could in a week of hauling cement, he decided to find a teacher and dedicate himself to wrestling.

Irma Gonzalez, one of the first luchadoras, came from a circus family. When her father disappeared after leaving to tour the United States, her family fell on hard times. In an interview she recounted her initiation into the profession as the result of necessity and luck:

> My papa went to the U.S. and left us. The checks didn't come anymore. He was a horseback rider, and he went touring in the U.S. with an American circus, but his checks stopped coming and we didn't have any money. But then I had an opportunity when I was thirteen years old. My [female] neighbor said to me, "Have you ever tried the luchas?" I said, "Well, I don't know about that," but I wanted to say yes. They just wanted me to fill a slot, because they were short [a luchadora], and if someone doesn't show up, the people get very rude and aggressive—they'll even burn down the arena. I said, "OK, if it's OK with my mother," but by then I had already asked her permission, so I really meant, "OK, then, let's go!"
>
> The friend who invited me said to me, "I'll take care of you, nothing's going to happen to you." And when we were there, they were slapping her around and . . . take care of me?!? How the hell was she going to take care of me?!? I could have taken care of her! So I wrestled without knowing a thing, *a puro valor Mexicano* [with nothing but Mexican courage].[7] Then I saw what they paid me, and I liked the environment, the people and all that, so I said, "Let's go, this is all right!" And I started to train, and went on to wrestle, wrestle, wrestle. (Interview with author, 1997)

While many veteran wrestlers became luchadores to escape from poverty, others had different reasons. Some started as amateur wrestlers and turned to professional wrestling as a way to extend their amateur careers. One retiree told me that he became a professional wrestler to win the affections of a female wrestling fan (whom he later married). For most veterans, however, the main attraction that lucha libre held was economic security.

Economic security was a concern of those who started after the 1960s as well, but they were more likely to foreground other reasons for entering the profession. By the time they started wrestling, the wrestling movie was a well established genre, and the stars of the ring and screen were known all over Mexico. In contrast to their elders, they knew what lucha libre was before they decided to do it. For those whose involvement began during childhood as fans of the sport, becoming a wrestler meant living out a fantasy. For these wrestlers, part of their professional socialization was coming to understand that it was, in the end, a job. As Guerrero del Futuro related in an interview:

> The way I used to see lucha libre, it seemed like something magical—to see the luchadores, with their shining costumes, their physiques, their masks . . . it seemed like a kind of magic. The secrets that they knew . . . I think it's like that for people. Like something that's beyond the everyday for everyone. Now that I'm a luchador, well, I see it more as a profession to which you have to allocate a lot of your time, a lot of time in the ring. That's what it's like behind the image.

But not all younger wrestlers started out as lucha libre fans. Some, like Ciclón Ramirez, became wrestlers because it seemed like a good job, but not because they liked to watch it:

> I hadn't seen anything more of lucha libre than the films of El Santo. I didn't like to watch it—I liked to wrestle. It's still like that. These days I don't, I won't go to the lucha libre. I'll stay home watching TV or with friends. It's funny. When I went to the gym for the first time to see how much they charged, just out of curiosity, I saw Mano Negra and I asked how much Mano Negra earned. And they told me, "Gee, Mano Negra makes 5,000 [pesos] now, 10,000 tomorrow, 3,000 on Friday, later 15,000 . . ." That mathematics told me "I want to be a luchador," but I didn't *like* it.

Many first-generation wrestlers described their entry into the world of lucha libre as a rebellion against family expectations. One, Furia Del Ring, told me that he would sneak off to the gym every day, telling his grandmother that he was staying after school to work on a gardening project. He would keep a bicycle parked behind the gym so that he could make a quick exit if she showed up, and he would rub his hands with dirt after class to lend credibility to his cover story. Muñeca Oriental became a luchadora despite the opposition of her father. As she recounted in an interview in 1997, she kept her training and her early career a secret from her family:

> I would say that it was mostly chance, right? Because I didn't even know much about that sport, and it didn't interest me, but I was staying with a friend (since I was having problems with my family), and she invited me to train. I liked it a lot. . . . It's that my papa is one of those people who wants or thinks that women should stay at home, having children. Before [discovering lucha libre] I had a lot of ambitions. I wanted to be a military nurse . . . but [my father] got in my way, saying no, that careers were for men.
>
> And so I started to train in secret, and after he found out and all, I was already very involved and he couldn't make me stop. That was enough, a week of training was enough for me never to want to leave the sport. Although it's hard, really hard, and I think it's even harder for women, but I don't know . . . maybe my desire to do something different, this need that I had to not just be a housewife.

In contrast, wrestlers who have an older relative in the business rarely face opposition from their families. It is quite common for children (or nephews, nieces, or godchildren) of a successful wrestler to follow their father or mother (or uncle, aunt, or godparent) into the business. This is not unique to wrestling but stands in marked contrast to some other sports, notably boxing. Whereas relatively few sons (let alone daughters) of boxers seem to go into that profession (in Mexico), lucha libre is full of dynasties. All six of Shadito Cruz's sons fight as the six "arms" (Brazo de Plata, Brazo de Oro, Brazo Cibernetico, Brazo de Hierro, Brazo, and—inexplicably—Robin Hood). All five of Ray Mendoza's sons became wrestlers, most of whom still fight as Los Villanos.[8] Hijo del Santo is said to be the only one of El Santo's ten children to go into wrestling, but some of his nephews are wrestlers (as was his brother). Some current stars are third-generation wrestlers.

Most second-generation wrestlers and their parents told me that parents don't like to encourage their children to become wrestlers but will support them if they wish to wrestle, as long as they also finish some postsecondary education. Even Hijo del Santo is said to have a degree in communications from the private Universidad Iberamericano. Second-generation wrestlers thus have, as a group, a higher level of formal education than their first-generation colleagues. Most wrestlers keep a day job, and even those who can wrestle full-time prefer to have an additional source of income. First-generation wrestlers might work as security guards, waiters, taxi drivers, or in other relatively unskilled jobs.[9] Some veterans hold administrative positions with their empresa in addition to their performance role. Many second-generation wrestlers, however, told me that they had degrees that qualified them for white-collar occupations, such as accountant or secretary, that they could fall back on if they were no longer able or no longer wished to wrestle.

Wrestlers know that the wrestling life is hard, and their livelihoods can be precarious. A wrestler's popularity can fall from one year to the next, and the sport involves intense training, constant travel, periodic injuries, and risk of permanent injury. Although there have been many wrestlers whose careers spanned three or more decades (unthinkable for most sports), wrestling takes a toll on the body, and most wrestlers retire before they reach their fifties. Knowing this, most wrestling parents insist that their children enter the business from a more secure position than they did. On the other hand, once a child (or niece, nephew, or godchild) shows a serious interest in wrestling, senior wrestlers usually support them.

Parental concern about the rigors of the profession is sometimes mitigated by the fact that having children join the business gives them more time together. Wrestling always involves travel. For wrestlers who are able to find work but are not connected with a major empresa, most travel is local—but in Mexico City, local can mean long distances indeed. Most of these wrestlers don't own cars, and many live on the outskirts of the Federal District, so the commute from home to an arena can take as long as three hours each way. Events usually start by 8:00 and can go on until 11:30 at night. Most public transportation stops by midnight, so wrestlers always worry about how to get to the arena and home again. As one put it, "the promoters worry a lot about how you're going to get to the lucha, but not at all about how you'll get back."

For other wrestlers, especially stars, a great deal of time is spent on traveling between states or touring other countries. Travel, especially international travel, is one of the perks of the the wrestling life. From the beginning of wrestling's professionalization in Mexico, wrestlers would tour wrestling territories in the United States for months at a time.[10] By the 1950s Mexican wrestlers, both men and women, were in demand in Japan. Later, they would tour other parts of Asia and Europe.

On the one hand, the opportunity to travel is attractive to wrestlers. Many luchadores told me that they were grateful to lucha libre because without wrestling "I would never have seen Japan" or "Indonesia" or "Kuwait." But constant travel is also stressful, especially for people with families. As Apolo Dantes, a third-generation rudo, explained in an interview in 1997:

> The life of a wrestler, when you're already a star wrestler, which is when you travel most, is really hard. Very lonely, too. You spend a lot of time alone away from your family, your home, your wife, your brothers and sisters, your parents. You have to endure it to be a wrestler, to be a star. Because it's very comfortable to be a *preliminarista* [in preliminary matches], where you wrestle once a week, and then you're at home. On Sundays you go out to the arena for two or three hours, and you go back. This is one kind of wrestler, but in my case, as a star and professional, I have to travel four or five times a week. Trips of two hours, four hours, to fifteen, twenty hours, in planes, in buses, in cars. . . . Sometimes a lucha can last half an hour, but it's twelve hours to get there to wrestle, and twelve to return. So that's tiring, too. You have to be ready to travel, wrestle, and return, because the next day you have to travel again.

One effect of so much travel is that professional wrestlers often have little time with their families. If their grown children enter the profession, they can have more time and more contact with one another. Irma Aguilar's main motivation to become a wrestler was the desire to spend more time with her mother, Irma Gonzalez. She remembered her childhood as having been lonely, because her mother was often away on tour.

> I just saw that she would leave, and she would leave me with my grandmother and my aunt, sad, since I had no siblings. I was an only child. I was so sad that she would fool me by saying, "I'm just going to the store, I'll be right back." Or she would tell my aunt to "take the kid to the park," and when I got back my mother would be gone. And sometimes the tours were months long—it wasn't any "I'll

be right back." No. She would go to Germany for two months, Japan was two months, too. Or here in Mexico she'd go to Monterrey, Guadalajara, and so we didn't spend much time together.[11] When she came back, I was so happy. She brought gifts, and took me here and took me there, but then in a little while it would happen all over again. So I was always sad. That's why I always wanted to go with her. And the only way to do it, she would tell me, the only way, was if I would wrestle. Because she would go to Germany, and I would say "take me with you," but no, the only way is by wrestling, no? That way they would pay my way, and there we'd go. (Interview with author, 1997)

Aguilar's debut took place under conditions that recalled that of her mother. She began to train while her mother was away on tour and was allowed to continue when her mother returned. After a few months, when Irma Gonzalez was again on tour, she was recruited to fight a match with her mother's friend and archrival Chabela Romero.[12]

I had trained only two or three months, but I remember that Chabela Romero was looking for a luchadora, because someone had backed out [of a match]. They were short a luchadora and were going around the gyms looking for a replacement. [The trainers at the gym told Romero not to approach her, saying,] "No, that's Irma's daughter," since my mother was her enemy. But she told me that, because of a commitment she had, she was short a luchadora. Well, she used me like a rag! . . . She swept the ring with me! I was a skinny little thing and had just learned [how to wrestle]. But since the other [luchadora] hadn't lived up to her commitment . . . she backed out . . . I don't know what happened . . . they needed another, whoever it was.

When her mother debuted, she discovered that she had a knack that the other luchadoras lacked. Irma Aguilar, however, found herself wrestling the ruda that many consider the best and toughest luchadora ever to fight in Mexico. When Irma Gonzalez returned from her tour, her daughter greeted her by shouting, "Mama, I wrestled, I already wrestled!" The two of them later toured as a mother-daughter tag team.

Having family in the business makes it much easier to find work. To get the attention of a promoter, wrestlers agree, you need to have a *palanca* (lever), someone on the inside of the business willing to pull strings for you. Parents, godparents, uncles or aunts, siblings, and cousins will act as palancas for relatives who want to enter the business. But while second-generation wrestlers acknowledge that relatives eased their entry into the business, they say that is not why they wrestle. The reason they give is of another order. Every second- or third-generation wrestler I spoke with said that they wrestled because "la llevo en mi sangre" (I carry it in my blood)—a self-evident, biological need. Whatever reservations wrestling parents may have about their children following them into a tough business, they tend to agree.

First-generation wrestlers give a wider range of reasons, of stories about why and how they decided to become luchadores or luchadoras. Some emphasize economic need, others emphasize a desire for autonomy or excitement. For others, becoming a luchador means fulfilling a childhood fantasy. But even if first-generation wrestlers cannot claim that wrestling is something they already carried in their blood, it is still something that enters their blood, that claims them physically. "Your body demands it," some would tell me. "If a day passes when nobody throws me to the mat, I just don't feel right."

Trainers

For all wrestlers, whether first or second generation, the training process has become more formalized since the 1950s. Whereas forty years ago, wrestlers could muddle through their first match, in the words of Irma Gonzalez, out of "puro valor Mexicano," lucha libre training is now fairly standardized.[13] No one becomes a wrestler before going through at least three years of training and passing the licensing exam given by the Commission of Lucha Libre (at least in theory). In other words, professional wrestling has become professionalized.

Lucha libre teachers are easy to find. In Mexico City alone, I knew of fifteen gyms where professional wrestlers trained students. Like lucha libre performance, lucha libre training takes place in several different kinds of spaces. Some schools are in small gyms that are affiliated with a specific empresa. In 1996, the EMLL began to offer beginning classes in the gym facilities in Arena Mexico, in addition to training sessions for employees.[14] Others are in gyms that offer complete weight training facilities but are known primarily as centers of lucha libre (and boxing) training, where several wrestlers hold classes during the week. Other spaces, like my gym, offered basic weight-room facilities and had one or two teachers come in a few days a week to give lessons. The trainers are wrestlers—some retired, some underemployed, some fully active as professionals.

The politics and ethics of training can be fraught for wrestlers and trainers. Luis Jaramillo would communicate some of the tensions in the relationship to me in a number of ways during the course of my training. He told his students that he was well known in the 1960s and 1970s, but only outside of the capital, because he had been unwilling to join the EMLL. As a result, he was marginalized in the Mexico City wrestling community. Outside of the Federal District, he used to partner with national-level stars, but he never achieved their level of renown. He felt that his place in the history of wrestling was unrecognized, but, he would tell me, he knew that he would gain his rightful place after his death.

Every day that we trained, Jaramillo would arrive near our 7:30 starting time, and shout, "¡Chavos, arriba!" (roughly, "Let's go, guys!").[15] That was the signal for his students to gather near the entrance and greet him, then either sit and chat with him or go back to their weight routine. He made a point of inviting new students to sit and talk with him, or (when there were no new students) he would call me over for a preclass chat. Sometimes he would ask me what I thought of lucha libre and what I planned to write about it. Sometimes he would talk about his personal philosophy, his history, or his opinions of contemporary lucha libre. One thing that he communicated to me time and again was his sorrow over the disloyalty of some of his old students. He said that he didn't mind, but that he had trained many stars who never give him credit in their interviews. Instead, they would say that they trained with more famous wrestlers. Indeed, when I interviewed professionals I realized that they often neglected to mention their less famous trainers. They would name famous maestros right away, but only talked about Jaramillo or a few others if I pressed them to tell me who they *first* trained with.

Some days, Jaramillo would lecture the class on some ethical or practical aspect of lucha libre. He would advise us not to look for trouble and to give up a wallet rather than fight off a mugger, even if we could. It would, he said, be a terrible thing to be responsible for killing or crippling a fellow human being, however deserving. On the other hand, he would say, if your life is in danger, "De que lloren en tu casa y que lloren en mi casa, que lloren en tu casa" [between people weeping in your house and people weeping in my house, better they should weep in yours].[16] Other times he would talk about training. He would warn us that there were a lot of incompetent trainers out there who would teach us how to do tricks in the ring, but not how to avoid injury. If we wanted to train with another teacher, that was OK, he said, but we should tell him. And even though it would be OK, it would be unhealthy to train too often without time to recover.

But it would not have been OK, not really. Many wrestlers train with more than one teacher and at more than one gym, but never concurrently. I think that when Jaramillo advised us against overtraining, he was also expressing anxiety that his students might leave him. He had reason to be anxious—the last time I visited him (in 1999), no one showed up for class. His advanced students were training in the same gym with a young member of the AAA, a wrestler called Mastín (Mastiff). "I don't believe in witch-craft," he told me, "but there's someone here who is very envious of me."[17]

Several wrestlers told me that it was good to train with more than one teacher to learn more techniques. But learning how to wrestle is not the only thing that a wrestler needs from a trainer. For wrestlers without family connections, a teacher is one's most likely palanca, and the ability of a maestro to act as a palanca depends on his or her connections with the rest of the familia luchística. A trainer with close connections to the EMLL or the AAA or one who has worked in different empresas can ask for (or call in) favors and activate relationships to get his students into an empresa. In return, a student (if successful) contributes to the trainer's prestige, in part by identifying him or her in interviews.

In the self-representation that takes place in interviews, wrestlers like to foreground their connections to prestigious teachers. The teachers most worth claiming are those who were or are wrestling stars, with one important exception. The most famous wrestling teacher in the country was the legendary Cuauhtemoc "Diablo" Velasco, who ran a school in Guadala-jara until his death in 1999. Velasco trained with the also legendary Raul Romero in Mexico City but returned to Guadalajara in the 1960s to start a wrestling school. Some credit him with the development of the specifically Mexican style of lucha libre, with its emphasis on agility rather than brute strength (others credit the Black Shadow, Alejandro Cruz). According to several older wrestlers, Velasco was known not as a particularly good or famous wrestler, but as a talented and systematic teacher. Because of

Velasco's importance as a trainer, Guadalajara is considered a center of lucha libre training, although Mexico City is the center of lucha libre performance.

No one ever told me that they sought a particular trainer because he or she would be a good palanca (although students at the EMLL school said that they hoped that their close association with the empresa would help them get in later). Most chose their first teachers by chance: they saw an advertisement in *Box y Lucha*, a friend invited them to a class, or they joined a gym for other reasons and decided to take wrestling classes offered there. But however wrestlers find or choose a teacher, all agree that at least three to five years of continuous training with a qualified teacher is necessary to be ready to work as a wrestler. A situation like my teacher's—wrestling for an audience without any prior training—is unlikely to happen now.

For women of Irma Gonzalez's generation, regular training wasn't even an option for novices. She noted in an interview that in the early years of her career, she and her female colleagues had to pick up techniques on their own:

> Nobody in particular trained me. You went around to gyms thinking, "Let's see what he wants to teach us." "Mister, would you please show me a lock?" There wasn't anyone in particular who would train us. [They would say,] "Ay, those broads, let's see if they can do *this!*" . . . But then, when we already were in the empresa, in Arena Mexico, there's a gym upstairs, and there's a person who is contracted by the empresa, and yes, I felt proud that I could already do all of the exercises that they do before they practice the locks, and all that stuff. (Interview with author, 1997)

Apparently, formal training has changed from a form of professional development to an obligatory means of initiation since the 1950s. Normally, after a wrestler has trained for several years, his or her trainer will let him or her know that he or she is ready to take the Commission of Lucha Libre's day-long licensing exam. The exam consists of a series of physical tests: aerobic endurance, falling skills, and familiarity with basic wrestling techniques. Trainees who pass are then licensed as professionals and register their characters with the commission. Once they are licensed in the Federal District, they can work anywhere in Mexico (if they can get a job).

From that point, especially talented or well connected wrestlers might be recruited by the EMLL or another large empresa, where they will make anywhere from $3 to $100 per match, fighting anywhere from once in a while to fifteen or more matches a week. The biggest stars can negotiate better terms, including a base salary to be paid whether they wrestle or not. The rest will work for one or more promoters, cobbling together as many matches as they can for whatever they can get. The pay per match can be $5 or less. For a raw beginner, it can be a bag lunch.

WRESTLING PERFORMANCE

An important element of the transition from trainee to professional is the wrestler's assumption of a character. Although trainees plan or fantasize about their characters long before they are ready to take the exam, they do not take on a nombre de batalla until they are near the end of their training. When a wrestler passes the exam, he or she registers as a specific character. Keeping track of characters and making sure that only one wrestler plays a given character is one of the responsibilities of the commission.

Wrestling characters are constructed along two axes: costume and persona, and ethical role. Wrestlers refer to the former as their *equipo* (equipment, costume) or their *personaje* (character, in the sense of a character in a movie). A wrestler's ethical position is called his or her *papel* (role). Following local usage, I will use *character* to refer to the combination of costume, name and persona, and *role* to refer to ethical identification. Some wrestlers play only one role, but others change sides during the course of their careers. From the point of view of the audience, a wrestler's moral stance is changeable, but his or her character is fixed. A wrestler is not thought to "play" a character so much as to "be" that character. Likewise, wrestlers never say that they play a given character, but that the character is their nombre de batalla.

Wrestling Characters

When professional wrestling was brought from the United States to Mexico, certain features of the genre were already well developed. Wrestlers played the role of heel or baby face, honest or dishonest as part of the performance. By the 1920s, contests between American and foreign wrestlers became popular in the United States (Mondak 1989, Wilson 1959). As

most scholars of U.S. professional wrestling have argued, the contest between American and foreigner became as central to the genre as the contest between good guy and bad guy (see chapter 1). In addition to native
and foreign, other social categories became the basis for wrestling characters in the United States.

That aspect of professional wrestling in the United States remains un-
changed. North American wrestlers still work primarily as representations
of social types. Most U.S. wrestlers mark a specific regional, ethnic, or class
identity through combinations of surname, clothing, hairstyle, and accent.
Most characters have names that sound like regular proper names, sometimes coupled with nicknames—for example, Hulk Hogan, Goldberg, Nature Boy Rick Flair, Gorgeous George, Jesse "the Body" Ventura, or Bruno
Sanmartini. Most of the rest have names that associate them with a class
status or professional occupation—the Blacktop Bully, IRS, or the Under-
taker. Through the linguistic cues of the name and the announcer's patter,
the paralinguistic cue of accent, and the visual cues of dress, wrestlers are
marked as elements of a social universe. U.S. professional wrestling thus
plays out as a melodramatic representation of social conflict.

During the 1930s and 1940s, when professional wrestling was brought
to Mexico, some of the structural assumptions of the U.S. version were
imported with it. In the early years, most wrestlers (like their U.S. counterparts) used their own names or nicknames in the ring (such as Firpo
Seguro, Black Guzman, Kid Vanegas or Dientes [Teeth] Hernandez). But
by the end of the 1930s, the kinds of characters that circulated in Mexico
began to diverge from the U.S. model. The first important shift was the
adoption of masks as a regular feature of costuming that in turn prompted
the elaboration of the discourse about secrecy and secret identities (see
chapter 4). Gradually other kinds of names and character types became
more important in the Mexican version of the sport. Second, while themes
of nationalism and social conflict remained an important part of lucha
libre, social types came to constitute only one of many categories of wrestling character.

The transposition of U.S. nationalist discourse into Mexican wrestling
required adaptation. In the United States, the genre had come to dramatize
two of the central tensions in U.S. society: the production of national
identity in the face of widespread immigration and the perception of the

United States as the "good" society under constant threat from a malevolent (but changing) enemy.[18] Neither of those tensions is central to the problematic of Mexican national culture. This is not to say that nationalist themes were or are absent or unimportant in lucha libre, but that they appear in ways that make sense in the local context.

Two themes have been central to twentieth-century discourses of Mexican national culture. The first has been that of mestizaje, the relationship between the indigenous and Iberian aspects of Mexico's culture and population, and their relationship to themes of modernity, civilization, and urbanization.[19] The second is the complex relationship between Mexico and the United States. In the 1930s (when the genre arrived) as now, the United States stood both as a model of modernization and as an overbearing and culturally alien imperialist power. As more Mexicans participated in lucha libre, the fact that they could outperform wrestlers from the United States in a modern, cosmopolitan genre became, in and of itself, a source of nationalist pride for its fans. As one reporter wrote in 1953, "There are excellent Mexican wrestlers, and for that reason the imported wrestler has to have, essentially, a quality capable of withstanding the competition with our own. This is one of the reasons that lucha libre is popular. Not for the locks, or for its scenes of pathos, nor for its savage violence in certain aspects, but because it supports national idols" (Seyde 1953a: 73).

In addition, in line with the U.S. model, luchadores, in some cases, performed as members of social categories that are salient in the Mexican context. Some wrestlers were marked as foreign, while others alluded to symbols of Mexican national identity. Still others made reference to a regional, professional or other identity category within Mexican society. At present, perhaps one-third to one-half of the wrestling characters in Mexico could be described as representations of social categories. The rest are not. The list that follows contains a selection of wrestlers, famous and not so famous, who were active in Mexico City in 1997 (plus two or three famous wrestlers who were retired or deceased). Taken together they represent the range of characters organized according to recurrent themes.

Proper Names

Apolo Dantes; Babe Richard; Martha Villalobos; Negro Casas; Xochitl Hamada; Ringo Mendoza; Americo Rocco

Asians

Gran Hamada; Sugi Sito; Ham Lee; Octagón; Muñeca Oriental; Kung Fu

North Americans

Shocker; Chicago Express; Vampiro Canadiense; Conan; Andy Barrow; Rambo

Other Foreign

Dr. Wagner; Karloff Lagarde; Americo Rocco; El Jeke

Regional

Rayo de Jalisco; Alacrán de Durango; Hermanos Dinamita; Sardo

Indians

Mexican

Canek; Principe Maya; Angel Azteca

Northern

Lady Apache; Jefe Aguila Blanco; Mohicana

Warriors

Black Warrior; Damian el Guerrero

Gangsters, Pirates, and Killers

Al Capone; Mano Negra; Rey Bucanero; Pirata Morgan; Killer

Cavemen

Cavernario Galindo; Yoni Guenguin; Mogur

Clergy

Fray Tormenta; Seminarista

Charros

El Mariachi; Mexicano; El Loco Valentino

Misc. Professions

Médico Asesino; Bombero Infernal; Maniac Cop; Los Payasos; Torero

Exoticos

Casandra; May Flowers; Divino Exotico; White Danger

Urban Youth Cultures

Heavy Metal; Los Vatos Locos; El Cholo; Super Caló

Animals

Aguila Dorado; Halcón Negro; Pantera del Ring; Tigre Blanco; Felino; Blue Panther; Lynx; Perro Aguayo; Lobo; Mastín; Scorpion; Mosca de la Merced; Búfalo Salvaje; La Briosa; El Tiburón; Fishman; Jurásico; Mastodonte

Futuristic

Guerrero del Futuro; Cibernético; Super Astro; Brazo Cibernético; MS1

Mass Media

Supercán; Ultraman; Power Rangers; Zorro; El Fantasma

Supernatural Entities

Angel de Plata; El Santo; Blue Demon; La Parka; Alushe; Bombero Infernal;
Juventud Guerrera; Cadaver, Satánico; Arkangel de la Muerte; La Diabolica

Forces of Nature

Astro Rey Jr.; Huracán Ramirez; Tinieblas; Mr. Niebla; Sismo; Elektra; Voltron;
Atlántis

Abstractions and Mental States

La Fiera; Fantasy; Violencia; Furia del Ring; Histeria; Psicosis; Filoso;
Discovery

Masks

Máscara Sagrada; Mil Máscaras; Máscara Universo 2000

Miscellaneous

Pierroth; Alebrije; Lizmark; Picasso

Although "Mexican" exists as an unmarked category in lucha libre (that
is, any wrestler not known to be a foreigner or portraying a foreigner is
presumed to be Mexican), some luchadores are specifically marked as
Mexican and identified with some symbol of national identity. Some, for
example, appear as *charros*—stock figures from the cinema's version of the
ranch culture of Jalisco. Others allude to Mexico's indigenous heritage.
Since one formulation of Mexican nationalism identifies the nation with its
indigenous roots, and the national struggle as one that begins with resistance to the Spaniards, wrestlers who refer to the ancient Aztec or
Mayan civilizations (Canek, Principe [Prince] Maya and Angel Azteca)
index national (rather than, or in addition to regional or ethnic) culture. In
addition, because national mestizo identity is understood to be rooted in
the (subordinated) indigenous sphere, wrestlers with particularly indigenous physiognomies, such as Ray Mendoza and Ringo Mendoza, are sometimes said to embody *lo mexicano*.[20]

A number of wrestling characters are identified with particular regions.
Canek and Principe Maya, for example, represent the Yucatán (as against

Mexico) at the same time that they represent Mexico against the European or North American other. Some regional identities are made explicit by the wrestler's name and costume—for example, Rayo de Jalisco (The Lightning Bolt of Jalisco), Alacrán de Durango (The Scorpion of Durango). In addition, several wrestlers (for example, Los Hermanos Dinamita) are always announced as being from an area, and they stress their ties to that area in interviews so that their identities become rooted in a particular Mexican place. The explicitly nationalist (or regionalist) coding of some of these wrestlers is reinforced by the musical themes that accompany their entrance—Mexican genres like mariachi or *norteña*, rather than rock or merengue. Some states are more likely to be represented than others: many wrestlers enter the ring as Jaliscences, very few (if any) as Chiapanecos. The regions of the country that are associated with mestizo ranch culture are better represented than the more heavily indigenous states of the south.

Wrestlers with identities rooted in national symbols are more likely to be técnicos, but may also be rudos. During performances, the audience will usually support the foreign técnico over the Mexican rudo. During battles between a foreign rudo and a Mexican rudo, however, the audience throws its support behind the Mexican, and the arena rings with chants of "Mex—i—co! Mex—i—co!" If a foreign rudo is involved in a series of escalating encounters leading to a grudge match (in Mexico the series of events up to and including the match is called a *pique*) his (or her) enemy will likely be one with an explicitly nationalist identity.[21]

Foreigners

The category of foreigner is important in lucha libre, but less so than it has been in U.S. professional wrestling. In the U.S. context, foreigners have either represented immigrant groups, or the current enemy—Germans during the two World Wars, Russians during the Cold War, Arabs and Persians in the 1980s and 1990s. The former group has included baby faces and heels, and actual immigrants or children of immigrants. Wrestlers in the latter group are usually heels (although they sometimes "defect") and are unlikely to be played by a real German, Russian, or Persian. Lucha libre also has its share of foreigners, but their nationalities and the meanings attached to their participation are quite different. The majority fall into two categories: gringos (mostly U.S. Americans, but also Canadians) and Japanese.

There are some exceptions. Since Mexico is known as one of the three centers of professional wrestling, wrestlers from a number of other countries pass through on tour or settle permanently to work. These include wrestlers from Brazil, the Caribbean, Central and South America, and England. There are also a few Mexicans who adopt a European, Middle Eastern, or other identity (Dr. Wagner, Americo Rocco, Karloff LaGarde, El Jeke). Although El Jeke (the Sheik) indicates his "nationality" through his costume, LaGarde and Rocco indicate it solely through their names. Neither they, nor Wagner (whose only German feature besides his name is a white, Germanic eagle on his white mask) speak with foreign accents (in fact, they seldom speak at all), or act in stereotypically German, French, or Italian ways. In the case of some "foreign" characters, then, their foreignness plays little role in their performance.

But most of lucha libre's foreigners are either gringos or Japanese. Mexico, Japan, and the United States are the three centers of lucha libre, and wrestlers from each country often tour the others. Lucha libre's very origin involved a tour of Mexico by North American wrestlers, and tours of U.S. territories were important to luchadores from the beginning of the sport's Mexicanization. By the late 1950s, wrestlers from the U.S. and Mexico organized tours of Japan, and Japanese wrestlers came to tour Mexico as well. Moreover, a small number of children of Japanese (and Chinese) immigrants became luchadores in the late 1940s and early 1950s. The presence of Asian, particularly Japanese, wrestlers in Mexico has less to do with geopolitics or the construction of cultural boundaries than it does with a dynamic internal to the genre.

In addition to the wrestlers who come from Japan to work in Mexico, a number of Mexicans take on Asian personae. They mark their character's nationality through elaborate costuming and modified technique. Their costumes are modeled after martial arts uniforms, or after a combination of samurai armor and Japanese anime, and most of them incorporate kicks and stances from Asian martial arts into their movement vocabulary. Xochitl Hamada, daughter of the Japanese-Mexican wrestler Gran Hamada, is an interesting variation on the play between Mexican and Japanese identities, as her name is simultaneously foreign (Hamada) and markedly Mexican (Xochitl is a woman's name that means "flower" in Nahuatl).

Japanese and other Asian wrestling characters, whether portrayed by

FIGURE 3
Muñeca Oriental
signing autographs

Mexicans or Asians, may be either técnicos or rudos. If anything, I saw more matches in which the Asian was the técnico. Asian identity is morally coded as positive or neutral, and an Asian rudo's wickedness is not usually linked to his or her nationality. Gringos, on the other hand, are more likely to be rudos than técnicos, especially if the wrestler's identification with the United States is made very explicit. For example, two of the most hated rudos working in 1996–97 (as gauged by audience reactions to their entrances) were Andy Barrow and Rambo. Barrow is from the United States, fights with a style more typical of U.S. professional wrestling than Mexican lucha libre, and sometimes announces his evil intentions by entering the ring carrying a large American flag. Rambo, dressed in combat fatigues and introduced as "the Vietnam Vet," plays a traitorous and underhanded coward in the ring. Most Canadian or North American wrestlers who toured Mexico while I was there were positioned as rudos.

Like other foreigner characters, gringos can be played by "real" gringos or by Mexicans. In addition, there are some luchadores who grew up in the United States, but whose parents or grandparents were immigrants from Mexico.[22] These reverse immigrants can be either rudos or técnicos. One, the Mexican-American wrestler Shocker, fought in a classically Mexican style, wearing a mask, and he was accepted as a técnico. He was unmasked sometime after I left the field, however, and now works as a bleached-blond rudo. Another reverse immigrant, Chicago Express, is also a rudo, and audiences respond to him (and, interestingly, Rambo) by calling him "Pocho" (a derogatory term for Chicanos and Mexican emigrants to the United States).

Ambiguously gringo foreigners may be or may become técnicos. For example, wrestlers who play North American Indians may be rudos or técnicos. The Cuban American Conan (who worked in the United States, as well as Mexico) has changed back and forth, while his sometime partner, the Calgary-born Vampiro Canadiense, started as a rudo but later became a técnico. Yet Mexican attitudes toward the United States in general are more ambivalent than hostile. One of the ways that ambivalence is expressed in lucha libre is by the use of English nombres de batalla, by técnicos as often as by rudos. While wrestlers including Fantasy, Discovery, or Blue Demon do not explicitly align themselves with the United States, they use English to invoke diffuse notions of modernity and exoticism.

Professions and Subcultures

Also in keeping with the U.S. model, many wrestling characters are based on social identities within Mexican society. A growing number of wrestlers are identified with particular youth subcultures: rockers like Vampiro Canadiense and Heavy Metal are crowd favorites. Others identify with gang culture from the U.S. border, using names like El Cholo and Los Vatos Locos. Super Caló and Mosca (Fly) de la Merced make reference to the street culture of the Mexico City.[23] Luchadores like Sexy Boy and Latin Lover emphasize their (ambivalently) masculine sexuality, while "exoticos" (see chapter 5) wrestle in drag. Both rockers and exoticos are among the wrestlers most likely to use an English name.

A few characters are based on professions, but unless warrior, gangster, clown, and pirate count as professions, they are few. All of the "professionals" (for example, a few "doctors," a team of cops, a soldier and Bombero Infernal [Infernal Fireman]) with which I am familiar are rudos (as are most of the pirates and clowns). In addition, there are religious figures, notably Fray Tormenta, a real priest, who wrestled to raise money for his orphanage in Teotihuacan. One of lucha libre's best known and best loved figures, the wrestling priest would sometimes say Mass with his mask in place. He also trained a number of the orphans under his care (whom he would refer to as his *cachorros* [cubs]) in lucha libre. He retired in 1998, leaving his mask to one of his former charges. At least some of the time, then, like U.S. professional wrestling, lucha libre too can make sense as a ritual combat between representative social types.

Beyond the Social

But if many lucha libre characters represent social types, the rest do not. At least one half of the characters circulating in lucha libre represent possibilities for agency that go beyond the merely human and social. Most of these seem to fall into three general categories: animals, powers-that-be, and figures borrowed from the mass media.

ANIMALS

Animal identities are usually performed through name and costuming (especially masking) alone—wrestlers do not, in general, adopt a different movement vocabulary if they play an animal character. Lucha libre fauna include fish and sharks, scorpions and flies, buffalo and eagles, dogs and mastodons. Some animals, however, are more common than others. The most popular animal characters also allude to symbols of Mexican national identity. Feline characters—panthers, jaguars, tigers, lions, lynx, and cats—are especially popular and recall (directly or indirectly) Mexico's pre-Hispanic past.[24] The first feline character, Caballero Tigre (Pedro Bolanos), made explicit reference to the Aztec "tiger/jaguar knights." The same could be said of birds of prey: eagles (although they are less common in the ring than hawks) are also associated with Mexican nationalism, both as the figure on the Mexican flag (with its reference to the Aztec myth of the foundation of Tenochtitlán/Mexico City), and the Aztec order of the

FIGURE 4
Fishman stalks
around the ring at
Arena Caracol

"eagle knights." Some animals might likewise be interpreted as regional symbols—scorpions are associated with Durango, sharks with Veracruz. But others—buffalo, dogs, horses, dinosaurs—have no such associations.

THE POWERS THAT BE

The ecosystem of the ring also contains a variety of larger forces that affect human lives. Some wrestlers represent elemental forces. Fray Tormenta, for example, means Brother Storm; Mr. Niebla, Mr. Fog; Tinieblas, Darkness. Other wrestlers appear as cyclones, hurricanes, and lightning bolts. Volcanoes and earthquakes, mountains and continents, and even metals are embodied in the contest of the ring. Nor are the entities limited to the natural world. Some of the most famous wrestlers in Mexico—El Santo,

Blue Demon, La Parka (the Grim Reaper), Vampiro—entered the ring as
beings from the beyond. Skeletons and cadavers, angels and demons, Egyp-
tian mummies, and even the Mayan elf Alushe are incarnated in the arena.
There is little correlation between the type of supernatural being and the
ethical role of the wrestler. El Santo began, after all, as a rudo. Blue Demon
(El Santo's sometime rival and sometime partner) was always a técnico.
Arkangel de la Muerte (the Archangel of Death) and Satánico are rudos,
but La Parka and Vampiro Canadiense are popular técnicos.

MASS MEDIA AND MISCELLANY

In addition to social types, animals, forces of nature, and supernatural
entities, many wrestling characters come from the world of mass media.

Some, such as Supercan (Underdog), Ultraman, or Zorro are based on television shows, cartoons, or comic books. Still others are oriented toward the future, to computers or outer space (SuperAstro, Cibernético, Astro Rey Jr., Guerrero del Futuro). Finally, there are a number of wrestlers whose names and costumes refer to abstractions, substances, or emotions: Histeria, Fantasy, Discovery, or Violencia. These, along with rockers and exoticos, are among the wrestlers most likely to use English names. Neither people, animals, forces of nature, nor supernatural, they enter the ring as concepts or adjectives.

The list of categories is not exhaustive, and there are many wrestlers who do not fit into any category that I could see: the portly Brazo de Plata (the Silver Arm), who uses his girth to play the role of virtuous and sympathetic clown; the rudo Pierroth (named for the commedia dell'arte figure), Lizmark (named after a cruise ship), Alebrije (a kind of colorful painted wooden or papier-maché figure), or Picasso. In addition, many characters fall into more than one category—in lucha libre as in life, identities are multiple and fragmented. Vampiro Canadiense is supernatural, but he is also a rocker (as well as Canadian). Los Oficiales are cops, but they are dressed as U.S. cops (one of them wears an LAPD insignia) and thus foreigners (except for Maniac Cop, whose face is a skull mask, and who is thus supernatural). Bombero Infernal is also both professional and supernatural. Panther plays as an animal and as a national symbol but uses an English name.

Lucha Libre as Magical Realism

The range of character categories constitutes an important difference between professional wrestling in the United States and Mexican lucha libre. Professional wrestling, in both contexts, is a drama about conflict and domination, a model of how people have power over one another. It thus makes an implicit argument about how social action happens, and what kinds of historical agents are effective in the world. In U.S. professional wrestling, actors on the historical stage seem to be imagined as social groups; hence confrontations take place between the working stiff and the egghead or the Italian and the hillbilly. North American wrestlers embody these types through their dress and their patter, much the way that people do in quotidian social contexts.

Lucha libre, however, seems to evoke a different cosmological order: one in which social groups have agency yet are not treated as the only forces that determine the course of history or daily life. In fact, class and ethnic conflict (important themes in U.S. professional wrestling) are relatively muted in lucha libre. Like magical realist fiction, lucha libre portrays a world in which human agency is limited and supplemented by the intervention of (natural and supernatural) forces beyond human control. Masking, in this context, is a convention that allows wrestlers to represent the abstract, mythological levels of reality. Lucha libre thus portrays a worldview that recognizes that human agency is ultimately constrained by the forces of history, nature, and the world beyond.

Incarnating the Character

The presence of costumes and characters makes lucha libre performance spectacular and enables the slippage between fiction and reality that constitutes the wrestlers as larger than life figures, "gods of flesh and blood."[25] Since the interplay of characters is so important to the genre, and the identification of the wrestler with his or her character so potentially profound, one would imagine that the choice and development of a character would be of enormous concern to wrestlers. What I found in interviews, however, was that although some wrestlers identify strongly with their characters, most downplay their importance. This is partly because characters are as likely to be granted to them or imposed on them as invented by them; many are either assigned by the empresa or inherited from someone else. Moreover, since characters are often recycled, many characters are repetitions of previous generations of wrestlers.

Characters, both masked and unmasked, are passed down (although masks are passed down more often), ideally (but not always) along kin lines. In the model case, a well-known wrestler will have one child who wants to take up the character. He or she then fights as a "junior" or "hijo de," either before or after the senior wrestler's retirement. If a wrestler leaves the character to a student or friend who is not a blood relation, the character should be called II rather than junior.[26] Ideally, whenever a character is recycled, it is conferred by the original wrestler to his or her successor: parent to child, friend to friend, or teacher to student.

In other cases, wrestlers are assigned characters by the empresa or even by the Commission of Lucha Libre. They can also be assigned new characters, masked or unmasked. For example, the man who wrestled as Ciclón Ramirez in 1997 had been through several transformations since he began his career:

> I went to Guadalajara together with El Pegaso and we met with [promoter] Ricardo Morales, and he helped us to design a UFO look. We wrestled for a while like that. When I went to the [Federal District] Commission for the license, they said that as UFOs no, better as pegasuses. So I worked in the EMLL, and I lasted a while as Pegaso I. But one day the empresa had me change my name to Ciclón Ramirez. The design [of the costume] is by Antonio Peña [then director of programming], the idea [for the character] is by Paco Alonso [president of the empresa].

His experience was fairly typical. Like most working professionals, he had nothing to do with creating his current character. It was one of several that he was told to play and meant little more to him than a set of work clothes. Since he fought as a masked wrestler, the audience was (one supposes) unaware that the different characters were played by the same man.[27]

The move from trainee to licensed professional to working professional often marks a change in the wrestler's relationship to his or her character. As trainees, wrestlers invest time and imagination in the design of a character. They may also invest money in a suitable equipo. Although he or she might base it on the advice of a trainer or fellow trainees, he or she will likely invent an initial nombre de batalla (unless he or she inherits the character). Once a wrestler is hired by an empresa, however, he or she can be assigned one or more characters over the course of his or her career. Moreover, wrestlers who are not hired by one of the major empresas and have to cobble together several gigs a week sometimes use more than one character concurrently. In general, then, wrestlers' characters are seldom freely chosen alter egos born of personal idiosyncratic taste. However, they *are* likely to index a wrestler's position in a larger wrestling world. Like family names, they mark connection (whether with parents, trainers, promoters, or training buddies) rather than personality or individual inclination.

Nevertheless, there comes a stage in a wrestler's career when he or she must learn to represent a character in the ring. Once a luchador reaches the professional level, wrestling technique and physical prowess, so carefully cultivated during formal training, are not enough: it becomes just as important for the wrestler to emote and to incarnate a character even (or especially) if it has been assigned. The characters, however, are often concepts with no particular content (aside from the costume). It is up to the wrestler to fill in the content, to give the character a recognizable personality.

The transition from athlete to athlete-actor can be difficult for many wrestlers. In the early 1990s, partly in response to the new competition from the AAA (see chapter 6), the EMLL went so far as to contract a drama teacher to coach some of their more promising wrestlers. According to the drama coach, Roberto Herrera, the wrestlers face a variety of problems moving from the gym to the arena. Some are very good in the ring but freeze when confronted with a microphone. Others are good at engaging with their opponent but don't know how to engage with the audience. For many wrestlers, however, the main problem is in connecting themselves with the character that they have been contracted to play.

In those cases, part of the work is to invent some sort of background, even if it is primarily an emotional background, for the character. For example, if the wrestler's character is demonic, he has them read *The Inferno* and *Faust*. He suggested that the wrestler Mephisto claim Faust's demon as his great-great-grandfather. For another wrestler, named after a type of fighter jet, he organized an excursion to a museum to view the airplane. If the wrestler's character is supposed to be enigmatic but the wrestler has a regional accent, he works as a dialect coach. In addition, he works with the wrestlers to develop a biography for their characters to use in interviews as well as in the ring. His services, however, are only provided to a small number of wrestlers who the EMLL management has decided to cultivate (Roberto Herrera, personal communication, 2006).

Becoming a wrestler means entering a profession in which the idiom of kinship and community is constantly reiterated. Even the spectacular costumes and characters which wrestlers bring to the ring may mark their relationships to an empresa or their kin. Or they may, just as easily, imply the existence of a kinship relation where none exists. The idea that wrestlers form a community, indeed a family, with responsibilities to one another and to the greater community is reiterated from the time a wrestler passes his or her licensing exam until she or he dies. On the other hand, the trope of family is somewhat misleading, as the structure of the work itself is highly competitive, highly stratified, and has become more so since the advent of televised wrestling in the 1990s. There is a world of difference between the experiences of the biggest stars, who can decide when to work and for whom, successful wrestlers who work for a stable empresa, and freelance wrestlers who go from promoter to promoter trying to put together enough gigs to continue to wrestle.

The Moral Order

As I explained in chapter 1, luchadores see lucha libre as a sport and themselves as athletes. Nonetheless, its theatrical and spectacular elements make it a peculiar kind of sport. One way to describe the ambiguity of professional wrestling is to admit that all sport is, in some sense, drama, but professional wrestling is sport in the mode of melodrama.[28] The term *melodrama* originally described a performance that consisted of recitation to musical accompaniment (T. O. Beidelman, personal communication, July 2001). According to Jesús Martín-Barbero, however, in the eighteenth century it came to refer to a genre of nonverbal popular theater in which emotional states were conveyed through conventionalized gestures (Martín-Barbero 1987). The term has since come to refer to performance genres that present a polarized worldview in which "moral struggle is made visible, announcing itself as an indisputable force," through an externalization of internal emotions (Joyrich 1992: 232). Whereas in tragedy the narrative conflict is located within a mind of a single subject, in melodrama it is played out between clearly marked characters.[29] A form of moral discourse, melodramatic narratives usually end with the triumph of good or, at least, the punishment of evil.

The narrative structure of professional wrestling is melodramatic in form. All matches but a few are organized as encounters between good and evil. In the words of Apolo Dantes, a third-generation rudo:

> The rudo or técnico is like the bad guy and the good guy in a movie, the villain or the heroine in a *telenovela*. It's life itself. It's cops and robbers. It's the corrupt politician and the policeman who goes after him, it's the one who defrauds a bank. It's life itself. It's the relationship that we have in everything . . . the good brother and the bad brother in the same family. It happens [*pues hay*]. And it's the same in the lucha. Like when you're watching a film, and the bad guy is hitting the good guy, and you get mad and you want the good guy to defend himself. It's a form that's always existed, and it's very common in Mexico.

Lucha libre is, however, a strange kind of melodrama because although audience members may enjoy seeing good triumph and evil get its come-uppance, they cannot assume that either will happen. There is no particular pattern of victories and defeats within a single event—the rudos win some matches and the técnicos win others. Moreover, while most members of the audience support the técnicos, there are always at least a few (and sometimes many) vocal spectators who cheer on the rudos. In Arena Coliseo, there is even a bleacher section reserved for the rudo cheering section. At some arenas (at least at the matches I attended) the cheering section for the rudos can be larger (or at least louder) than the cheering section for the técnicos. Thus, although most of the public identifies with good, as embodied by the técnicos, they do not expect that everyone will agree, nor do they expect good to triumph, even in the last instance.

In contrast to character, wrestlers see the roles of rudo and técnico as crucially important to the genre. Many veteran wrestlers insist that the proliferation of elaborate characters in lucha libre is a relatively recent, historically contingent phenomenon; as I noted in the last section, the number of wrestlers who work under their own names has declined steadily since the 1940s. The same veterans, however, claim that the rudo-técnico contrast has always been a part of lucha libre. According to Eduardo Ramón Bonadas (the first Huracán Ramirez),[30] there have always been rudos, because there have always been wrestlers willing to cheat.

> Well, there have always been sneakier wrestlers, no? Ones who while you were wrestling and when the referee doesn't notice, would pull down your trunks a little, or would bite you—use some trick to beat you. Those are what are now called rudos. And the técnicos are those like I was, a *baby face*, that is, one of the mellow ones. We would play them a dirty trick, but always in response to what they had already done to us. We defended ourselves. We had to defend ourselves. (Interview with author, 1997)

But rudos are not merely "sneakier wrestlers" who like to cheat. Rudismo is a consciously chosen and carefully cultivated role that depends on the effective and creative performance of a complex set of conventions. To be a successful técnico likewise depends on much more than mere obedience to rules. The two roles, rudo and técnico, are constructed in relation to each other, but also in relation to the audience, authority, competence, and solidarity. This section will explore the different contrasts that together produce the discourse of the rudo and the técnico.

The terms themselves, *rudo* and *técnico*, do not mean *bad* or *good*, nor do they have the mocking quality of the equivalent English terms (*heel* and *baby face*). The dictionary definition of *técnico* is "a person who is qualified to realize specialized work, generally practical or in support of professional work" (Colegio de México 1996: s.v. *técnico*). In other words, a *técnico* is a skilled worker, a technician. This primary meaning refers to the técnico wrestler's reliance on the repertoire of locks and counterlocks that can be used to defeat an opponent. Thus, in contrast to the English baby face, it implies not naïveté on the part of the wrestler but skill.

However, the term *técnico* has a secondary, politically significant meaning in Mexico. Since the late 1970s, it has marked one side of two opposed tendencies within the PRI, *técnicos* (technocrats) and *politicos* (politicians). It marks a split between a politics based (in theory) on rational management, and one based on negotiation of personal loyalties.[31] Moreover, although the técnicos may be seen as a tendency within the PRI, the técnico tendency (which privileges efficiency and modernization) was important in the ideological justification for the continuation of the PRI regime, which consistently portrayed itself as a force for rational modernization (regardless of the use of tactics that could be seen as militating against such rationality). In a sense, then, support for the técnico wrestler might be read as a kind of support for the government, or at least for a vision of modernization that the Mexican state has endorsed.

Rudo also has a range of meanings. It is "that which acts brusquely, carelessly, with excessive impetuousness or certain violence; that is not polite, is discourteous, too severe or hard . . . That requires a great deal of physical force, and assumes a certain violence" (Colegio de México 1996: s.v. *rudo*). Another connotation, though, is that of an urban tough guy: someone from the city, with little formal education, but plenty of street smarts. The rudo, in this sense, is both product and master of the rough urban environment. Rudos and técnicos might thus be seen as two competing models of urban comportment, contradictory notions of what is appropriate behavior in a situation of perpetual and disorienting modernization and urbanization.

While wrestlers do not always choose their characters, they generally do

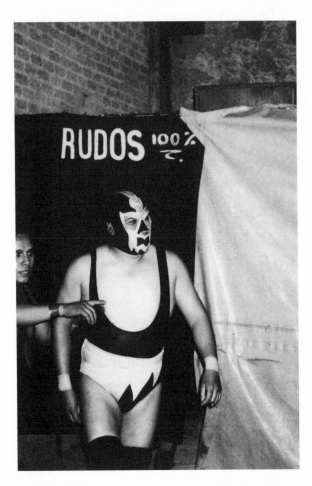

FIGURE 6
Rudo making
an entrance

choose their moral identification. During the first year or two of training, wrestlers aren't really supposed to perform a role, but a preference for one role tends to emerge in the course of the training process. Wrestlers often change roles over the course of a career; in fact, the ability to perform both roles is considered to be a mark of true professionalism. Nevertheless, the preference for one role or the other is considered something deeply linked to the wrestler's temperament. As Apolo Dantes put it, "a lot comes from your personality, what you feel you want to project to the people. In my case, I start to wrestle hard and everybody gets involved and wants to mess with me."

Thus, in contrast to character, although a teacher, friend, or promoter might advise a wrestler, no one should assign a wrestler's role.[32] A técnico is a técnico and a rudo a rudo. Each role carries its own price along with its own rewards. The técnicos are rewarded with the affection of the public, with cheers, requests for autographs, and general adulation. They pay a price, however, in that they are always supposed to respond in kind—to give autographs when requested, to be friendly and approachable, however tired they feel or inconvenient it may be.[33] The rudo's job is to make the audience angry, to court the public's abuse, and thus the rudo is under no such obligation. Many of the rudos whom I interviewed contended that theirs was the more challenging role, and more central to the structure of the genre. As the ex-rudo and referee Babe Richard recalled in an interview in 1997, "It's easier to wrestle as a técnico. The rudo has to have a way to make people become impassioned. He has the spectacle, the sport, the profession. The técnico, respecting his image . . . [he has to have] spectacularity, charisma. But I think to be rudo is harder. He carries the spectacle."

Others say that the técnico role is harder because the técnico has to know "more luchas," that is, he or she must have a wider range of locks and other techniques to draw on in the ring. Some thought that because of the technical demands of the role, it was better to start as a rudo and consider changing sides once one's skills improved. Most agreed with Guerrero del Futuro that "the salsa of lucha libre, the *sabór* [spice] is the rudo." Rudos are attracted to the role of villain because it feels more artistically satisfying.

A competent professional wrestler must communicate a moral position to his or her audience, and (because of the structure of the performance) he or she must do so primarily through nonverbal means. This section examines the performance of moral difference in lucha libre. How does one tell a técnico from a rudo? On the most obvious and explicit level, the difference between them is that the técnico "follows what are supposed to be, and what are perceived by the audience, as the rules" and the rudo is "the wrestler who breaks these supposed rules in order to gain what the audience should consider an unfair advantage" (Birrell and Turowetz 1984: 276). In fact, the difference between the two roles is actually constructed at a number of levels. But it begins with movement vocabulary: different ways to enter the ring, different preferred techniques, and different orientations of their bodies in the space of the arena.

Movement and Morality

The técnico role is characterized by grace. Like a matador, he or she has to *moverse bonito* (move prettily, nicely). The role demands a high degree of

FIGURE 7 A *salto mortal* from the ropes misses its mark

acrobatic skill, as the técnico spends more time on the ropes or in the air than does the rudo. Técnicos should enter the ring by vaulting or somersaulting over the cords instead of just stepping over or between them. They should wear their opponents down through graceful aerial maneuvers and pin them with cleverly constructed submission holds—perhaps with a signature lock like El Santo's *de a caballo* (horseback), or the priest Fray Tormenta's *el confesor*.

The rudo, on the other hand, is more earthbound and makes greater use of brute force—hitting, lifting, and dropping an opponent, or using simple pins set up through earlier damaging moves. In addition, the rudo is expected to show more emotion—anger, fear, cowardice, or pride. In the words of the ruda La Briosa, "the técnico trains more, spends more time at the gym. Rudos are more free, we let ourselves be driven more by temperament" (quoted in Pacheco 1990: 319).

One of the most challenging parts of the rudo's job is to learn to do things badly, for as the retired técnico Shadito Cruz explained in an interview in 1997:

> When [the rudos] take their place [in the ring], they can't do it nicely. Things have to come out wrong so the people see who is going to be the rudo and who is going to be the técnico. They yell, they make faces until the people see who's

going to be the rudo and who's going to be the *limpio*.[34] The limpio tries to do everything well and prettily so that people will applaud him. And the rudo has to do things badly, with insults so that the people hate him.

One aspect of the técnico/rudo difference, then, is the contrast between skill and brutality. It is not a defining contrast, however, since there can be a number of different ways for a wrestler to display him or herself as a técnico or as a rudo. Although técnicos are expected to be graceful and rudos brutish, there are elegant, skilled rudos, and earthbound, clownish, or violent técnicos.

Wrestlers and the Public

In the last match, between Solar I and Mr. Niebla vs Karloff Lagarde and Mano Negra. Lagarde ran out of the ring, almost crashing into me. He ran to the southwest corner, and sat in one of the empty chairs, while an old couple on the west side taunted him. Finally he rose, and strode up to them, telling them to "shut up." Solar ran to chase him away shouting "Leave them alone, they are our public. They are decent folk (*son gente decente*) like me. You will have to respect them!"

FIELD NOTES, APRIL 1997

Beyond the technical aspects of performance, one of the most important signs of moral identification is the interaction between the wrestler and the public. The audience should identify with the técnico, and the técnico should identify with the audience, thus the técnico's job is to engage their sympathies. Even if provoked, a técnico cannot, must not respond to the audience with hostility. Rudos, on the contrary, do. Their job is to anger the audience and to provoke their hostility: they tell hecklers to shut up, they exchange insults with old women at ringside, and they display physical aggression toward the audience.

Wrestling matches do not take place exclusively within the ring. Wrestlers get thrown from, jump from, or leave the ring during the course of most matches. In some of the larger arenas, especially those used by the AAA, a barrier separates the area immediately surrounding the ring from the front row seats, but that is not the case in most arenas. From Arena Mexico to three-hundred-seat locales in the outskirts of the Federal District, wrestlers are often thrown from the ring directly into the front row.

Spectators usually recognize the setup, get up, make a quick dash to the side before the wrestler lands, and then regroup as soon as it is safe to do so.

Whenever the action leaves the ring, rudos and técnicos interact directly with the audience. The técnicos usually avoid actually falling on top of the fans, and the fans (unless they are pro-rudo) assist them in getting back up, pat them on the shoulder, or shout words of encouragement. When técnicos move around the arena, they stick to the aisles. The rudos, on the other hand, violate the boundaries between the wrestlers and the audience. They crash into the front row and knock it over, or land and sit in one of the vacated seats. A rudo might walk to the back of the arena by stepping from armrest to armrest of the occupied chairs. In the most extreme cases, the rudo may physically attack a spectator.[35]

I witnessed one such incident at an event in a tiny arena northwest of the Federal District that I attended with two wrestlers (a rudo and a técnica) and their five-year-old daughter. During the last match, a slight fellow with a neatly trimmed beard, looking like a lower-level office worker on his day off, became especially worked up. He jumped to his feet as soon as the rudos entered the ring and began to scream insults at them. He didn't say anything unusually offensive (calling them thugs, and shouting "no puedes"—you can't do it—and "you're worthless," giving them the horns), but he did so with unusual intensity, shouting and gesticulating while a woman I supposed to be his wife sat calmly next to him. Finally, one of the rudos, Fishman, threw one of his opponents directly into the heckler, knocking him over (along with a number of chairs whose occupants, anticipating trouble, had already moved aside). The little man jumped back up and went right back to his shouting, now mocking Fishman for how little damage he had done.

Afterward, when I discussed the match with the two wrestlers, they both strongly condemned Fishman's actions. As the técnica pointed out, "people like that support the spectacle. They're good for [the rudos] as well as for us." Her husband, the rudo, maintained that rudos who pick fights in the audience are unprofessional. "It is a rudo's job to anger the audience, but it should be done through his treatment of the técnico. He shouldn't have gotten angry at the man." I asked if he was really angry, if it hadn't been part of the show, but they insisted that he had been angry and out of control.

FIGURE 8
Lucha libre fan,
just before being
knocked over by
Fishman

Cases of direct aggression against the audience are thus a gray area in rudo performance. Rudos are supposed to display disrespect toward the audience, but to keep the display within certain bounds. They aren't necessarily supposed to feel disrespect toward the audience.[36]

Authority and Legitimation

The way the técnico and rudo roles are most often defined (by commentators, analysts, and spectators) is that the rudo cheats and disrespects authority, and the técnico respects authority even when its representatives are flawed. As one audience member explained, when asked why the rudos were entering the ring when the referee had told them not to: "They're rudos, they respect nothing." Técnicos, in contrast, respect authority. But while that may represent a general pattern, it does not actually constitute a rule. Rudos play by the rules at least some of the time, and técnicos may break the rules without compromising their status or the audience's identification with them.

Authority in lucha libre is personified by the referee. Like wrestlers, referees are a fundamental part of the performance. Also like the wrestlers, different referees have different styles and different moral postures. Some, like Güero Rangel of the EMLL, are known as "honest" referees, who calmly enforce the rules against rudos and técnicos alike. Others, like El Tirantes of the AAA, openly favor the rudos and help them to cheat. Authority is thus portrayed as only partly reliable, only sometimes legitimate. In addition, even neutral referees "allow" the rudos a latitude that they do not allow the técnicos, since breaking the rules is in the nature of their role.

Most referees are former wrestlers. When age or chronic injury make performance too painful, tiring or dangerous, some wrestlers become referees to be able to stay in the wrestling world. Sometimes the transition is planned long in advance. A wrestler asks the empresa he works for to switch him over and then may take several months to work on a transition from one role to the other. Others find themselves called upon when another referee fails to show up at a match (like many of the veteran wrestlers were called upon to wrestle) and are subsequently offered the position by the empresa. Like wrestlers, referees must be licensed as such by the Commission of Lucha Libre, but unlike wrestlers, none of the referees that I interviewed had formal training in their new role before they took their licenses. In the words of Rafael Maya:

> As a wrestler, I saw the referee as the one who says what we could or couldn't do. When I got up to referee for the first time, I put that into practice. I don't know if I did it well or not, but the commissioner told me that I did it well. So to do what I did, by the regulation book that we had fifteen, seventeen years ago . . . there were not so much rules as norms. So I did know about that, and that's what I put into practice. Eye gouges, strangulation, when someone touches the cords, that no one should attack me or the public, I put it into practice and it worked. (Interview with author, 1997)

Enforcement of the rules is only one part of the referee's role. Given the nature of Lucha Libre, it is the part of his or her role that carries the *least* "real" authority, since a degree of rule breaking is already scripted into the performance. There are, however, two more aspects of the referee's role in which his authority is taken seriously by the wrestlers. First, the referee's most important responsibility is to stop the match if a wrestler is really injured. Since acrobacy has become an increasingly important part of lucha libre over the past two decades, the chances that a serious injury could occur have increased as well.[37] A good referee should be able to tell if a wrestler is injured, even if the wrestler doesn't feel it. A referee also has to know what a bad fall looks like and to be able to tell the difference between performance and injury.[38]

But the other part of the referee's role is to judge the public's response to a match and let the wrestlers know if they need to change their rhythm. Rafael Maya again:

> When they're wrestling, for example, and one of the wrestlers is in a painful hold, and you're here, and you see the public's not with them, you have to say to them, "C'mon guys, pick it up, let's have some action. The public is bored, they want more movement." And then if they don't do it, well, that's their problem afterward, if they don't call attention to themselves, they aren't delivering what they can really do. So it's one of the many tasks of the referee, [to see to it] that they give a good lucha. More than anything else, that's the base: a good lucha, a good spectacle. That they both demonstrate what they learned in the gym of the art of self-defense, of submission holds, of locks and counters, apart from their spectacular aerial moves, et cetera, depending on the situation. But even so, if you see they're doing badly, you have to activate both, tell them, "Action, guys, let's go!" (Interview with author, 1997)

The idea that the referee represents authority is taken seriously, at least by the Commission of Lucha Libre and some in the wrestling family. Like respect for the audience, respect for the physical integrity of the referee was one of the three fundamental rules of lucha libre propounded by Rafael Barradas in 1953. During his tenure, no one was exempt from respecting the rule—not even the referees themselves. On the other hand, the referee is responsible for making sure that the wrestlers give the public an interesting spectacle. As illustrated by a story that Rafael Barradas recounted to me in an interview in 1996, the two obligations are sometimes in contradiction.[39]

> When the wrestler El Santo was approaching the end of his career, many of his colleagues went to great lengths to hide the fact that his strength was fading—

that he was just a mortal being. Barradas recounts that at one event in the Arena Bravo, he saw El Santo give the referee, Ray Hernandez, what at first looked like a casual brush. The referee flew out of the ring and landed in the front row seats.

I was horrified. El Santo did what you just don't do! So the commissioner, Dr. Reynaldo Garcías, said to me, "Mr. Barradas, I know what to do. I suspended El Santo, I've pulled him out of the arenas." I said, that's right, El Profesor is going to be suspended for such and such time. Why? Because he didn't respect the referee.

Soon after, the referee came to see me, and he said "Mr. Barradas, please don't suspend El Profe." (Because we all called El Santo "professor.")

"Why not?"

"Because I wanted to help him. Seeing as he can't wrestle very well, he doesn't have much energy, I threw myself out of the ring as if I were a wrestler, as if I had been touched by a hurricane. But I left on my own power."

So I said, "Do you think you helped El Profesor with that kind of thing? You made me suspend him. So you're suspended, too—for double his time!"

The ethical position of the referee, particularly in relation to the public, is contradictory. On the one hand, the battle between good and evil, honesty and mendaciousness, decency and indecency, is mediated by the referee. To some degree, both the public and the referees understand that the referee represents the authority of the commission and, indeed, the idea of legitimate authority itself. However, since part of the rudo's role is to cheat, part of the referee's role is to tolerate the rudo's contempt for his authority or to fail to see the rudo's underhanded actions. The public responds to the figure of the referee in two ways: Members of the audience, especially those at ringside, often "assist" the referee in making calls. When a rudo pretends to have been fouled, fans surrounding the ring wave their forefingers in the air and cry out, "No es cierto" (It's not true). When a rudo fouls a técnico, the arena rings with howls of "fauuuul!" Longtime fans will even approach the ring and explain a complicated or ambiguous series of events directly to the referee.

Referees, like wrestlers, are divided into good guys and bad guys, although (in general) the division is less formalized or official than that between wrestlers. Also, although there are referees who openly side with the rudos, most do not. In fact, the referees that I interviewed viewed pro-rudo referees as irresponsible and unprofessional, calling too much attention to themselves and undermining the spectacle as a whole. But even evenhanded referees must sometimes fail to punish rudos for their misdeeds. The attitude of the public is thus contradictory. On the one hand, they act as if they expected the referee to enforce the rules fairly and are willing to assist him in doing so. On the other hand, even if they don't openly favor the rudos, referees must fail to uphold the rules and allow the rudos to exploit them. The insults directed at referees, notably "puto" (fag, rent boy) and "vendido" (sellout), signal their role as embodiment of corrupt or ineffectual authority. Moreover, all referees, even those who cultivate a persona of honesty and authority (like the EMLL's Güero Rangel), will be vilified by the public whenever the rudos are winning.

Yet the referees I interviewed insisted that they were evenhanded in the ring, and the commission, through its prohibition against attacking the referee, positions them as legitimate authorities. Referees who were rudos when they were wrestlers often make an effort to change their image in order to fit the role of authority figure. Some switch to the técnico role during the year before their retirement, while others simply change their behavior with the change in status.

The change from rudo to referee is not always easy, as Estela Molina, the first female referee reveals. Molina performs as a strict and commanding authority figure, but for twenty-five years she wrestled as a ruda. In an interview with a reporter from *Box y Lucha* (1997a: 20), she complained that in taking on the role of the referee, she gained little in public sympathy but lost her ruda prerogative to answer back:

> People are very offensive, they shout at us and are aggressive toward us. I find myself dealing with every person and they have opinions about everything that it's better not to think about. And I feel very bad, because as a luchadora, well, then I answered back and defended myself because it was part of my role as a ruda. But now, I have to hear them and keep quiet. I'd like to answer, but I remember that I'm a referee and I have to control my impulses.

Moreover, in some cases the transition from rudo to authority figure may never be completed. For example, one referee, Babe Richard, switched to the técnico side during the six months before his retirement from wrestling. As a referee, however, he acts both inept and corrupt. Rudos and técnicos alike make a great show of ignoring his instructions and defying his authority, while he makes a great show of blindness and credulity whenever the rudos cheat. The odd thing about referees, then, is that they figure simultaneously as representatives of legitimate authority and as the foci of the public's outrage over corruption. The figure of the referee simultaneously upholds and undermines the idea of legitimate authority in general.

Despite the prohibition against it, it is not unusual for rudos to attack the referee during or after a match. Like the rules against insulting the audience or fighting outside of the ring, it is a rule more often honored in the breach. When rudos attack the referee, it is usually an overt, intentional act of aggression. They might grab him by the legs and drag him around the ring, chase him or kick him. Sometimes a rudo will mock the referee's authority by holding a pin to the count of two, then releasing it with the boast, "It's not over until I say so." Yet referees are not safe from técnicos either. Técnicos are sneakier in their attacks on the referee. For example, a referee might stand behind a técnico, just as a rudo, standing atop the corner ropes, is ready to jump onto him or her. When the rudo jumps, the técnico shifts out of the way so that the rudo lands on the referee (who, as soon as he can get up, angrily disqualifies the rudo). In another scenario, several rudos gang up on one técnico. As each rudo rushes at the técnico, he throws them. Finally, the técnico, apparently caught up in the series of rapid-fire throws, "accidentally" grabs and throws the referee as well.

While rudos and técnicos differ in the kinds of attacks they use against referees, they usually attack the same referees: ones who openly or covertly favor (or are unable to control) the rudos. Attacks by rudos thus read as punishments meted out to an unreliable ally, or an ally whose loyalties are divided between the rudos and the rules. The técnicos, on the other hand, snipe at a referee who refuses to live up to his or her responsibilities as the embodiment of legitimate authority.

But as with movement vocabulary, attitudes toward authority and fairness do not define the técnico role. In fact, técnicos engage in a wide range of rule-breaking or -bending activities. Some violations are explicable as acts of righteous rage, as when they attack the rudos before the match is officially announced or try to rip off an opponent's mask. The audience cheers such acts as understandable reactions to previous provocations. Yet even in cases of clear, shameless fraud, fan loyalties do not change, and técnicos continue to be técnicos, as the following example illustrates.

Pista Arena Revolucion, April 3, third fall of second match. Mano Negra Jr. and La Flecha (técnicos) vs. Tigre Cota and Rencor Latino (rudos). Tigre Cota and Mano Negra Jr. are tagged in by their partners. Each runs to the ropes and bounces off the cords, but they slam into each other on the rebound, and knock each other out. Both are lying on the canvas, dazed. La Flecha tries to enter the ring, but the referee signals for him to stay put. He instantly obeys. Rencor Latino, meanwhile, has entered and is moving toward the fallen wrestlers when the referee catches him and begins to reprimand him. He argues with the referee, starts to leave, then moves to enter again, and the referee scolds him some more. As the rudo is arguing with the referee, La Flecha slips back into the ring. He rolls Mano Negra Jr. onto his stomach and places him on top of Tigre Cota. Then he quietly leaves the ring and, once outside, calls to the referee who turns, sees the semiconscious técnico on top of the semiconscious rudo, and counts the pin. The audience, having witnessed this blatant display of underhandedness, cheers happily. (Field notes, May 1997)

When La Flecha slipped into the ring, he did not act out of rage or passion (as técnicos are allowed to do). The referee was not favoring his rudo opponent. He simply and blatantly took advantage of the fact that the referee's back was turned, and he cheated. Yet the response of the audience was to cheer him as a técnico—in other words, it did not not undermine his status as a good guy. Clearly, respect for abstract ideals of fairness and justice, while part of the técnico toolkit, is not an absolute requirement for the role.

Solidarity

There is, however, one more crucial difference between rudos and técnicos. Unlike técnicos, rudos cannot reliably coordinate their actions. When they fight in teams, all kinds of blows miss their mark and fall on an ally. For example, there is a standard team attack, where two (or more) wrestlers put each of their opponents in a headlock and then rush toward each other to ram their heads together. Very often, if two rudos attempt to execute the move, the técnicos slip out of the lock at the last second and the rudos crash into each other. If the roles are reversed, and the rudos escape, the técnicos recognize each other and stop short. In another trope, a rudo stands outside of the ring, casually locking an enemy's elbow against the ropes as he faces the audience. The rudo doesn't notice when the técnico escapes and substitutes the arm of another opponent. The rudo will continue to apply the painful armlock, oblivious of the victim's identity. When the rudos recognize each other, when they see they have hurt (or been hurt by) an ally by mistake, they lash out at each other. Técnicos, in contrast, recognize each other and stop in midaction if they are about to hurt a teammate. If they crash into each other by accident or through rudo manipulation, they apologize, hug or slap one another on the back, and return to the fray. They assist each other, avenge each other, protect each other. The hallmark of the técnico, then, is solidarity.

In the United States, the roles of baby face and heel are normally left implicit, and the only way for a casual observer to know who is the good guy and who is the bad guy is through their actions and gestures during the match, and by the commentator's and audience's response to those actions. Serious fans know which is which because they know each wrestler's history, but it is possible for a native English speaker who is indifferent to wrestling to watch a match and never realize that the moral coding is going on at all. In Mexico, in contrast, wrestlers explicitly belong to one of two "bands," the *banda de los rudos* or the *banda de los técnicos*.

The space of the ring itself (and by extension, the arena) is morally coded—there is a técnico corner and a rudo corner. When the wrestlers enter the ring, the rudo(s) should enter first, followed by the técnico(s), and then by the referee(s).[40] The wrestlers go to their respective corners, and the referee follows them with a ritual pat-down of their costumes (ostensibly to make sure they are not concealing a weapon). The announcer then climbs into the ring and introduces the combatants. The introduction invariably starts with "In the corneeer of the rrrrrudos . . ." and "in the corneeeer of the teeecnicos . . ." respectively. There is no pretense that their divergent behaviors are the product of casual individual idiosyncrasy. Both teams act out of loyalty to a more globally defined side, and their affiliation is announced at the beginning of every match. Thus, while behavior toward the public and the referee and differences in technique are important in producing a contrast between técnicos and rudos, the distinction itself is grounded in allegiance. Técnicos are técnicos because they are on the técnico side. Rudos, likewise, should be loyal to the rudo side, even though treachery is one of their characteristics. Although the técnico represents good, there is no expectation that virtue will ultimately vanquish evil.

Lucha libre presents good and evil, not as mutual exclusions, but as mutual necessities (Rapport 1997: 90)—less like the difference between God and the devil than between two antagonistic moieties.

Since moral identification is displayed as a public matter, changes in ethical identification not only need to be narratively explained (as they are in U.S. wrestling) but also have to be ratified officially when the wrestler in question enters the other side's corner to be introduced (in a subsequent match). This is important, because even though the choice of roles is believed (by wrestlers) to emerge out of an inner "truth," wrestlers do change sides. Indeed, some wrestlers say that the ability to fight well in either role is the mark of a true professional. Although an unsuccessful wrestler might change roles without much fanfare to see if his or her luck changes, for more successful wrestlers, changes in ethical identification (unlike changes of character) are usually public events, and subjects of narrative justification.

If a rudo is supposed to change to a técnico, the shift often begins when the rudo takes advantage of an unexpected opportunity to fight on the técnico side, for example, intervening when other rudos go "too far" in attacking a técnico. Other times, an especially popular rudo (like Perro Aguayo, Vampiro Canadiense, or El Santo himself) will simply switch in response to popular demand (or at least a promoter's perception of popular demand). El Santo accomplished the transition in one night by appearing in the Arena with an image of the Virgin of Guadalupe on his silver cape (Roberto Herrera, personal communication, 2005).

Rudo-to-técnico transitions are narratives of salvation or recuperation. The rewards of becoming an admired técnico are self-evidently attractive. Técnico transitions to rudismo, however, are narratives of corruption and need to be carefully justified. It is in these dramas that the relationship between the three levels of performance—real life, character, and role— are drawn into sharp relief. The character must be made immoral through the commission of unmistakably immoral acts. Yet behind the character's transformation lie the motivations of the actual wrestler, motivations that situate the character's actions and may resignify them as moral within a broader context. However, as the story that follows will illustrate, the relationship between "reality" and "performance" is more fluid and ambiguous than it may initially appear.

When I first started following matches in Mexico City, one particular rudo stood out—a stocky man in a white mask with white German eagle insignia on one cheek, white trunks, and white boots. The classical minimalism of his costume coupled with an exquisite sense of timing and gesture made Dr. Wagner Jr. one of my two favorite bad guys. I liked Apolo Dantes for his snide humor and charm, but I liked Dr. Wagner Jr. for his charisma and understated menace. His father, Dr. Wagner Sr., was a rudo of my teacher's generation, long retired. Since Dr. Wagner Jr. still wore the mask first worn by his father, his full name was a secret, even though his background was known. He had once been part of a trio, along with Hijo de Gladiador and Gran Markus, called the Ola Blanca (the White Wave—all three wrestlers dressed in white), but in 1996 he worked solo or with different partners at different matches.

In late 1996, a wrestler called Silver King also appeared frequently in the EMLL arenas. Compact and muscular, with a Roman nose and wiry black hair, he struck me as a competent (if unspectacular) técnico. His costume was even less elaborate than Dr. Wagner Jr.'s: boots and trunks, nothing more. The color of his costume changed from show to show. He had once been a member of a trio called Los Cowboys that had fought against La Ola Blanca for the 1994 World Championship Trios belt of the Consejo Mundial de Lucha Libre.

On January 12, 1997, Silver King participated in a *batalla campal* between twenty-two wrestlers that I watched at Arena Coliseo. The wrestlers eliminated each other one by one and then returned to fight as trios in the order in which they were eliminated. Of the last twelve, seven were rudos and five were técnicos, so in the penultimate match the young rudo Astro Rey Jr. fought on the técnico side. Although the rudos on the other side accused him of betrayal and threatened revenge, Astro Rey fought well as a técnico. He officially switched sides afterward and was announced as a técnico at the beginning of his match a week later.

From the beginning of the batalla campal, however, it was clear that the central drama turned on Silver King. During the batalla campal he avoided elimination by staying outside of the ring, ignoring shouts from his fans of "Get in there, Silver King!" He returned for the final match as the captain of

FIGURE 9 Dr. Wagner

the técnico team, which consisted of himself, Mano Negro Jr. and Super Astro, facing Scorpio Jr., Black Warrior and Bestia Salvaje. According to the rules of the match, a side could win a fall by pinning the captain or both of his teammates. As the wrestlers took their places, a cheering match started in the audience, some shouting "Silver King, técnico!" and others "Silver King, rudo!" It was clear from the public's reaction that Silver King had acted in morally ambiguous ways in previous matches, and that everyone knew that his loyalties were no longer clearly with the técnico side.

During this match, his actions were far from ambiguous. When Super Astro, abject, tagged his hand, he refused to enter the ring, despite more shouts of "Get in there, Silver!" from the crowd. After tagging the unresponsive Silver King repeatedly, Super Astro tried to tag in Mano Negra Jr.

instead, but the referee wouldn't allow him to enter (since Silver King had already been tagged). At one point, Silver King even held Super Astro's arms while the rudos hit him. Then the two of them argued, gesturing broadly—Super Astro pantomiming accusations, and Silver King pantomiming denial. Super Astro finally gestured for him to leave, shouting, "We don't need you!"

As the actions of Silver King became more outrageous, more and more of the audience left their seats, trying to approach the ring to cheer the other técnicos or reproach him. They were held back or led away by security guards and other arena employees. Finally, during the last round, Silver King climbed over the ropes, ran to the rudos' corner, and did a sudden pratfall in front of Black Warrior. He lay there thrusting his legs in the air, waiting to be pinned. Black Warrior complied, ending the match in favor of the rudos. The public was exhilarated with outrage, whistling and shouting obscenities toward the ring. The security guards, who had moved in from the back during the last round, surrounded the ring to keep the crowd away.

For the next few weeks, Silver King was in a liminal state, officially a técnico, but acting in favor of his rudo opponents. They, on the other hand, would not accept him as one of their own. Some matches would end with all of the other wrestlers ganging up on him. If the job of the rudo is to generate emotion, to anger the crowd, he was succeeding wonderfully. Still, I wondered why he wanted to exchange the public's admiration for their contempt. Even if it was simply a decision on the part of the EMLL management, why turn Silver King into a rudo? Then, one day, as I was leafing through a back issue of Box y Lucha (1996b: 12), I found an explanation. According to the reporter, since early that autumn, the EMLL programmers and Dr. Wagner Sr. had been trying to work out a way for Silver King to team up with his *brother*, Dr. Wagner Jr. The only obstacle was that they were on different sides. One would have to change.

That made sense of Silver King's transformation, for the image of brothers hitting brothers is considered troubling in lucha libre. As one of the Hermanos Dinamita told me (explaining why he became a rudo after his older brother switched sides), "Es desagradable pegarle a tu sangre" [it is unpleasant to hit your own flesh and blood]. It is regarded as distasteful, inappropriate, even corrupt for family members to confront each other in the ring. Masked wrestlers have been known to refuse matches by claiming to be brothers. Some consider allowing masked siblings to wrestle each other (where the audience does not know their relationship) to be a form of corruption. As one reporter editorialized that year:

> I don't know if there is an agreement between promoters to have brothers face off against brothers, but this sickness . . . is provoking a certain doubt among the fans about what their rights are. I once cried out that these confrontations damaged not only the families of these contenders, but also the example that they give on television to the children. Nobody listened to me. And if the Commission of Lucha Libre of the Federal District, which knows perfectly well the names of the [masked] luchadores and their origin, doesn't put a stop to those bad examples, its credibility, I insist, will be at risk. I don't have the least idea what the reason is for this idiocy that degrades the spectacle, but neither do I understand the complicity of the commission in failing to put a stop to it. (*Box y Lucha* 1997a: 22)

In this context, Silver King's conversion took on another meaning (at least for regular readers of *Box y Lucha*). The narrative of disorder, in which he turned on his friends and offered himself up to his enemies, was staged in order to restore order in the real world. The discourse of treachery hid a deeper discourse about the transcendent power of kinship in the familia luchística. Sure enough, within a couple of weeks, Silver King and Dr. Wagner Jr. joined together as a tag team. About a month later, they challenged Apolo Dantes and Satánico for the middleweight title and won. Silver King put on white briefs and boots to match his brother, and for a while the two of them teamed up with Gran Markus to form a new Ola Blanca.

Epilogue

A few months after Silver King's incorporation into the rudo band, I was chatting with Jaramillo, who was grouching about his disloyal alumni again. To my surprise, one of the wrestlers he mentioned was "the guy who goes around as Dr. Wagner Jr." He was, he said, an old student of his who paid off the original Dr. Wagner and his wife for rights to the character. If my teacher was right, he was not Dr. Wagner Sr.'s son at all. Were he and Silver King brothers? Is Silver King Dr. Wagner Sr.'s son? I don't know. I thought that the drama of Silver King's turn, his betrayal, had been a fiction staged in order to exemplify the higher value of family unity in the backstage, "real" world. But if my teacher was right, then the genealogy that underlay the drama was yet another fiction. The virtue that was enabled by the fiction of corruption was, in fact, another fiction—this one made possible by the mask of Dr. Wagner.

Old or young, creole or mestizo, general or laborer or lawyer, the Mexican seems to me to be a person who shuts himself away to protect himself. His face is a mask and so is his smile.

OCTAVIO PAZ, *THE LABYRINTH OF SOLITUDE*

4

THE WRESTLING MASK

On February 3, 1984, El Santo, the most popular wrestler in the history of the sport in Mexico, was interviewed on national television by the "Walter Cronkite of Mexico," Jacobo Zabludovsky.[1] He was invited, along with his long-time colleagues Wolf Ruvinski, "Mocho" Cota, and Blue Demon, to discuss the eternal question of the nature of lucha libre performance: whether it was a "sport" or merely "circus, tumbling and theater." The sixty-three-year-old wrestler had retired a year before, ending a career that spanned four decades as a pop-culture hero, and had been working occasionally as an escape artist, against his doctor's advice. He had starred in fifty-six movies, won more championships, and captured more masks than any wrestler before or since, but he never exposed his own face to the world until the prerecorded interview was broadcast that night.

That night, in front of what must have been millions of viewers, El Santo removed his mask. For the first time since 1942, he revealed his face to his public and let them know his "real" name: Rodolfo Guzmán Huerta. Two days later, while doing his escape act in the Teatro Blanquita, he suffered a fatal heart attack. Hijo del Santo (Son of El Santo), his youngest son and heir to his mask, was wrestling in Acapulco when it happened and wasn't told until he stepped out of the ring. El Santo was waked and buried with his mask in place, as he requested in his will (Morales 1998).

Eleven years later, also in February, the Mexican government launched a new offensive against the Ejercito Zapatista de Liberación Nacional (EZLN). As part of that offensive, on February 9, the attorney general's office released a photograph of a man they claimed (rightly or wrongly) to be the movement's charismatic leader, the ski-masked figure known only as Subcomandante Marcos. Metaphorically ripping off his mask, they revealed him to be nothing more than Rafael Sebastian Guillén Vicente, former university professor and son of a Tampico furniture dealer. Government officials claimed that the photograph's circulation in and of itself was an important victory. The next day's *New York Times* quoted an unnamed official who insisted (rather prematurely) that "the moment that Marcos was identified and his photo was shown and everyone saw who he was, much of his importance as a symbol vanished. . . . Whether he is captured or not is incidental" (*New York Times* 1995: 1). On the face of it, the statement was absurd. Although Guillén was clearly not indigenous (a fact that officials used to undermine the EZLN's claim to represent the indigenous Maya of Chiapas), there had never been any pretense to the contrary. His identity was revealed to be what everyone more or less expected, although Alma Guillermoprieto (1995) observed that the unmasking temporarily lessened his sex appeal.

As a politico-military gesture, however, it did make sense seen as a familiar trope from lucha libre. Marcos's response, in fact, echoed an incident involving Hijo del Santo that happened some years before. In the middle of their divorce, the wrestler's soon-to-be–ex-wife sent photographs of what she claimed was his unmasked face to the press. The son of El Santo responded by denying that he was the man in the photographs. Since there was no way to know unless he unmasked himself, her claim was impossible to prove (Rugos 1994: 24). That was precisely the reaction of Marcos to the government's ploy. Within days he relayed a message to the Mexico City press in his familiar epistolary style:

> *P.S. that rapidly applauds this new "success" of the government police*: I heard they've found another "Marcos," and that he's from Tampico. That doesn't

sound bad, the port is nice . . . *P.S. that despite the circumstances does not abandon its narcissism"* So . . . Is this new Subcomandante Marcos good-looking? Because lately they've been assigning me really ugly ones, and my feminine correspondence gets ruined. . . . [signed] The Sup, rearranging his ski mask with macabre flirtatiousness. (quoted in Guillermoprieto 1995: 44, emphasis original)

Like the son of El Santo, he was able, through simple denial, to reestablish his imperiled sex appeal, his revolutionary credentials, and, most important, the charisma of his mask.

Masks, masking, and unmasking are themes that pervade not only lucha libre, but also Mexican cultural discourse as a whole. This chapter is an exploration of the power of the mask in lucha libre and in the broader Mexican context. My aim is to draw out connections between lucha libre and the national culture in which it is embedded and to which it contributes through the medium of the mask.

Masks have been a part of lucha libre since the 1930s. By the 1950s the wrestling mask came to symbolize the sport itself. The mask is a metonym for lucha libre, worn by perhaps half to two-thirds of Mexico's wrestlers. Although a few wrestlers in the United States have used masks, they have never come to be used very much, let alone come to represent the very essence of the performance genre. Yet in Mexico the mask and play with the mask are very important to the genre, for the mask is more than just an element of costume. In this chapter, I will explain how the mask functions in lucha libre: both by its capacity to shift the rules of performance and by its capacity to align wrestling performances with other discourses about culture and nation.

LA MÁSCARA AND LO MEXICANO

Many people, both in and outside of the familia luchística, have called attention to the connection between the use of masks in lucha libre, and their ritual use by indigenous peoples in Mexico. By connecting lucha libre to the indigenous world, the mask is seen as central to the Mexicanization of the genre. In the words of the artist Sergio Arau: "In the United States, wrestlers started to use masks, but it didn't stick, and they stopped, using makeup instead, because it's more normal, more Hollywoodesque. But in Mexico, I say, and as I suppose the anthropologists say, it seems more logical that we use masks, because all our ethnic groups . . . employ masks in their rituals" (quoted in Alipi 1994: 25).

Aligning lucha libre with indigenous ritual simultaneously aligns it with an important trope in the discourse of national culture in Mexico. The revolution of 1910–20 stimulated a shift in thinking about the Mexican national subject. As part of the postrevolutionary nationalist project, the paradigmatic Mexican came to be imagined as mestizo, rather than creole —the product of racial and cultural mixture between Spanish and Indian. The conceptualization of the mestizo subject was, moreover, explicitly gendered, as the mestizo was imagined as the son of the Spanish father and Indian mother.[2] The indigenous thus became identified as the locus of *Mexico profundo*, the ground of Mexico's irreducible cultural identity. Yet the indigenous was not identified as the Mexican national subject per se. Claudio Lomnitz Adler (1992: 2) has written, rather, that the dominant discourse constituted "an argument about the individuality of the Mexican process: the soul of Mexican culture is Indian and its political body is destined to be ruled by mestizos against the Europeanizing process of the lackeys of foreign imperialism." To link the urban practice of lucha libre to indigenous ritual, then, could have the effect of legitimating it as a *nationalist* practice.

INDIGENOUS USE OF RITUAL MASKS

The use of masks in traditional rituals or dramas is indeed widespread in rural, indigenous Mexico. In calling these practices "traditional" or "indigenous," I do not mean that they are timeless and unchanging. But as products of complex historical processes of syncretization, such practices function as signifiers of tradition (whether indigenous or mestizo), and are used to assert communal identities and rights (by signifying difference from the national or urban culture, or signifying participation in an underlying "deep" culture common to all Mexicans).

In the ethnographic literature, traditional masked performances are reported to take place across a large geographic and cultural range in Mexico. Most uses of masking in Mexican ritual appear to fall into two categories of performance: satirical or parodic genres (or roles), and what Francis Gilmore (1983) calls "combat plays." For example, variations on the role of "sacred clown" have been reported in indigenous communities from

Chiapas to Sonora. These include the Yaqui *p'askola* (Lutes 1983), who dance at a variety of saints' festivals; the Mayo *pariseiro*, who crucify Christ in the passion play (Crumrine 1983); and the *k'ohetik* in Chiapas, who appear during the festival of Carnival to parody the town officials (Bricker 1973). The role of sacred clown is generally interpreted as an inversion ritual, in which the clowns deliberately violate community (and natural) norms in order to make them explicit, or as a way to criticize the powerful without risking retaliation.

The sacred clown role seems to be confined to communities that are unambiguously considered indigenous—rural communities where most people speak a language other than Spanish, and Catholic religious practices and beliefs are heavily mixed with local, heterodox ones. Another parodic use of masks, however, is widespread in both indigenous and mestizo contexts: the *pastorela*. Pastorelas are performed all over Mexico during the month before Christmas. The form originated in the sixteenth century as a tool of Catholic missionization. In its oldest version, it portrays the journey of the Three Kings to Bethlehem (Sanchez Hernandez 1986).[3] In most parts of Mexico, it takes the form of a satirical play that couches social critique in burlesque parody. Pastorelas can (in theory) be performed by anyone, are composed for the occasion, and allow for a great deal of improvisation by the actors. Thus pastorelas can include everything from small-town productions that mock the local power structure to professional productions that criticize key figures in the national government. Although masking is not essential to the genre, at least some actors in most pastorelas wear masks.

Another way that masks are used in traditional performance is in the set of ceremonies that Frances Gilmore (1983) labels "combat plays." One particularly interesting example, in relation to lucha libre, is a fertility ritual performed in Nahuatl-speaking communities in the state of Guerrero called the *danza del tigre* (tiger dance). A petition for rain that takes place in May, the dance is performed by young men of the community who dress as jaguars, wearing painted clothing and heavy wooden or leather masks. The youths fight each other with rope whips in order to shed one another's blood as a sacrifice, so "that by shedding human blood, the jaguar deity will release his own blood in the form of rain which then fertilizes the maize crop" (Saunders 1998: 38–39).

More widespread than the danza del tigre is a class of dramatic ritual that portrays the victory of the Spanish over their non-Christian enemies. Like the pastorela, these rituals were originally performed in the context of Colonial evangelical efforts. The most widespread version, called Moros y Cristianos (Christians and Moors), is performed all over Latin America (as well as Spain) and celebrates the Reconquista. One variation, La Conquista, portrays the Spanish victory over the Aztecs, and a third, Los Tastoanes (from *tlatoani*, a Nahuatl term for leader or noble) combines elements of La Conquista with elements of the Easter passion play. In all three variants, participants are divided into two morally marked sides, one side representing the Christians, led by Santiago, and the other representing the Moors or Indians. Although the Christians always vanquish their enemies by the end of the ritual, Olga Nájera-Ramirez (1997) argues that (at least in the case of Los Tastoanes) the Christian victory represents incorporation, rather than defeat of the other side. In a number of variants, the villagers or townspeople who act as the non-Christians wear masks. In Moors and Christians, the mask may be as simple as a bandana and sunglasses, or a fake beard (Gilmore 1983). In Los Tastoanes, some individual characters (such as a morally ambivalent character called Cireneo) and the masses of tastoanes wear masks specific to their roles.

Masks are thus most likely to be used in two kinds of performances in traditional contexts: those in which participants mock powerful figures or violate community norms, and those in which participants engage in ritual combat (or both). In this sense, they resemble lucha libre in both its melodramatic-agonistic and its ludic aspects. When used by those who violate community norms—sacred clowns, Moors, tastoanes—the mask helps to perform a necessary separation of the community member from the morally problematic actions of his or her character. But the mask empowers performance on a more profound level as well.

Early (but persistent) anthropological theories of the mask held that masking was a universal phenomenon originally rooted in the inability (or unwillingness) of the masker's audience (and to some extent the masker him- or herself) to distinguish between the entity represented by the mask and the masker representing the entity.[4] This position, rooted in the Lévy-Bruhlian notion of an ontological difference between the perceptual orientation of "primitive" and modern societies,[5] has come under attack (Halpin

1983, Pernet 1992) for both theoretical and empirical reasons. But more recent work suggests that, indeed, there is a special relationship between masking and the performer's sense of identity, albeit one that is quite nuanced.

John Emigh (1996), for example, discovers a continuum of identification in the masking practices of several genres of Hindu drama (in Orissa, India, and in Bali). In some genres, masks are understood to facilitate "visitation" by the sometimes dangerous divine beings that the masks are believed to contain (in both senses of the word). During performance, a performer might or might not enter a trance state, which would allow the supernatural entity to act directly, using the dancer's masked body. That need not happen for the performance to take place—if the entity does not take over, the performer can follow the script. In other genres, masks represent characters (rather than divinities), which dancers inhabit by "referencing the aesthetics of ancestral visitation" (Emigh 1996: 125). In other words, there are different ways in which masks can be inhabited by maskers (and maskers inhabited by masks), even within the same dramatic tradition, including trance visitation, mimicry of visitation, and interpretation based on visitation.

Although I have found no reference to a tradition of trance possession and masked ritual per se in Mexico, there does seem to be a variety of ideas about the relationship between the masker and the mask. In some masked performance, such as that of the Mayo *p'askola* clown role, the mask may be seen as an instrument of spiritual empowerment for the masker.[6] On the other hand, the masks used in Moorish and Christian combat plays are not treated as loci of the supernatural, nor do people pretend that they don't know who the dancers "really" are. The same is, of course, true of the more conventionally theatrical pastorela. In all cases, however, the mask allows the masker a moral authority or moral immunity, freeing him or her to take on or embody a critical role.

THE WRESTLER'S MASK

The connection between traditional masked performances and lucha libre, however, is indirect at best. The use of wrestling masks in the United States predates their use in Mexico. In 1915, a wrestler calling himself "The Masked Marvel" debuted in Manhattan. The wrestler, later revealed to be

Mort Henderson, set up a series of escalating challenges until he was unmasked by Ed "Strangler" Lewis. After that, several different U.S. wrestlers played the role of the Masked Marvel for short periods (Jares 1974). The Masked Marvel "himself" was never really a character, but a gimmick.

The Mexican wrestling mask, however, was designed by a shoemaker in Mexico City in 1934. Antonio H. Martinez moved from Leon, Guanajuato, to Mexico City in the late 1920s, where he became one of lucha libre's earliest fans. According to his son Victor (the current proprietor of his shop, Deportes Martinez), Antonio Martinez was a special fan of the wrestler Charro Aguayo. The two eventually met, and when Aguayo found out he was a shoemaker, he asked him to design a boot for luchadores who, until then, were using boxing shoes.[7] Martinez soon became known among wrestlers as a source for wrestling boots. Later that year, a U.S. American wrestler who fought under the name Cyclone MacKay and wanted to use the Masked Marvel gimmick in Mexico approached him. MacKay asked Martinez if he could make him a "hood." As Victor Martinez (son of Antonio and current proprietor of Deportes Martinez) recounts, when his father asked MacKay what he meant, he replied that he wanted "a hood, something you can put on, tie on, like the Ku Klux Klan or something like that" (interview with author, 1996). Thus, the first wrestling mask was not carried from the villages of Jalisco or Guerrero to Mexico City. It was invented by an urban, mestizo shoemaker at the behest of a North American performing in a genre recently imported from the United States. It alluded not to the ritual practices of indigenous Mexican communities but to the Ku Klux Klan.[8]

For about a year, the Masked Marvel was the only wrestler to use a mask. Then, in 1936, a Mexican wrestler named Jesus Velasquez, started wrestling as El Murciélago (The Bat) Velasquez. Wearing a leather mask and an elaborate cape, he would carry a bag into the ring from which he would release a swirl of bats. In the wake of his success (and a wave of popularity of masked comic-book heroes), more luchadores put on masks.[9] By 1955, dozens of wrestlers wore masks, prompting *Box y Lucha* to publish a two-part photographic feature on "mask mania" (*Lucha Libre* 1955a: 17–18, 1955b: 18–19). When Mexican wrestlers took up the mask, they transformed it from a temporary gimmick to an integral part of the performance.

According to Victor Martinez, the first Martinez mask was made of two pieces of suede, but it didn't fit well and was uncomfortable to wrestle in, so

FIGURE 10
Victor Martinez, son of the inventor of the lucha libre mask, at work in his shop

the shoemaker started to play with the design. The classical wrestling mask, developed by Antonio Martinez and used to this day, is made from four pieces of solid color cotton synthetic (presently spandex) blend sewn together to cover the entire head except for the eyes, nose, and mouth. In the back there is an opening, with a tongue, that is laced like a tennis shoe to hold the mask in place. There is usually contrasting trim around the eye, nose, and mouth holes, and some type of insignia or pattern. The form of the wrestling mask changed little for several decades after its invention. Before the 1990s, the most radical change in design was a trend in the 1970s toward leaving the lower jaw uncovered. Since lucha libre returned to television in the early 1990s, however, more elaborate variations with horns, beaks, fringe, and other projections have become more common.

Rodolfo Guzmán Huerta was one wrestler who adopted the mask in the early 1940s. Born in Tulancingo, Hidalgo, but raised in Mexico City, he followed two of his older brothers into professional wrestling in 1932. He wrestled as a rudo under his own name (Rudy Guzmán) without much success until his promoter suggested that he wear a mask. In 1942, newly masked, Guzmán billed himself as El Murciélago II, but when the original threatened to sue him he changed character again. Later that year, still a rudo, he covered his face with a silver lamé mask and entered the ring as "El Santo, el enmascarado de plata" (The Saint, the man in the silver mask, after the comic-book character Simon Templar). With that, his wrestling career took off. In 1958 he starred in his first movie, and in 1962, he changed his role from rudo to técnico. Then he spent the rest of his life as a professional symbol of the triumph of good over evil.

The spread of the use of masks in the late 1940s and 1950s coincided with the advent and growth of the wrestling movie: low-budget films turned out by the dozen after the end of the golden age of Mexican cinema in the 1940s (see chapter 6). The most famous masked wrestlers were recruited to the film industry, which, in turn, bolstered and widened their fame. Certain masks—that of El Santo, that of Blue Demon, that of Huracán Ramirez (among many others)—gained iconic status, and an etiquette developed around protecting the honor of the mask and the anonymity of the wrestler. El Santo, in particular, was known for his exemplary care of his mask and his secret identity. He wouldn't even let his guard down during his work in the movies.

The following anecdote, recounted to me by an acquaintance, a television executive whose uncle had worked for the Churubusco film studios, illustrates the extent of El Santo's care of his anonymity. When my friend was a child, his uncle would take him to visit the studio along with his cousin. One of those times, when he was eight years old, they went to watch the filming of an El Santo movie. The wrestler arrived at the studio every morning with his mask in place and would keep it on throughout the day, even during meals. The uncle tried to convince El Santo that it was safe to come without his mask until it was time to shoot—after all, hundreds of people worked in the studio, and no one would associate an anonymous worker with the great El Santo. The wrestler finally agreed, and one day left the mask off as he went to lunch.

The uncle, however, had noticed on other days that El Santo always ate the same thing for lunch, and so when lunchtime arrived he looked for a stocky man eating *chilaquiles* with chicken and cream. He then bribed his son and nephew to go up to the stranger eating the chilaquiles and say to him: "Santo, we really admire you." They did, and to their surprise and confusion, the man jumped, clasped his face, and ran off "shrieking like a showgirl."

In El Santo's case (and perhaps that of other wrestler-actors as well), viewers never heard his voice either. As he was allegedly too busy to memorize scripts (or perhaps lacked a suitable voice), his lines were always dubbed by an actor in postproduction.[10] The total effect was to conceal not only his face, but also his voice. Thus, in a sense, he was a body double of himself. "El Santo" *was* the mask and the torso. He both was and was not Rodolfo Guzmán, for the mask transformed both the wrestler and the performance.

The mask transformed lucha libre. It associated the wrestling performance with the idea of a unified Mexican national culture rooted in a pre-Hispanic past. That association is strengthened by the many feline or eagle identities, echoing both the pre-Columbian *caballero tigre* and *caballero águila* (jaguar and eagle knights) and today's danza del tigre. In addition, the mask helps to foreground some elements of performance and to mute others, for although there is no unambiguous tradition of "visitation" in traditional Mexican masquerades, the presence of a mask changes the dynamic of the relationship between the character (en)acted, the actor, and the "script" of the actions. As Emigh writes (1996: xviii–xix):

> In working up a role, the unmediated self of the actor, the mask (persona) that is to be acted and the text that is to be spoken within the flow of action form a triad. The tendency in most Western theater today is to begin with the confrontation of actor and text and to work towards the persona—a term which in common usage has come to mean character as well as mask. [In masked theatrical forms] this process begins, instead, with the confrontation of actor and mask. . . . The text and mise-en-scène . . . will be shaped by this encounter and will often be improvised within the boundaries established by aesthetic form and social occasion.

In lucha libre, then, the mask changes the relationship between the wrestler, the wrestler's "script," and the wrestler's character, first of all, by objectifying the wrestler's character in a material and visual form. This is one way that lucha libre has tended to privilege the visual and gestural over the verbal. The pre- and postmatch interview and hyperbolic exchange of insults, so important to narrative development of U.S. professional wrestling, are rarely used.[11] The identification of the wrestler with his or her role, even for wrestlers who do not mask, seldom depends on what they say or how they say it. In lucha libre, the body and mask signify. The voice seldom does. Moreover, the transformation of the wrestler/actor into the character happens whenever he or she puts on the mask whether or not he or she changes his or her behavior.

In addition, the use of masks opens up the possibility of a set of rules of play that are *about* masks. These include rules regarding actions in the ring, and a set of metarules: who can be masked, what mask they can use, and the etiquette that protects a wrestler's anonymity. As we saw in chapter 2, lucha libre performances are organized by a combination of formal regulations (the size of the ring, the rules for disqualification, and rules for different types of matches) and tacit conventions (e.g., there should usually be a rudo side and a técnico side). In the rules about masking, both metarules and rules of play include both formal mandates and tacit understandings. The section that follows will set out the rules of masking, and their implications for wrestlers who wear the mask.

RULES OF THE GAME

Metarules

There are two metarules governing masking. The first of these is quite formal: Any wrestler who wishes to wear a mask in the ring must be so licensed by the commission. Moreover, the commission is said to hold masked wrestlers to a higher standard on the licensing exam, because, it is argued, the mask will protect a wrestler from deserved humiliation if he or she wrestles badly. The wrestler will have less incentive to wrestle well and will thus cheat the audience. The second rule, while less formal, is taken at least as seriously: A masked wrestler must never publicly expose his or her unmasked face, or disclose his or her identity. On the one hand, this means that the wrestler must enlist the collusion of people who must know the wrestler's secret (family, close friends, business associates and so on). On the other, it means complying with a set of rituals for negotiating the border between wrestling space and quotidian space.[12] A masked wrestler should don (and remove) the mask in a space where his or her face will not be noticed and associated with the mask. The mask should be off when he or she leaves his or her home, but ideally, it should be in place when he or she arrives at the arena. This is not a problem if the wrestler owns a car, but most wrestlers do not own cars. They must arrive at and leave the arena in taxis or public transportation, and so have to negotiate the masking in a taxi, or a couple of blocks away from the arena. To pull it off, to achieve the transformation, requires a sense of timing, and a faith in the anonymity of most interactions in the city—a sense that taxi drivers don't notice the faces of their fares, or bystanders and bartenders the face of the guy who came in to use the bathroom. It also implicitly depends on their collusion— that they understand the importance of the wrestler's anonymity and will respect his or her responsibility to maintain it.

Rules of Play

Inside the ring, the mask is treated as a fetishized object that represents the wrestler's honor. The masked wrestler cannot let his or her face be seen under any circumstances. This opens up a range of possibilities of play, since in lucha libre (especially for the rudos) it is often as good to humiliate an opponent as to defeat him or her. A wrestler can humiliate an opponent by exposing his or her face, but to do so is grounds for disqualification. Thus, a wrestler can pursue dominance through victory or exploit the fetishistic value of the mask and pursue it through humiliation. Between those two extremes, wrestlers can tear each other's masks without actually removing them. While that doesn't mean disqualification or exposure for either wrestler, it does cost one wrestler an expensive, custom-made mask.

A wrestler thus unmasked is disempowered. Until the mask is returned he or she can't fight, but can only clutch his or her face and wait—either for a partner to retrieve it or to be led to the dressing room to put on a fresh one. The unmasking trope, then, can be played in several different ways to build the narrative of a given match. Here I will give two examples.

A torn or stolen mask in the second round works as a setup for revindication in the third. I saw one dramatic instance of this in a match that featured the técnico Solar II, teamed up with two other técnicos against a group of three rudos led by his rival Scorpio. In round two, Scorpio managed to unmask Solar, who rolled himself out of the ring, covered his face, and crouched miserably in the corner. His teammates were unable to recover the mask, so he stayed there until a small boy led him away to the dressing rooms, his hands still covering his face. The referee declared the técnicos the winners of round two by disqualification. As soon as round three started (while Solar was still absent), the rudos ganged up on the remaining técnicos, two of them kicking and punching one, while the third kept his partner at bay. Then, just when it looked hopeless for the técnicos, Solar reappeared with a sparkly new mask, leapt into the ring, and energetically took on all three of the bad guys at once. Revitalized, his partners joined in and quickly pinned the rudos to win the match.

Self-unmasking is another tactic used by rudos, based on a ploy in which the wrestler spontaneously clutches his groin and drops, moaning, to the ground, in hopes that that the referee will disqualify his opponent for fouling him. In the masked version, while the referee is ostentatiously otherwise engaged, the rudo undoes his own mask and thrusts it into the hands of a puzzled técnico. Then he writhes around clutching his face, just as the referee turns, sees them, and disqualifies the técnico.

However, the most important way in which the mask itself becomes part of the narrative is through something called a *lucha de apuesta* (betting match). In the lucha de apuesta, a wrestler will bet his or her mask or hair on the outcome of the match, against the opponent's mask or hair. Some hair, long trademark manes identified with particular wrestlers, is relatively valuable, but since it grows back, hair can never have the value of a mask. Once a wrestler loses a mask, he or she loses anonymity. His or her face, name, and birthplace are publicly revealed, first in the arena, and later in the press. Even more important, he or she loses the right to use a mask thereafter. In the metarules of lucha libre, to change from one character to another, from one mask to another, is not considered dishonest, but to cover a face (and an identity) once it has been uncovered is fraud.

The wrestler who has agreed to lose a lucha de apuesta is paid a bonus by the event's promoter, since they usually draw a large audience. Sometimes a lucha de apuesta takes place because the empresa wishes to promote the career of the winner. Sometimes it takes place either because the loser needs money or is planning to switch empresas (where he or she will fight under another name chosen by the new empresa), or has tired of the responsibility of remaining incognito. Luchas de apuesta take place after a period of several months of heightened rivalry between two wrestlers (called a *pique*), during which time they exchange threats and escalating challenges. During the fight itself there is no real risk to mask or hair, since victory and defeat have been agreed to in advance. However, that does not mean that nothing is at stake for the wrestlers. The masked wrestler is taking a genuine risk when he or she agrees to lose, for loss of a mask might mean loss of charisma, loss of the ability to move the public. The moment of revelation clarifies the relationship of a particular wrestler to a particular mask.

A wrestler who takes up the mask has to confront the problem of how to inhabit it, how to make another's face his or her own. As in other forms of masked theater, Emigh explains (1996: xviii), "the unworn mask begins as something clearly set apart: an inert and disembodied other. The actor confronting the mask is nakedly and pathetically himself (or, increasingly, herself). For the actor, the otherness of the mask becomes both the obstacle and the goal. He or she must redefine the sense of self in order to wear the other's face and be true to it in spirit, thought and action."

At the moment of unmasking, the wrestler faces a new task: that of transferring the charisma that the mask had accrued to pure bodily gesture. He or she loses the illusion of being more than human, beyond the everyday obligation of having a name and a history. The wrestler must transfer to his or her human body the redefinition of self that he or she developed to wear the mask. In that moment, the wrestler's future becomes a matter of speculation, and the wrestler's career is put at serious risk. The ritual of unmasking might reveal that the mask was the key to his or her success. On the other hand, he or she might be able to transcend the unmasking and prove (in the words of the wrestler Conan the Barbarian) that "the mask doesn't make the wrestler, the wrestler makes the mask" (Fascinetto 1992: 27).

Meanwhile, the mask of the winner is invested with the charisma of the mask of the loser. A wrestler's official career history always includes a listing of masks and hair as well as championships won, and everyone knows that the masks (depending on whose mask) are worth far more than a championship. A really big star (especially if he or she is masked) has to be able to claim several masks on his or her shelf as evidence of his or her prowess and willingness to risk the irretrievable. But since the matches are fixed, the conquered masks really represent a decision made at some earlier time by the empresa to advance the winner's career. They are thus a testament to the wrestler's position in the empresa.[13]

The fact that anonymity and the charisma of mystery can be irrecoverably lost gives them a heightened value. Even though many careers continue after an unmasking, it is widely believed that many more do not. In the words of one reporter: "In the moment in which wrestler takes off the mask, people fall like a plague on the ring. All want to know the unmasked, but with the passage of time, people cool down and forget about the fallen. Oh tragedy! He loses his anonymity and loses his public" (Valentino 1993: 4).

The lucha de apuesta is therefore a mechanism by which the mask is invested with significance. To unmask a wrestler increases the value attributed to the mask of the winner. The very possibility of unmasking, and its irrevocability makes all masks worth something. The care with which the rules around masking are observed empowers the mask both to conceal and to transcend. It allows the mask to be the vehicle for other meanings.

One of the ways in which the mask helps wrestling to signify is by foregrounding linked discourses of kinship, nation, mortality, and permanence. As stated above, when a wrestler is unmasked his or her name and place of birth are published the following week in magazines like *Box y Lucha* and *Superluchas*, as well as the sports section of some newspapers. By extension, the wrestler's personal history and genealogy become definitely knowable. Unmasking reveals the wrestler's embeddedness in the social world. Yet the relationship of masking to kinship is not only one of concealment. It can also be one of display, or selective revelation.

Masked characters are the most likely kind to be passed down from parents to children. If a parent is or was a successful masked wrestler, one of his or her children may inherit the mask, inheriting, in a sense, the parent's social identity. The original wrestler has the right to decide who will use the mask, even if he or she was unmasked and unable to use the mask during the rest of his or her career.[14] The effect of this is a kind of hypercontinuity—El Santo, Rayo de Jalisco, Dr. Wagner, Blue Demon, and others whose careers started in the 1940s appear to be with us still, still wrestling at the same arenas.

In practice, the transmission of masks from parent to child is gender-specific; I only know of masks that passed from father to son, uncle to nephew, or godfather to godchild. Women are less likely to mask to begin with, and I know of no woman's mask that has been passed to a second generation. The person who dons a classic mask may not, in fact, be the son or nephew of the original, but it is conventionally expected that he will be. If the father's mask was very prestigious, taking up the mask may be a heavy burden. Heirs may worry about failing to preserve its prestige and charisma. Hijo del Santo, for example, did not put on his father's mask until he had proved himself as a wrestler under the nombre de batalla "El Korak." Although there are many wrestling families, those who do wear masks seldom refer to themselves as legends. They can't. Aside from rare exceptions, only by masking are wrestlers able to convert themselves into national or regional symbols, and only through masking can they appear to efface time.

A QUESTION OF HONOR

One of the clearest dramatizations of the importance of the mask in embodying continuity was a lucha de apuesta of the mask of Hijo del Santo against the hair of Negro Casas that took place on September 19, 1997. Both Hijo del Santo and Negro Casas are heirs of wrestling lineages, men who were (according to the announcer when the match finally took place) "formed genetically for the *lucha profesional*." Negro Casas is the son of Pépe Casas, a técnico of the same generation as El Santo who was at the time a referee for the AAA/PAPSA. He has uncles in the business, and a brother who wrestles as the masked Felino. Negro used to be a rudo, but had fought as a técnico for the past few years. His past notwithstanding, Negro made a wonderful técnico: elegant, acrobatic, and expressive, with a trademark mane of lush black hair.

Hijo del Santo, on the other hand, had been fighting as a rudo since the previous December, a switch that angered some of his public. According to the wrestling journals, one of the ostensible reasons for his going over to the dark side was his longstanding hatred of Negro Casas. The two wrestlers had engaged in an escalating series of attacks and counterattacks, challenges and counterchallenges since the New Year. This lucha de apuesta, which the EMLL press release titled "A Question of Honor," was to settle accounts once and for all, with only one pin. The match was to be the final event of a gala celebration of the sixty-fourth anniversary of lucha libre's arrival in Mexico.

It had not been a good year for live lucha libre. Ticket sales had been low, and I had seen many matches take place in arenas that were half full at best. The EMLL had closed down the smallest of its three arenas in Mexico City that June, and there were rumors that they were going to close the Acapulco arena as well. For this match, however, tickets were sold out by 1:00 in the afternoon. By 4:00, the streets were full of fans and scalpers seeking each other out and bargaining over tickets. The 18,000-seat arena was absolutely full, and (I later heard) people stood outside all evening waiting to learn the outcome of the final match.

In front of such a large and enthusiastic audience, all of the wrestlers did their best to shine. The preliminary match between minis was elegantly paced, climaxing with a beautiful corkscrewing "suicide leap" out of the ring by Cicloncito Ramirez onto Damiancito. The next match was equally dramatic and risky. In the third, luchadora Lola Gonzalez (who had announced her intention to retire some weeks before) won the last match of her twenty-two-year career against her Japanese rival Bull Nakana. A pair of muscular young men wearing reproductions of Aztec stone masks escorted her into the ring. After the match, she was sent off with gifts and tributes from her colleagues. Bull Nakana gave her a porcelain doll and wiped away tears as the others made speeches. In the next match, when Rayo de Jalisco made his entrance accompanied by mariachis, his rival Cien Caras grabbed a guitar and broke it over Rayo's head. As they usually do, the matches moved from relatively orderly preliminaries to increasingly chaotic, violent, and prestigious later bouts until the time came for the final.

Because Hijo del Santo had been fighting as a rudo, the moral coding, the symbolic weight of the event was unclear to me. Although I knew that Hijo del Santo, no matter what, still signified as the son of his illustrious father, I also knew that Negro Casas was going in as the técnico, as the representative of decent folk. I had also read in *Superluchas* (1997: 24) that Hijo del Santo was going to star in his own television series on Channel 13.[15] Each of the two had threatened to retire if he lost, so I wondered if it wasn't Hijo del Santo's way of moving on to an acting career (although I knew about the scandalous retirement match between Conan and Perro Aguayo, after which neither retired). But any doubts I might have had vanished as we waited for the match to begin.

Suddenly, on the screen above the ring, we could all see the silver mask, the shoulders covered by the matching cape. I couldn't tell where he was standing—a dark space with metal beams in the background. And then he spoke: "Today will be the fiftieth defense of this mask. El Santo and Hijo del Santo are *united*. And I will show you why I carry this mask with pride— Because *I am the son of El Santo*."

After he finished his speech, he entered the ring, *lowered on cables from the rafters of the arena*. The silver lamé mask covered his head as always, but instead of his usual cape, he wore one that, while still of silver lamé, had three vertical strips of green, silver (standing in for white), and red (the colors of the Mexican flag). Echoing his father's switch from the rudo to the técnico role thirty-five years before, in the silver space, instead of the flag's eagle insignia, he wore an image of the Virgin of Guadalupe.[16] As he waited in the ring, Negro Casas's theme song, Jose Luis Guerra's "El Costo de la Vida," came over the loudspeakers, and Negro's face appeared on the overhead screen. He spoke from the dressing room, responding to Hijo del Santo's challenge: "Santo, your hour has come. Tonight the threats will end, the challenges will end, and you too will end. I will show your face. Arena Mexico and all the world will know who is your master—I, sir. Tonight the legend ends . . ."

But by then it was clear that Negro Casas didn't have a chance. The symbolic weight that Hijo del Santo carried into the ring was too much: aligned verbally and iconically with his late father and the spiritual mother of the Mexican nation, descending into the ring like the holy spirit, he overwhelmed the distinction between mere rudo and técnico.

For the first few minutes, the two men stayed near the center of the canvas, engaged in an intense and focused exchange of holds. Negro Casas grabbed Hijo del Santo and dragged him toward the corner ropes as the arena started to echo with whistles and cheers, cries of "Santo, Santo," and a few of "Negro, Negro." He hung Hijo del Santo by his feet from the corner ropes, backed up, and then slid feet first across the canvas into his chest. Then he took the abject wrestler down, dragged him to another corner, and slid into him again. He repeated the whole thing once more, but then on the fourth attempt, Hijo del Santo was ready. He ducked to the side at the last second, and Negro slid all the way out of the ring. Hijo del Santo righted himself on the ropes and leapt through the air onto his opponent. They got up from the ground, both a little groggily, and reentered the ring.

From there, it went back and forth for a while. Hijo del Santo tried to put Negro Casas into an a caballo hold (his late father's signature move), but he escaped. Negro managed to hang him from the ropes again, but Hijo del Santo pulled himself up to sit on the corner, and then leapt onto Negro. He tried to apply the a caballo again but couldn't pull it off, so he shifted his body until he held Negro's arm between his legs and, using his body as a fulcrum, pulled the arm downward to apply a painful shoulder lock. Negro immediately spread his fingers and wiggled his hands in the conventional gesture of surrender, and the referee declared Hijo del Santo the victor. Negro Casas stood up, grabbed a microphone, and complained that El Santo had cheated by taking advantage of the fact that he had recently recovered from a broken clavicle, that El Santo had applied the lock to his injured arm, but to no avail. The official barber came out, wearing his official jacket—a blazer with a big pair of scissors in a blue circle printed on the back. Negro Casas grabbed his scissors and started to cut his own hair, throwing the locks contemptuously out of the ring. The barber started to shave the sides of his head, the lights went up, and it was over.

Negro Casas's defeat was inevitable because it was only *his* defeat. It was not the end of a legend, as Hijo del Santo's would have been. The prematch interviews (which were not the norm in lucha libre) accomplished the identification of the mask of El Santo with such powerful national symbols as the flag and the Virgin of Guadalupe. Negro Casas could be the son of Pépe Casas, but he could not *be* Pépe Casas, and Pépe Casas was not El Santo. Hijo del Santo, in contrast, proclaimed his unity with his late and illustrious father. Only masked wrestlers can truly inherit a parent's very identity at his retirement or death, and only they must carry the full burden of the parent's image.

In this sense, the wrestling mask is an inalienable possession in the sense put forth by Annette Weiner (1993: 6): possessions "imbued with the identities of their owners which are not easy to give away . . . certain things [that] assume a subjective value that places them above exchange value." The mask makes possible a transfer of charisma and power from the older generation to the younger, an instance, perhaps, of "cosmological authentication" (6). The dynamic by which masks pass through generations portrays "the need to secure permanence in a serial world that is always subject to loss and decay" (7). The mask, in this sense, effaces time, effaces generations, effaces mortality.

With the exception of second-generation stars like Hijo del Santo, wrestlers express the same ambivalence toward their masks as they do toward their characters. Most do not experience the mask as a means of transcendence. Trainees who wanted to mask said that they wanted to emulate their idols or liked the way masks looked or wanted the protection from humiliation that anonymity offers. Those who didn't want to mask sometimes jested that "only the ugly ones wear masks." But for a trainee or novice wrestler, the first mask is also tangible evidence of their commitment to and desire for a wrestling career. Thus, when some of my classmates showed off their first masks, it was an exciting moment. The masks, products of their own imagination, marked them as real wrestlers. They were beautiful, captivating objects, each one custom-made by hand (by Victor Martinez, in the shop that his father founded for those who could afford him, or by other mask makers working out of their homes or small shops for the rest).[17]

No one, however, claimed to believe in any essential difference between those wrestlers who masked and those who didn't. Moreover, like other aspects of character, the only opportunity to wear their own masks in the ring would very likely come during the transition between being a trainee and being a novice professional. If they were later assigned a mask by their empresa, the relationship between wrestler and mask would probably be merely one of costume.

Since the 1990s, this alienation of most wrestlers from their masks and characters has been reinforced by changes in the politics of copyright.[18] Before lucha libre returned to television in the early 1990s, rights to a given character were usually assumed to belong to the wrestler who embodied it. Once retired, or even before retirement, a wrestler could pass that character on to an heir or sell the rights to it or impede its use by others. Since then, however, empresas themselves have started to copyright characters and mask designs. Antonio Peña, the founder of AAA/PAPSA, was involved in a number of copyright disputes with wrestlers during the time of my fieldwork.

When one of the stars of the AAA/PAPSA, Máscara Sagrada, left the empresa in 1996 to join a rival empresa, PromoAzteca, he claimed it was because Peña had cheapened his image by promoting a slew of Máscara

Sagrada spinoffs (Máscara Sagrada Jr., II, etc.), as he put it, "neither sons, nor nephews, nor nothing" (*En Caliente* 1996). Peña responded by sticking another wrestler into the costume, and so two Máscaras Sagradas circulated in the arenas, each empresa claiming theirs to be the authentic one—PromoAzteca because their Máscara Sagrada is the man who appeared as Máscara Sagrada for several years, the AAA because Peña claimed to hold the copyright. In effect, he redefined a practice once considered fraudulent—presenting an unknown wrestler in a star's mask—as the legitimate disposition of intellectual property. The conflict between the AAA and PromoAzteca (see chapter 6) redefined the mask and character as forms of property fully alienable from the wrestler.

THE MASK AND ITS CIRCULATION

Whether the mask can or should be considered the inalienable property of the wrestler, the fact is that masks circulate. They circulate as concrete objects and as symbols. This section traces the paths of circulation of masks and of The Mask.

If you walk down Calle Doctor La Vista or Calle Peru during a weekday, Arenas Mexico and Coliseo are not hard to find. But if you walk there when the arenas are open, they are impossible to miss, for as you approach the arena you hear melodious cries of "*Máscara, máscara*, get your favorite wrestleeeer." Lining the sidewalk along the block are women and men standing next to blankets on the ground, or stands of wire racks, that are covered with brightly colored wrestling masks, copies of the designs won by the thirty or so most popular wrestlers of the moment. They range in style from the minimalism of El Santo's plain silver covering to the elaborate beaks and horns of Mosca de la Merced or Violencia. They come in all sizes, from keychain ornaments to full-sized masks to fit an adult. The mask makers have shops in the old neighborhoods of the city, like Tepito, or in the outskirts like Nezahualcóyotl or Itzacalco. While the fabric is very different from that used in professional-quality masks (usually a heavyweight, sometimes padded, synthetic instead of lightweight cotton/lycra blend) the method by which they are made is not that different. They aren't custom made, but the souvenir masks are handmade by homeworkers who sell them for anywhere from about US$1 for a key chain ornament to $4 or $5 for a full-size mask. Inside the arena, another mask vendor circulates

FIGURE 11 Vendor selling masks inside the arena

with racks of masks for sale. Most are bought for children, who wear them in the arena so that star wrestlers' faces are echoed in miniature during the program. They are ubiquitous in Mexico City (and most of the country). Sold in public markets as well as the arenas, worn by children at play, or collected by adults, the souvenir masks represent one instance of the wrestling mask's circulation.

In a second instance of circulation, young men in rural Guerrero purchase wrestling masks to use as liners to protect their faces from the rough wooden or leather jaguar masks they use when they perform the danza del tigre (Janina Möbius, personal communication, 1997). The wrestling mask is often regarded as the extension of pre-Columbian cultural forms into the modern city. In this instance, however, it exemplifies the selective adoption of modern technologies into self-consciously traditional indigenous cultural performance. This kind of appropriation seems to have taken place as early as the late 1950s in Zinacantan, Chiapas. One of the photographs in Vogt's classic 1969 ethnography shows a ritual dancer wearing a wrestling mask.[19]

In addition to its circulation as an object, the wrestling mask also circulates as an icon, and the drama of unmasking circulates as a trope. In the culture of what Martin Needler (1998) has labeled the "classical Mexican political system," unmasking constituted a powerful and positive symbolic act. As Needler and others have portrayed it, the system itself was an elaborate masquerade: a one-party state, set up as if it were a multiparty democracy. While competing political parties are legal under the post-revolutionary constitution, the PRI and its precursors contrived to exclude other parties from political power through a complex combination of tactics including monopoly on or manipulation of national and popular symbols, patronage, cooptation of dissent, sponsoring ineffectual "opposition" parties, electoral fraud, and violence.[20]

Under the Mexican constitution, the presidency carries nearly unlimited power, but since the constitution forbids reelection, the power of individual presidents is limited to one six-year term. Until 1999, the selection of the PRI's candidate was the prerogative of the president himself, and since the PRI's candidate was guaranteed the election, the process gave the president the right to appoint his successor. The party was, however, always made up of various factions that would maneuver for position in advance of an election (at the local as well as national level). The identity of the PRI candidate was a matter of secrecy and speculation until the president announced his decision, an act called the *dedazo* (the finger) or *destapa* (which means both unveiling and unmasking). In the act of revelation, the president's successor (known thereafter as the *destapado*—the unmasked) would be invested with the prestige of the president himself. The destapa would come, however, only after a series of behind-the-scenes maneuvers by different factions and political tendencies within the party. Once the candidate's identity was revealed, all factions would be expected to give him unconditional support. The electoral campaign itself consisted of a series of presentations of the candidate to the public (a public ritually constructed through such presentations; Lomnitz and Adler 1993). Since it was not possible for any other party to win the election, the election itself was not a ritual of selection, but of the ratification or manifestation of a decision that had already been made.

This aspect of the political system, then, strongly resembled a lucha libre match. In lucha libre and in presidential elections, much is at stake. Different factions struggle for dominance, different wrestlers maneuver for position within their empresa. Decisions are made about who will be brought into the spotlight, and who will have to wait their turn (or be satisfied with having taken their turn). The match is performed for its own sake, not as a means of determining winners or losers. As in the elections, the outcome of the match is predetermined, and the result is the manifestation of decisions that had already been made at another level of the system. But even though the ending is predetermined, *how* the match is played out, how much grace or force is displayed (by wrestlers, or by party members mobilizing blocs of voters, or suppressing the opposition in support of the destapado) makes a difference for future matches.

Lucha libre came to Mexico during the same period that the classical political system was consolidated under Presidents Elias Calles and Lázaro Cárdenas. Its development paralleled that of the PRI's hegemony, during which time Mexican citizens voted in elections in which their performance as voters was at stake, but not the election's outcome. I do not believe that lucha libre was organized as a deliberate critique of the PRI. The sport was integrated into the bureaucracy of the Mexican state through the Commission and the Unions early in its history, and the EMLL demonstrated its commitment to the PRI over the years. The empresa arranged benefit matches for PRI candidates and organized its wrestlers to march in May Day parades until the PRI lost the mayoral election in 1997. The trainer in the empresa, El Faisán, identified himself as a "PRI militant." In short, the promoters who worked in Mexico City's dominant empresa were not likely to have been critical of the hegemony of the PRI. The resemblance between the two genres of performance was not formally articulated by wrestlers or even by Mexican social commentators who have written about lucha libre. Nevertheless, the parallels invested lucha libre with an implicit and potentially subversive, political significance.

ENTER SUPERBARRIO

As I recounted in the introduction, on the morning of September 19, 1985, a massive earthquake struck Mexico City. Confronted with tremendous damage and a slow and misleading government response, residents of the city experienced a moment of unity and common purpose as citizen brigades organized to dig survivors out of the rubble. In the year that followed, groups of grassroots activists organized to protest the inadequacies of the government's response and demand housing for those left homeless (whether by the earthquake or by economic circumstance). In 1986, a number of these groups formed a coalition, the Asemblea de Barrios, which emerged as an independent political force in its own right.

In the year before the election of 1988, when, for the first time since the early 1940s, the PRI faced a serious challenge for the presidency from the breakaway PRD, the Asemblea decided to run a candidate of their own, the masked wrestler Superbarrio. Thus it was that on November 17, the Asemblea unveiled Superbarrio in front of the Monument to Benito Juarez in the Alameda Park. Unlike the PRI's candidate, he was not, strictly speaking, a destapado. His trademark mask stayed in place. Since the first formal act of a destapado was, traditionally, to offer his resignation to the ministry where he worked, Superbarrio went to Arena Coliseo a few days later and asked to enter the ring before the first match. There he asked the lucha libre public to accept his resignation from his position as luchador.

Superbarrio is both a real figure and a piece of political theater. He debuted in June 1987, several months before he announced his candidacy. At the time, according to Marcos Rascón (now a PRD representative, and generally credited as Superbarrio's "intellectual author"), the wrestler was never intended to be a permanent fixture in the movement, just a temporary gimmick to use in a couple of demonstrations. Yet nearly two decades later, Superbarrio remains a fixture of the Mexican Left. Moreover, when Superbarrio began his struggle for housing rights in Mexico City, another wrestler independently decided to don a bright green mask to march in protests against the proposed Laguna Verde nuclear reactor in the state of Veracruz. Ecologista Universal and Superbarrio were thus the first two "social wrestlers"—people (perhaps wrestlers, perhaps not) who take up nombres de batalla and wrestling masks to represent social causes. Mujer Meravilla, SuperAnimal, SuperGay, and Superniño all emerged in the 1990s to fight for the rights of women, animals, gays, and street children respectively.

Why did social wrestlers make sense in Mexico? The answer lies in the complex layers of signification that were already at play in lucha libre by the late 1980s. First (as I will discuss in chapter 6), lucha libre had come to stand as a synecdoche for the culture of the urban popular classes and a set of claims valorizing that culture as a site of Mexican authenticity. Second (as I will also discuss in chapter 6), the meanings attached to lucha libre in

FIGURE 12 Ecologista Universal and Superanimal perform a parodic "destapa" of a Green Party candidate for local office

the ring were supplemented by the meanings attached to the luchadores of the cinema. The wrestler could thus symbolize the triumph of justice over corruption. But in addition to the wrestler's symbolic weight as the hero and representative of the poor (or of civil society in general), the social wrestler could articulate the interpretation of the Mexican political system that was latent in the live performance and rework it as an explicit critique of the PRI. Superbarrio, Ecologista Universal, and the other social wrestlers used the wrestling mask as a sort of reverse Brechtian device: a means to call attention to the artifice and alienation not of the theatrical production, but of the dominant system itself. Lucha libre's potential as political theater even lay in the name of the genre: *lucha*, glossed as "wrestling," also means "struggle." Social wrestlers merely shifted the ground of struggle from the arena to the *lucha social*.

Lucha libre performance inverted the trope of masking as it was used in the political ritual of the Mexican state. Whereas the presidential candidate was ritually empowered through unmasking (in a gesture that implied both the generative power of the president and the heretofore hidden powers inherent in the person of the candidate), lucha libre locates power in the mask itself. In lucha libre, masking implies the assumption and maintenance of an empowered identity, and unmasking signifies divestment and humiliation. Transposed to the context of Mexican opposition parties, the lucha libre mask empowered figures like Superbarrio.

According to Marcos Rascón, the Superbarrio figure was inspired by a theatrical intervention that he helped to organize with a group of housing activists in the early 1980s. It was, he recounted in an interview, "a typical accident."

I was a fan when I was a little boy in Ciudad Juarez, and it's one of those things that gets interrupted, no? Your fandom, as a boy, changes and stops. But in 1983, we started political work in the center of the city, and the first place we started to organize was a *vecindad* [tenement] that was right behind Arena Coliseo. . . .[21] The landlord was one of the classic rich men out of a cartoon. He was a Lebanese man, a Mr. Atala, who would arrive in a black Buick, like from the 1950s, with a bowler derby, and full of rings, with a proper black suit, with a bow tie. And he would get out of the car and go into the vecindad to collect the rent himself, and he arrived with his assistant or secretary who was like "El Licenciado," with his briefcase. So he would start to knock on doors, and he was the boogieman, he was the horror . . . the first lucha that we had to fight was to end people's fear of Mr. Atala.

So you had Mr. Atala and El Licenciado. And El Licenciado was like . . . not only economic power was going to fall on you, but also the law. So it was horrible. And it was a vecindad full of balconies, with many places to hide. You would enter by 19 Calle Chile and leave by 20 Calle Leon Rubio, no? So you could cross, entering by the little entrance on 19 Chile, and the moment you enter, there were three patios full of apartments, 800 apartments, and it was filthy. And since you could leave through the other side, obviously, it was full of gangs of kids who were robbing people in the Center, and the police would chase them, and they would duck in there, and leave by the other side. It was like the Casbah.

And in the middle of all that violence and tension, Mr. Atala would come to collect the rent. He was so tough that he dared to do it. And then it was usual for him to perform his own evictions. He would arrive and "chun!" he would give them the "get out!" and they practically went and threw the people's stuff into the patio, and nobody interfered. It was shocking, but nobody interfered.

So it was a little bit remembering [his childhood] and a little bit of it being in the lucha libre environment, where a lot of people attended the luchas or were fans of the luchadores. It coincided with the fact that in July of 1983, El Santo died, and this was a reason to resuscitate him.[22] So the older women, I said to them, why not, when Mr. Atala comes to collect and evict, have El Santo suddenly appear on the balconies. Let's buy the whole uniform and have El Santo appear saying, "halt right there!" (Interview with author, 1997)

Four years later, the Asemblea de Barrios membership decided to create their own wrestler, to represent them in the fight for housing. One of the Asemblea's tactics was to organize physical interventions to prevent evictions. The idea for Superbarrio emerged after one such demonstration, in which a large group of people prevented an eviction in the neighborhood of La Merced. After the demonstration, some of the Asemblea membership met and "remembered what we wanted to do in 1983. We began to talk, and the Superbarrio thing came out. And from there, with the ladies who came to the meetings, some went to get the tights, others the trunks, others to find the mask."

Superbarrio's costume references a number of pop-culture icons. In addition to his association with lucha libre and El Santo, and the allusion to Superman, the costume's colors allude to a television character called El Chapulín Colorado (the Red Grasshopper). The Chapulín, a creation of the comedian Chespírito, is a comic antihero who fights crime and protects the innocent, but his triumphs are always due to the unintended consequences of his clumsiness. The Superbarrio figure thus simultaneously references the "cultural imperialism" of the North American comic book and the Mexican mass-mediated figure of the sympathetic incompetent, as well as the cinematic and live incarnations of lucha libre.

Superbarrio himself gives a different account of his own origins, which further separates his quotidian identity from his function as Superbarrio:

I was evicted for the first time when I was eight years old, and the second time when I was eleven. I have felt the unfairness of the landlords, the abuse of police, those I have lived. Afterward, when the earthquake happened, I was one of the affected, and I participated in the neighborhood organizations of the Center. Now I'm a street vendor. One day, June 12, 1987, at about 7:30 in the morning, when I opened the door of the house to go to work, a red light blew into my room and whirled everything around in my room. When it calmed down, when the light disappeared and the wind stopped blowing, I had on the mask and clothing of Superbarrio, and a voice said to me: You are Superbarrio, defender of the poor tenants and evicter of the voracious landlords. With all the concern that I had over the evictions and for the people who came to complain that they had been evicted, it was the response to that mortification that had happened to me so many times. (Cuéllar Vasquez 1993: 54)

Like the "El Santo versus Mr. Atala" action, Superbarrio was supposed to be a short-term tactic, meant to add a ludic element to the Asemblea's organizing efforts. He became a permanent fixture, however, once the Asemblea discovered the effect that he had on politicians, who were unnerved by the presence of a masked man. As Rascón told me:

A very common way that demonstrators arrive at public offices is to send a commission. Now, in this transition, where the commission enters the office of the functionary, there's a change of attitude. They start ready to do battle and as soon as four or five enter, there's a guy behind a desk, who says, "What is your problem?" You arrive and everything is a sanctuary, with photographs of the president . . . and someone suddenly wants to know "What do you want?" You have to express yourself well. . . . In that terrain, in that little parcel, many movements are left humiliated, we might say, no? But when suddenly Superbarrio enters the struggle (*lucha*), and Superbarrio appears in the office, the functionary behind his desk feels absolutely disoriented, out of order. He's the one who starts to stutter, who stumbles and knocks things over . . . Because he knew by the presence of Superbarrio that we were mocking him.

Superbarrio created two problems for the party functionary and more generally for the state. First, his presence at meetings keyed the event (in Erving Goffman's sense) and made it difficult for politicians dealing with the Asemblea to dominate the meeting.[23] But in addition, Superbarrio created a problem in terms of the post-1968 strategy of the PRI of neutralizing dissent by coopting and assimilating the leadership of potential opposition.[24] In order to be coopted one must have an identity that is embedded (or can be embedded) in personal relationships. Superbarrio's "real" identity is still not a matter of public record. Some say there are many Superbarrios; I've heard some claim that Rascón is Superbarrio, and others say he's really Carlos Monsiváis. He is also said to be a former wrestler, forced into retirement by chronic injuries some years earlier. But in another sense, Superbarrio doesn't exist as an individual at all, and since in order to be coopted, one must have an identity, the mask granted Superbarrio the power of incorruptibility.

Whereas Superbarrio was born of collective effort, the wrestler who embodies Ecologista Universal invented the character himself, because he wanted to contribute to the struggle against the Laguna Verde nuclear reactor. He was, in fact, a wrestler, struggling with problems with alcoholism and depression. When I interviewed him, asking him about the character's origin, he said that his life changed when he saw a television documentary on the monarch butterfly (which migrates to and from one forest in the Mexican state of Michoacan). Seeing the butterfly's long migration motivated him "to reflect, to take a moral inventory. What had I done? Like the insect, I fought for life." Inspired, he decided to develop a wrestling character who could leave the ring and participate in the struggle for the environment. To find a name, he looked in the dictionary. "I went to the dictionary and found *ecología, ecologismo . . . ecologista.* Since the lucha for the defense of nature is universal, I needed a universal vision, so I chose Ecologista Universal." He designed a costume that would symbolize his new commitment: a green cape bordered with yellow flowers and lined with white ("The flowers represent hope, because they become fruit. Green and yellow represent nature and the sun, white represents the purity of the sky"), and a single black glove ("The costume represents the cycle of life, so the black glove represents death").

Ecologista Universal's approach to political activism has been less playful than that of Superbarrio. His actions have made use of forms of protest traditionally associated with Catholic religious ritual: pilgrimage and fasting. For example, he fasted against NAFTA in 1991 and again in 1993. After the 1992 gas explosion in Guadalajara, he walked across Jalisco, Michoacan, Hidalgo, Queretaro, Mexico, Tlaxcala, and other states to inform people about the explosion and connect it to the movement against nuclear power. He also carried a wooden cross from Jalapa, Veracruz (his home), to Laguna Verde to protest the power plant itself. He toured for clean elections in 1994 and walked from the Angel de la Independencia in Mexico City to Chiapas for peace. However, he also participated in more theatrical forms of ritual protest, fighting lucha libre matches against his enemy El Deprededor (The Despoiler) and (along with Superanimal) performing a destapa of a Green Party candidate by pulling a pillowcase off of his head in

1997. As a result of his very visible political activities, he has been beaten up several times during his campaigns. Thus, he says that his visibility makes him vulnerable; his mask makes it easier for thugs to identify him. But the mask also makes it easier to gain supporters. "It makes it easier to present the struggle as universal, to say, "I am the people, I exist, and I do not agree with what is going on." (Interview with author, 1997)

CONCLUSION

The lucha libre mask is not simply a gimmick, not simply an element of costume. On the contrary, the mask has been of crucial importance in the constitution of lucha libre as a signifying practice. The presence of the mask has several interrelated effects. First, it has an impact on performance itself by serving as the motor for a range of narrative tropes. Symbolizing the masked wrestler's honor, it provides the pretext for attacks on that honor and for its defense. Because it is so central to the performance, and because it is beautiful, the mask serves as a metonym for the genre itself. And because of its centrality, the mask connects lucha libre with other discourses of nation, class, and culture in which masks (whether actual or metaphoric) are important.

Many writers and artists have asserted that the masks of lucha libre demonstrate a continuity between indigenous Mexico (whether pre-Hispanic or contemporary) and the urban present. The lucha libre mask is not, however, a direct continuation of rural tradition. Its history is rooted in the urban, modernizing environment of Mexico City in the 1930s, and its link with indigenous practice is filtered through the nationalist discourse of the postrevolutionary state. Nevertheless, the association of masks with the civilizations of the pre-Columbian past, the "México profundo" of the indigenous present, and the modern, urban practice of lucha libre empowers the latter with a complex set of symbolic, affective associations. It allows lucha libre to represent a model of national culture that transcends the division between the modern and the indigenous.

But the mask has a symbolic function beyond that of unifying the urban and the Indian. The centrality of masking in lucha libre allows the elaboration of a primarily visual, corporeal conversation about myth and secrecy, and about the relationship between personhood, individuality, and role. Insofar as lucha libre is a conversation about social agency, the mask provides a symbolic means of communicating a series of propositions about mid- to late-twentieth-century Mexican political culture. For over sixty years lucha libre set up a mise-en-scène in which the battle between good and evil was always arbitrated by corrupt authorities. It provided a space for a playful commentary about the political system as a whole. The mask allowed it to add a crucial element—it portrayed the struggle for power as a dialectic of concealment and disclosure. The act of hiding a wrestler's face with a mask both personalizes and depersonalizes. It allows the male wrestler to become a transcendent, mythic figure, even as it may mark him as the heir to his father's or uncle's very identity. It portrays masking as an empowering act and unmasking as a disaster. The discourse of the lucha libre mask thus provided a parodic contrast with some of the central metaphors of the twentieth-century Mexican state. In a system in which "unmasking" was used to empower the presidential candidate, lucha libre insisted on recognizing that power was found behind the scenes, before the matches. Because of the importance of the metaphors of masking and struggle, lucha libre was easy to adapt as a form of parodic political commentary.

5

A STRUGGLE BETWEEN TWO STRONG MEN?

As I showed in chapter 1, scholarly treatments of professional wrestling in the United States and Canada are divided in their evaluation of the genre's politics of class and nationalism. Some academics argue that professional wrestling's message is essentially counterhegemonic and explain it as a dramatic critique of the pretensions of liberal capitalism. Others argue, instead, that it is a conservative form that dramatizes and helps to reinforce ethnic boundaries, presenting political dissent as unpatriotic. In the evaluation of its gender politics, however, there appears to be no such division. Most writers take the gendered meanings embodied in wrestling for granted, beyond the level of analysis. Those who do attend to gender argue that it performs a male chauvinist worldview, despite the participation of women as wrestlers (Mazer 1998, Ball 1990). In a departure from most analyses, Sharon Mazer has proposed that its central theme is the display of diverse forms of masculinity, and that the presence of women and less masculine men only underlines this central point. "Despite its apparent transgressions," she writes (1998: 100), "and even though women are always visible in the margins and to the audience—professional wrestling is always a performance by men, for men, about men. Both its ethos and its aesthetics are explicitly centered on the idea of masculinity as something at once essential and performed."

If we accept Mazer's contention that professional wrestling is a representation of hegemonic constructions of gender in the United States, we might ask if the same could be said of lucha libre. The question of how gender is represented and what statements about gender are made (explicitly or implicitly) in lucha libre is particularly interesting in light of the extent to which discourses about masculinity in Mexico intersect with those of national culture. Is lucha libre, then, centrally about hegemonic constructions of masculinity in Mexico?

My first experience with live lucha libre certainly led me to think so. The event took place in an arena in Ciudad Nezahualcoyotl, and I went with an Ecuadoran sociologist who had lived in Mexico for the previous six years. Ciudad Nezahualcoyotl (called Neza for short) is the largest of the "mushroom cities" that grew up around the Federal District, seemingly overnight. Built in a drained lakebed, its population grew through informal settlement from virtually nothing in 1945 to 675,000 in 1970 (Vélez-Ibañez 1983). It has continued to grow, and is now at well over 1 million residents, listed as the fourth-largest city in Mexico.[1] Most residents (the majority of whom emigrated from the Federal District or other states) survive through their engagement with the informal economy. It is known to outsiders (including wrestlers) as an impoverished and dangerous area. It is also a place where lucha libre is a vibrant part of the local culture. In 1969 there were three wrestling arenas, compared with five movie houses (Vélez-Ibañez 1983: 74). The main arena, Arena Neza, is relatively close to the border of the Federal District, and it was there that we went to sit in the concrete bleachers surrounding the ringside seats.

I remember very little of the performance itself beyond the entrance of the first wrestler. In one smooth motion, the lithe, lycra-clad masked man vaulted over the ropes into the ring. After that, it was a blur of movement—difficult for me to follow, much less analyze.

I was therefore eager to hear my friend's interpretation of the performance, which he gave me a few days later over coffee. Like Sharon Mazer, he maintained that lucha libre was centrally about masculinity. More specifically, it was, he said, a dramatic celebration of "machismo." By linking lucha libre with machismo, he connected the performance to a system of male dominance, widely attributed to Mexican culture (and to other Latin American and Iberian cultures) that equates masculine self-worth with the oppression of women and humiliation of other men. My own position, however, is different. Although I agree that ideas about gender that may be glossed as machismo are at play in lucha libre, a number of counterdiscourses struggle with machismo for dominance in the ring. The representation of gender in the ring is complex and nuanced and cannot be accurately described as the theatricalization of *machista* ideology. This is the case because, regardless of the importance of machismo as a discourse (or as lived experience) in Mexico, it is not all encompassing. Contradictory ideas about gender circulate in the arena because they circulate in Mexican society as a whole.

MACHISMO AND DISCOURSE

In the academic literature on the ideological construction of nationalism, it has been widely argued that men and women have been differently situated in the nationalist discourses of the nineteenth and twentieth centuries. A commonplace observation is that nationalist ideologies interpolate the national subject as male, while treating women as the repositories of tradition, symbolically equated with the national territory. The construction of the male subject, moreover, is predicated on a series of exclusions, and on the simultaneous construction of a "healthy" hegemonic masculinity. The fact that women are "more traditional" might be seen as a good thing, to be encouraged or even enforced, or it might be seen as an obstacle to modernization (or as both). However, either the masculinity of the national subject is unproblematized, or he is problematized as pathologically feminine and in need of masculinization. In this context, Mexico presents an unusual case, because intellectuals concerned with the problem of national culture have tended to problematize the Mexican male as the repository of an ambivalent tradition and to represent Mexican hypermasculinity as pathological.

This formulation was first developed in Samuel Ramos's influential 1933 work *Profile of Man and Culture in Mexico*. His central argument was that Mexicans suffered from a collective inferiority complex because they had no culture of their own. Mexican (elite) culture consisted of borrowings from Europe, wrenched from their context. The (male and mestizo) Mexican, caught between the archaic, devalued, anticulture of the Indian and the secondhand culture of Europe, thus experienced his culture as a lack, which he hid behind a wall of defensiveness. In this sense, Ramos argued, every Mexican was, at heart, a *pelado*, an uncouth, uncultured, urban street tough. Like the lower-class pelado, every Mexican (male), no matter his class position, covered his sense of inferiority with a glorification of masculinity, which he equated with power. "From here," Ramos wrote, "is derived a very impoverished idea of manhood. Since [the Mexican] is, in effect, a being without content or substance, he tries to fill his emptiness with the only value that is within his reach: that of the macho" (quoted in Monsiváis 1981: 105).

At the time that Ramos used the term, *macho* meant male in the strict sense, used to refer to a male animal (such as a ram or a billy goat), and insulting if applied to a man (Gutmann 1996: 250). But in Octavio Paz's widely read 1961 work *The Labyrinth of Solitude* (which was, in a sense, a response to or continuation of Ramos's project), the term was used to refer to a social type. The problematic, archetypal Mexican male subject in Paz's writings was not the pelado (member of a particular social class), but the macho as such: aggressive, invulnerable, and insensitive.

Paz centered his analysis of the gendered symbolics of nationhood on the verb *chingar*. *Chingar* could be translated as "to fuck," but it implies not only penetration, but violence and violation. While *fuck* may imply violation, it can also be used to describe more consensual or mutual relations. *Chingar* describes the actions of a violently penetrating actor. Paz argued that the verb referenced the key idiom of power in Mexican culture by creating a difference in status between the active and passive agents, between actors and their victims. The person who suffers the action of *chingar*, he wrote, "is passive, inert and open, in contrast to the active, aggressive and closed person who inflicts it. The *chingón* is the *macho*, the male; he rips open the *chingada*, the female, who is pure passivity, defenseless against the exterior world. The relationship between them is violent and is determined by the cynical power of the first and impotence of the second" (Paz 1962: 81).[2] Masculinity itself is an inherently agonistic field of power that is exclusively open to males, and whose primary idiom is penetration. It is open to males because they are anatomically "closed," and closed to women because, inherently penetrable, they are "open."

The specificity of the term *chingar*, Paz argued, distinguished a general Iberian (especially Andalusian) honor/shame system from Mexican machismo. Under the terms of honor/shame systems in general, male status, glossed as "honor," depends (at least in part) on the ability of a group of male kin to maintain control over the sexuality of their kinswomen. Women's capacity (and willingness) to uphold their kinsmen's honor by assuring that they are seen to be controlled by their fathers, brothers, or husbands is glossed as "shame." In the specific case of Mexico, however, the sex/gender system is tied to the trauma of national identity. Machismo, argued Paz, is the gendered symbolic and material inheritance of the primal scene of the Mexican nation, the Conquest, here understood as the rape of the Indian mother by the Spanish father. "To the Spaniard, dishonor consists in being the son of a woman who voluntarily surrenders herself: a prostitute [*hijo de puta*]. To the Mexican it consists in being the fruit of a violation [*hijo de la chingada*]" (Paz 1962: 80). In the national Oedipal drama, power is conflated with the penetrative masculinity of the conquistador. The essayist tradition of Paz and Ramos (which has become part of public discourse both in and outside of Mexico) thus connected an exaggerated masculinity based on competition, violence, and resentment with the central problematic of Mexican cultural identity.

But whereas the essayist tradition construed the figure of the macho as a problem or a wound, in other realms the macho was celebrated. As Ilene O'Malley has argued, the cult of machismo (itself perhaps a response to the randomness and ubiquity of violence during the revolution) was assimilated to the ideology of the PRI by the 1940s. The macho also flourished in the film industry of the 1930s and 1940s and beyond as a paradigmatic figure of mexicanidad, where he was incarnated in particular actors (Jorge Negrete, Pedro Armendariz, Pedro Infante, David Silva) and particular roles: the charro, the boxer, the revolutionary. These roles depicted a romantic notion of the macho as the real, earthy Mexican, indifferent to risk, indifferent to death. However, as Carlos Monsiváis (1981) and Matthew Gutmann (1996) both have noted, although the macho has served as a symbol of national identification (at least in some contexts), he was simultaneously portrayed by the middle classes as a class other. As Gutmann puts it, "authoritative discussions of machismo . . . have all made connections between the macho, who represents the masculine pole of life . . . and the broader social and political world of twentieth century Mexico . . . and from the beginning, the portrayal of machismo (or its *pelado* forerunner) has been uniquely linked to the poor, unsophisticated, uncosmopolitan and un–North American" (1996: 255).

Likewise, ethnographic studies of Mexico and other parts of Latin America have also, with few exceptions, studied the poor, the uncosmopolitan, un–North American (or un-European). This situation is neither surprising nor unique to Latin America. It has, however, had implications for the ways in which the articulation of class, gender, modernity, and national culture have been represented in the ethnography of urban Mexico. In the ethnographies of the 1960s and 1970s, machismo came to be identified with a kind of violent or histrionic masculinity connected to particular social classes. Oscar Lewis, in his studies of the Mexican urban poor (most notably in *Children of Sanchez*, 1961), categorized it as an element of the culture of poverty, a cultural complex whose characteristics included "a relatively high incidence of abandonment of mothers and children, a trend toward mother-centered families, and a much greater knowledge of maternal relatives, the predominance of the nuclear family, a strong predisposition to authoritarianism . . . a belief in male superiority which reaches its crystallization in *machismo* or in the cult of masculinity, a corresponding martyr complex among women, and, finally, a high tolerance for psychological pathology of all sorts" (1961: xxvi–xxvii).[3]

Although Lewis did not claim that machismo per se was the exclusive property of the lower classes, he asserted that its "peculiar patterning" might determine whether it was part of the culture of poverty or just part of "Mexican" culture. "For example," he wrote, "in the middle class, *machismo* is expressed in terms of sexual exploits and the Don Juan complex whereas in the lower class it is expressed in terms of heroism and lack of physical fear" (xxvii). Nevertheless, as Gutmann has argued, the definition of machismo that Lewis elicited from one of the Sanchez sons, equating machismo with the refusal to back down in a fight, became a reference point for much subsequent literature on masculinity (not only in Latin America, but for settings as far removed as Polynesia).[4] Some ethnographers have challenged the accuracy of accounts (like those of Lewis) that portray machismo as a cultural ideal among the Mexican lower classes, pointing out that, in some contexts, the term *macho* is derogatory, used to describe men who are either old-fashioned or lack the traditionally manly qualities of responsibility or solidarity (Gutmann 1996, Romanucci-Ross 1973, Lomnitz Adler 1992).

Another strand of ethnographic writing (on Mexico and other parts of Latin America) has sought to reevaluate the meaning of machismo by analyzing it as a sex/gender system that expresses an underlying cultural logic. In the end, the main contribution of most of these studies has been to document or elaborate Paz's contention, in *Labyrinth of Solitude*, that the existence of the macho depends on the existence of two other figures: the woman and the failed man, the maricón (fag). Those who have attended more closely to the role of women in the system have argued that machismo is, fundamentally, a system of male dominance over women; that the system is grounded in a set of expectations of female behavior (public chastity, acceptance of suffering, idealization of motherhood) that distinguish good women (*mujeres abnegadas*—women who deny themselves) worthy of protection from unworthy "whores." Evelyn Stevens (1973) argued that this complex, "Marianismo" (emulation of the Virgin Mary), constituted "the other face of machismo."[5] More recent contributions foreground instead the importance of relations between males, arguing that "machismo is not exclusively or even primarily a means of structuring power relations between men and women. It is a means of structuring power between and among *men*" (Lancaster 1992; see also Prieur 1998, Kulick 1998, Carrier 1995).

In these latter accounts (and in line with Paz), masculine identity is understood to be inherently agonistic, so while women are necessary to the self-construction of the macho (in ways that I will clarify below), they are not sufficient to it. The performance of the macho—impenetrable and dominant—is equally dependent on the existence of the man who fails to defend his manhood and allows himself to be penetrated by other males. Sexual relations between males are, therefore, conceived as acts of dominance and subordination. As Paz observed over forty years ago, the penetrator is thus "regarded with a certain indulgence," whereas the "passive agent is an abject and degraded being" (Paz 1962). The penetrable male—called *maricón* or *jota/joto* in Mexico, or *cochón* in Nicaragua—thus functions as the symbolic endpoint in a continuum produced through ongoing competition between men.[6] As Roger Lancaster writes (1992: 237): "Every [male] act is, effectively, part of an ongoing exchange system between men in which women figure as intermediaries. To maintain one's masculinity, one must successfully come out on top of these exchanges. To lose in this ongoing exchange system entails a loss of face and thus a loss of masculinity. The threat is a total loss of status, whereby one descends to the zero point of the game and either literally or effectively becomes a cochón."

Like the Nicaraguan cochón, the Mexican maricón, as various writers have noted, is "homosexual," but within this system, homosexuality is inscribed not by object choice, but by willingness to be penetrated by other males. He is ontologically feminine because he is "open," penetrable. Since any man might become a maricón, the macho must continually reaffirm his position of *impenetrability* through displays of virility, violence, and risk taking.

LUCHA LIBRE AS MACHISTA RITUAL DRAMA

According to Sharon Mazer, professional wrestling in the United States is a ritual presentation of a North American ideology of masculinity, one that is simultaneously essentialist and constructivist. Rather than offering a "presentation of masculinity that is singular and conservative," she claims that the genre "presents two or more contradictory possibilities [of masculinity] poised against and coexisting with each other. Masculinity is both a choice and an essence, an option and an imperative" (1998: 117). The masculinity of the wrestlers is essentialized by two mechanisms. First, she argues, the presence of women in the ring provides an unbreachable limit—an other against which the masculine selves can be measured. Second, professional wrestling portrays male bodily contact as asexual contact: "The prohibition against sexualizing the contact between men is unspoken, but nevertheless emphatic. . . . Professional wrestling thus offers participants the actual or vicarious pleasures of participating in physical contact between men in a sanctioned arena while at the same time inhibiting or denying the possibility that those pleasures might be sexual" (110). The heterosexualizing presence of women and the desexualization of physical contact between men serve, she argues, to define the limit of masculinity. Male wrestlers must, in the end, show that however they act, whatever they wear, they have not violated that ultimate limit. It is, Mazer says, "imperative for each wrestler that his drag be dropped at some point to display and celebrate the essential man within" (116). Professional wrestling thus presents an account of North American masculinity that is complex and allows for diversity yet rests on the exclusion of women and denial of homosexuality.

The presentation of masculinity in lucha libre is similarly complex and contradictory. No one in the wrestling family ever told me that lucha libre was about machismo per se, although several wrestlers and others regarded lucha libre as an essentially masculine activity. Some told me that the pleasure of lucha libre for the audience should lie, in part, in seeing the *cuerpo corpulente* (thick muscular body) of the implicitly male luchador. Others described the performance itself as "a struggle between two *men* to show which of them is the stronger."

Yet the ways in which gender is represented in Mexico do not mirror the ways in which gender is represented in U.S. professional wrestling. First, it would be difficult in Mexico to argue that the contact between wrestlers is not sexualized, since male-male sexual contact (like wrestling) is perceived as a matter of domination (and, to some degree, vice versa—physical domination is implicitly sexualized). Lucha libre thus shares certain features with a speech genre known in Mexico as the *albur*. The albur is a double entendre, used in a kind of competition, in which the speaker tries to linguistically align himself as the penetrator in relation to the listener. "Each of the speakers tries to humiliate his adversary with verbal traps and ingenious linguistic combinations in which the loser is the person who cannot think of a comeback . . . These jibes are full of aggressive sexual allusions, the loser is possessed, is violated by the winner, and the spectators laugh at him" (Paz 1962: 82).[7]

One way to look at lucha libre performance is as a visual, physical albur. The goal in lucha libre is not to knock the opponent out, or score a point against him, but to render him immobilized, helpless, and (perhaps) ridiculous. During the match itself, wrestlers play with humiliating one another —one example of this is the routine in which one wrestler rips off another's mask, a trope Jose Joaquin Blanco (1990: 31) calls the attempt to "despoil the most cared for and coveted virginity on earth."

As I have described, a match ends in one of three ways: the winner may pin the loser's shoulders to the mat for the referee's count of three, the winner may put the loser in a submission hold (in which case the loser has to show that he or she is suffering and acknowledge submission by rapidly waving his or her hands with fingers outstretched), or one side may be disqualified by the referee for violation of a rule. There are a number of different holds that can be used to end a match, and most involve a degree of intimate and immobilizing bodily contact. In the often-used *rana invertida* (inverted frog), for example, the loser is pinned on his back with his legs bent and feet off the ground. The winner immobilizes him by grabbing his opponent's wrists and pressing his body against the back of the loser's thighs, sometimes accompanying the gesture with loud grunts and thrusting motions as he tries to increase the effectiveness of the hold.[8] In El Santo's signature de a caballo move, the winner straddles the loser's back in a squatting position. He drapes the loser's arms over his thighs and pulls his head backward, which hyperextends the loser's back until he submits. But whatever techniques are used, victory depends on rendering the opponent spectacularly powerless, robbed of agency. Within the terms of machista discourse, the loser is placed in a feminine and violated position.

While wrestlers themselves would not necessarily agree that they are participating in a pantomimic rape, the sexual subtext is revealed in the audience response. Strenuous holds elicit cries of "¡ay, papá!" and other subtly (or not so subtly) homoerotic responses. In the battle between two machos, the winner, in the words of one spectator "makes [the loser] his woman." Salvador Novo noted as much in his 1940 essay *Mi Lucha (Libre)* (the title is a pun on *Mein Kampf*). Of the wrestling match, he wrote:

> We already know that one of the two will defeat the other. It is even possible to suppose (and this supposition, far from robbing the spectacle of artistic merit, confers on its organizers an admirable tragic talent that is Olympic in more than one sense) that one can predict which of the two opponents turn it is to receive, like a submissive wife, the weight of his opponent on his chest and back. When that happens, we already know that all is consummated. But while that happens, that is, during the delicious process that Havelock Ellis would call the tumescence—what brilliant improvisations we see! (Novo [1940] 1964: 600)

In this sense, lucha libre provides a spectacular affirmation of the equation between being a man and being on top.

There are practices within both performance and reception of lucha libre, however, that problematize this reading, since, in the match between two strong men, the symbolics of gender are given an ironic twist. The battle is one between two machos, but the *real macho* is not the técnico (for whom most spectators will cheer). It is the rudo who recognizes no authority but power, who epitomizes the rule of violence and domination over the rule of law. In other words, in a system in which hypermasculinity is equated with exploitation, it is the rudo who better performs the macho role. In this sense, the técnico is the representative of an alternative model of masculine authority, in Anne Rubenstein's phrase, the "counter-macho" (Rubenstein 2003: 226).

The técnico can be understood as the "countermacho" in another sense as well. In a 1998 article, Marit Melhuus synthesized the literature of male sexuality with that of "Marianismo," to describe the cultural logic of a central Mexican mestizo gender system. Because her argument integrates a number of observations about sexuality and gender in Mexico in a way that is somewhat novel, it is worth summarizing here. It is grounded in her own research on (presumptively heterosexual) women and men in San Felipe, a provincial capital north of Mexico City, and Annick Prieur's work with "jotas" in Ciudad Nezahualcoyotl, where I first saw lucha libre. Prieur's subjects are "vestidas": males who cross-dress and are attracted to conventionally masculine men by whom they wish to be penetrated. In using both sets of data to examine "the interconnections between heterosexual and male homosexual discourses" (354), Melhuus argues that San Felipe and Ciudad Nezahualcoyotl (and, by implication, the entire Mexico City *clase popular*)—in fact, all of central highland Mexico (including wrestling fans and luchadores of both sexes)—share the same sex/gender system.

Melhuus defines *machismo* (following local convention) as a gloss for male dominance in a system where men and women belong in separate, mutually constitutive hierarchies of power. The hierarchy is quite distinct. Men are situated on a continuum of masculinity, with the dominant penetrating, impenetrable macho at one pole, the maricón at the other. Between the two poles, however, are degrees of masculinity.[9] Women, on the other hand, operate within a dichotomy—not of more and less feminine, but between decency (or respectability) and indecency. If Melhuus's analysis of the central Mexican gender system is correct, it has implications for the gendered symbolics of lucha libre, for luchadores are differentiated (through victory or defeat, but also throughout the course of the match and to differing degrees) not only in reference to the masculine status continuum of macho-maricón. They are also, before the match, divided into a dichotomy of técnico and rudo, decent and indecent. In other words, if Melhuus is correct in her analysis, in lucha libre both gender hierarchies are integrated in a single performance. The struggle between two strong men is simultaneously organized as a struggle between two women.

THE GOOD, THE BAD, AND THE FEMALE

According to Melhuus (following Stevens and others), the female hierarchy of virtue is predicated on the two mutually exclusive grounds of virginity/impenetrability and motherhood. Women resolve the contradiction between the two through identification with the Virgin Mary, but that identification is grounded less in the latter's status as virgin than in her status as mother. Although a woman ideally achieves respectability through motherhood in the context of a sanctioned marriage with a husband who is able to provide for her and her children, it is acknowledged by the women of San Felipe that that is not always possible. It is expected that women will sometimes be *fracasada* (ruined, i.e., seduced and abandoned) or *abandonada* (abandoned by a man who did fulfill the role of husband/father for a time, but left her for another woman). In such cases, a woman's status as mother may in and of itself grant her respectability.

Since the performance of masculinity requires both the control/protection of kinswomen and displays of virility (with other men's kinswomen), both decent and indecent women are necessary to the construction of the masculine continuum.[10] Both necessary and dangerous to the production of masculine identity, women, in this system, are the site of male vulnerability. At the level of representation—of the circulation of symbols—this problematic (a dilemma widely cited in the literature on honor-shame systems) takes a particular form in the popular culture and national mythology of Mexico. The dramatic form that receives widest circulation in Mexico, the telenovela, is conventionally structured as a struggle over the love of a good (or at least salvageable) man between two feminine archetypes: the humble, affectionate, chaste, honest heroine, and the often wealthy, evil, manipulative *mala mujer* (evil woman).[11]

In telenovelas (as in some, though not all *historietas*, small, inexpensive comics that are very popular in Mexico),[12] the moral coding of a woman depends on her relationship to and influence on a man. This particular aspect of the mala mujer is apparent in the construction of the archetypical mala mujer, "La Malinche," who achieved her infamous status in the pantheon of national symbols by collaborating with the conquistador Hernán Cortés. Malintzin, as she was named, or Doña Mariña, as she was called by the Spaniards, was a slave, bilingual in Nahuatl and Mayan, who was given as a gift to Cortés by the Mayan lords of Tabasco. She became both his mistress and his translator. Instrumental in the later course of the conquest, she came, over time, to figure as a master symbol of betrayal and destructive xenophilia.

As the corrupted Indian, La Malinche stands in symbolic contrast with the Virgin of Guadalupe, the indigenized apparition of the Virgin Mary who (in contrast with the whorish Spaniard-loving Malinche) appeared as a mother figure to "The Indian" Juan Diego. The figures of Guadalupe and Malinche thus link the contrast between decency and indecency with central myths of national origin. The Virgin of Guadalupe represents not only respectable, circumspect, maternal womanhood, but also the successful and legitimate integration of the Spanish and indigenous aspects of Mexican culture. La Malinche, on the other hand, connects sexual impropriety and ambition with a traitorous love of the conquering foreigner. In ordinary conversation, the epithet *malinchista* (or *malinchismo*) is used to mean one who prefers the foreign over the Mexican, usually in connection with middle- or upper-class consumption patterns. If the macho is stereotypically lower-class and ultra-Mexican, the insufficiently Mexican Malinchista is stereotypically middle- or upper-class.

Another aspect of the symbolic construction of the mala mujer is that, although sexual availability is important, representations of the indecent woman define her not only (or even primarily) by her sexuality, but also by her public activity (Paz 1962, Melhuus 1998, Castillo 1998).[13] As Debra A. Castillo observes, stories about bad women and prostitutes in Mexico "describe a national culture in which presumed gender boundaries for women and the transgression of these boundaries are deeply embedded features of the social fabric. . . . Women who infringe upon the public space remain scandalous, and this continuing scandal . . . resides initially in the impact of a female-gendered human being in an unexpectedly public space, quite apart from questions of sexual availability" (1998: 3). At the level of representation, in different kinds of fiction, then, sexual availability functions as a metaphor for transgressing the boundary of the public.

Melhuus uses her ethnographic data to argue, however, that in the moral system of San Felipe, women's public activity (in particular, work outside of the home) may be judged contextually. It is indecent for a married woman to work outside the home because she undermines her husband's honor on two grounds: her money-earning activity implies that he cannot provide for his family and her visibility implies that he cannot control her movements (and thus her sexuality). However, the social meaning of work is different for abandonadas and fracasadas. All women, regardless of marital status, can achieve respectability through suffering as mothers. Motherhood and suffering are seen as intrinsically connected and intrinsically virtuous, and this allows certain behaviors to be contextually defined as decent or indecent. It is fully respectable for a single mother to work to support her (fatherless) children as long as her work can be construed as a sacrifice undertaken for their benefit. The central Mexican sex/gender system has a morally legitimate place for the category "single mother," but, Melhuus argues, it lacks a morally unambiguous place for the childless "single woman."

It is in this particular that Melhuus explicitly connects her data on small-town Mexico with Prieur's material on Ciudad Neza. Prieur's informants are lower-class males who refer to themselves as vestidas or jotas, who seek to attract and keep conventionally masculine partners by cultivating a feminine self-presentation (which she glosses as "stealing femininity"). She interprets the vestidas' appropriation of feminine signs as part of an elaborate ruse in which they pretend that they are female so that their partners can pretend that they are heterosexual. Melhuus links her material on San Felipe women with Prieur's vestidas by arguing that, in the sex/gender system of central Mexico, the structural position of the single woman is taken by the autonomous-yet-penetrable jota. She acknowledges that "in urban contexts, and in particular, middle class contexts, [the single woman] would be recognizable, indicating, perhaps, shifts in the ways of configuring gender" (38). But by placing Prieur's informants into the same symbolic order as her own, she implicitly places the "respectable career woman" outside the bounds of local gender configurations in Ciudad Neza as well as San Felipe.

The picture that emerges in the works of writers from Paz to Melhuus is of a coherent, consistent Mexican gender system, lived by all of the lower classes (and perhaps by *all* Mexicans), in which real men dominate and penetrate, good women scrupulously observe the distinction of public and private (so far as they are materially able), and jotas, in their inevitable failure to defend their boundaries, prop up the masculinity of the machos. But an examination of lucha libre—its performance, its reception, and its subculture—casts doubt on the adequacy of this account. If lucha libre is, indeed, a story that Mexicans tell themselves about themselves, the story it tells about gender is more contradictory than the story told by many analysts of the Mexican gender system. Lucha libre is a performance that is open to multiple readings on the axis of representations of gender, even when it is performed by two men. To complicate matters further, many matches cannot be described as a struggle between two men. Not all wrestlers are male, and not all male wrestlers are unambiguously men. The sections to follow will look at different performers in the arena who cannot credibly perform in a battle between two machos but are wrestlers nonetheless.

A STRUGGLE BETWEEN TWO *MEN*?

De Los Otros

Lucha libre is a space in which the macho–maricón continuum is represented not only in the relative positioning of men competing over who is "more" macho but also by men who have abdicated their masculinity. In Mexico such men are referred to by a number of terms: *homosexual*, *gay*, *joto* (jack or page, as in a deck of cards), *marica* (sissy), *puto* (male whore), *raro* (queer), maricón (big sissy), or, euphemistically, as *los otros* (the others). In the literature of male-male sexual practices and identities in Latin America, some writers have suggested that local ideologies of sexual difference, in which the homosexuality of the penetrated male supports (rather than undermines) the masculinity of the penetrator, allow a space of tolerance that North American and northern European societies lack. Lancaster, for example, has claimed that gay bashing does not make cultural sense in the Nicaraguan context since cochones pose no threat to masculine subjectivity. While Nicaraguans may respond to the cochón with "amusement or contempt . . . bullying . . . intimidation, sometimes blackmail . . .

rough play," cochones face "neither organized, lethal violence, nor panicked attacks" (Lancaster 1992: 247). Prieur (1998) makes a similar point when she suggests that Mexican society is more tolerant of gay visibility (as opposed to gay activity) than Norwegian society. In other words, they suggest that the visible maricón or jota (like the prostitute) is accepted (albeit within certain limits) in Latin American societies because he underwrites the masculinity of the macho (see also Carrier 1995, from whom I borrowed the heading above).

I find such arguments unconvincing, for gay men in Mexico face widespread hostility that goes well beyond "amusement" into culturally specific forms of contempt that include lethal violence.[14] However, the hostile attitudes toward and beliefs about gay men that several people (wrestlers and others) communicated to me differed in significant ways from those common in the United States. First, as many have asserted (Paz 1962, Lancaster 1992, Kulick 1998, Prieur 1998, Carrier 1995), the contempt that many Mexicans express toward homosexual men is directed at men who allow themselves to be penetrated. The act of penetration is transformative only for the receptive partner. It places him, but not his partner, into the category of "maricón." The man who only ever penetrates other males is not "just" a man, as some have argued. But he is (in the words of one middle-class Mexican woman) "just a *cabrón*, but not a maricón."[15] The man who allows himself to be penetrated, on the other hand, is guilty of having failed to defend himself, having allowed himself to be exploited. The fact that the maricón lets himself be exploited not only makes him the object of pity; his refusal to defend himself makes him potentially dangerous. The maricón is thought to be intrinsically traitorous because *no tiene palabra* (his word is no good). He doesn't defend himself (by definition) and so is not to be trusted.

JOTOS IN THE RING

The figure of the maricón/joto appears in lucha libre as a category of wrestler called *exotico*: a male luchador who wrestles in drag. The exotico's movement vocabulary is campy, often silly, seldom dignified. They intersperse their wrestling moves with skipping and preening, sometimes flirting with or kissing the other wrestlers. While it is certainly possible to read exotico performance as an antigay slur, that is not the only possible reading. The parodic wrestling performance of the exotico can also be understood as a challenge to the discourse of the degraded maricón.

I have never heard the term *exotico* used outside of the context of lucha libre, although it recalls the terms raro (queer) and *exotica* (referring to cabaret dancers, particularly in the 1940s and 1950s). The first exoticos appeared in the 1940s. Sterling Davis, a wrestler from the United States, worked in Mexico as Gardenia Davis, a rudo who would throw gardenias to the crowd when he entered the ring. He was followed by another wrestler, Lalo el Exotico. Like Gorgeous George (whose character was inspired, in part, by Gardenia Davis), the two men played preening dandies. More luchadores took up the role afterward, using names like Babe Sharon and Orchidea.

Until the late 1980s, exoticos seem to have insisted on a separation between their roles and their real-life identities. When interviewers would ask Rudy Reynosa, the best-known exotico of the 1970s and early 1980s, about his behavior outside of the ring, he would insist that the act was just an act. The only pre-1980s wrestler I have heard of who did self-identify as a "joto" worked the circuit in the 1950s, but as a luchadora.[16] That changed in the mid-1980s, however, when a pair of wrestlers trained by Reynosa debuted as exoticos. In contrast to previous generations of exoticos, they made no attempt to deny a connection between their role in the ring and their daily lives, publicly identifying themselves as *homosexuales*.

LOS EXOTICOS

> An *exotico* is a person who is delicate, who has fine manners. This doesn't mean that he doesn't know what lucha libre is, because for them to give you the professional wrestler's license . . . you have to know how to do intercollegiate wrestling, Greco-Roman wrestling—you have to be 100% prepared.
>
> MAY FLOWERS 1997

> We Los Exoticos are homosexuals, and that's how we fight. We don't experience a conflict of being men and women at the same time. We represent a double persona at the same time.
>
> CASSANDRA, QUOTED IN FASCINETTO 1992: 192

I first saw exoticos in the ring in Puebla in 1994 in the match between two three-man teams described in chapter 2. The técnicos were led by a wrestler called Seminarista. Rumored really to be an ex-seminary student, he wore a rosary printed across the chest of his gray lycra body suit. The rudo team consisted of their captain, El Loco Valentino, a dandified charro in baby-blue tights and a large black sombrero, and two men wearing garish make-up and frilly bathrobes, which they shed to reveal flowered one-piece women's bathing suits. It was a violent match in which Loco Valentino beat Seminarista to a bloody pulp, while the latter refused to submit. Finally, the exoticos, Adrian and Cassandra, interweaving wrestling techniques with displays of limp wrists and puckered lips, pinned each of Seminarista's teammates in especially lascivious-looking holds. The match ended with Seminarista lying abject and bloodied on the canvas, while the victorious drag queens pantomimed the rape of his partners.

Adrian and Cassandra performed a style of wrestling that shifted the role of exotico away from Gardenia Davis knockoffs toward a potentially more subversive presentation. The style began during the 1980s, when Rudy Reynosa started to carry the exotico act a little bit farther than his predecessors. In addition to the displays of vanity that marked Gardenia Davis and others as feminine, Reynosa began to harass his opponents in the ring with kisses and flirtatious gestures, all the while maintaining that his exotico style was just an act. Around 1986, however, he trained two young wrestlers to perform with him as a team called Los Exoticos. These two, May Flowers and Pimpernela Escarlata, changed the exotico role, for unlike their predecessors they publicly embraced a gay identity.

May Flowers began training as a wrestler around 1984 and debuted as an exotico a year and a half later. Attracted by the glamour and the wardrobe, the fine clothes and finer manners, he studied the movement vocabulary of his contemporaries: Bello Greco, Sergio Hermoso, and his mentor Reynosa. When he and his partner Pimpernela made their debut, they added more explicitly feminine accessories to their costumes: "Pantyhose, makeup, hats, gloves . . . if the exoticos from before wore glamorous clothing, what we wore was even more glamorous" (May Flowers, interview with author, 1997). May Flowers, Pimpernela Escarlata, and Rudy Reynosa formed a trio: Reynosa, short and wide, played the clown. Pimpernela Escarlata played the skilled wrestler, and May Flowers played the acrobat, throwing himself off the cords.

In their interviews, May Flowers and Pimpernela Escarlata (unlike Reynosa) made it clear that they were really gay, and that the role of exotico came to them "naturally." According to Pimpernela Escarlata, to take another role would have been an act of fraud, impossible to pull off in front of a discerning audience. In an interview with Lola Fascinetto, he recounts:

> I used the mask on three occasions, *m'hija*. When I started in *lucha libre* I began wrestling as a man with the title "Vans," but later the people figured out that I wasn't a man, because they know, they aren't stupid, "That's a *joto!*" they shouted. It made me ashamed, and in order to throw them off the scent, I put on another mask of a man with another name: El Playboy. But sincerely, I couldn't do it, *m'hija*. So I put away the men's masks, and I went out camping it up (*joteando*) as an exotico. (Pimpernela Scarlata, quoted in Fascinetto 1992: 188)[17]

The Exoticos changed the exotico style from a representation of a tendency to a representation of a social category and celebrated lucha libre as a means of upward mobility for themselves specifically as homosexuals. Both May Flowers and Pimpernela Scarlata worked in gay bars in their hometown of Torreon, Coahuila, before they became wrestlers (May Flowers as a barkeeper, Pimpernela as a drag performer). Conflating sexuality with class status, May Flowers has described lucha libre as a way past the limited options available to him: "Not just any homosexual travels or is given the luxury to say I'm going to this or that part of the world, much less those in our condition . . . coming from a very humble environment" (May Flowers, quoted in Fascinetto 1992: 187).

Instead of separating their wrestling personae from their personal identities, they present themselves as "homosexual" (their term, sometimes interchangeable with "gay") role models: ambassadors from the liberated capital to the closeted provinces. As Pimpernela Escarlata recounted to an interviewer, when they went to Villahermosa, Tabasco: "We gave advice to the gays there, because many of them, for X problems with the family, with work, school, were ashamed and went pretending that they weren't gay, but when they see us up in the ring, photographed in magazines and they know about us from the news reports, then it's like they feel like they have more freedom to be themselves" (Pimpernela Escarlata, quoted in Fascinetto 1992: 192).

In fact, the exoticos have served as role models, at least once. One young gay man from the northern state of Tamaulipas told me that he had seen the Exoticos perform in his hometown when he was a young teenager, struggling with his sexual identity. Watching the exoticos wrestle and actually defeat their opponents was, he claimed, an affirming experience, and one that helped him to come to terms with his sexuality. While I don't know whether this is a common experience for gay youth in Mexico, it indicates that the Exoticos' performance does allow for the possibility of positive identification for some fans.

On the other hand, the exotico role is treated as a subcategory of rudo, and the audience generally responds to them as such. This means, however, that even though the fans of the técnicos jeer them, they have the support of the prorudo faction. In some arenas, a sizable section cheers them on with semi-ironic cries of "¡Arriba los maricones!" and "¡Da le maricón!" (Hooray for the maricones; Give it to 'em, maricón). Although they act out the stereotype of the effeminate queen—as Pimpernela Escarlata put it, "joteando"—they do not necessarily act out the stereotype of the cowardly traitor. As a team, they demonstrate more loyalty to one another than would most rudos. Even when they get in each other's way, they present themselves as willing to forgive each other. For example, in November 1996, May Flowers lost his hair in a "suicide match" to the masked rudo Pierroth.[18] After defeating several other duos, he and Pierroth faced each other. By his own account he had Pierroth in a double nelson when Pimpernela Escarlata entered the ring to deliver a flying kick to Pierroth. He missed, hitting May Flowers instead, and Pierroth was able to take advantage of the moment and pin the exotico.

Since they are rudos, it is not strange that Pimpernela plucked victory from his partner's grasp. Driven by rage or a will to dominate, rudos often miss their target and land their blows on an unfortunate ally. What was strange was May Flowers's reaction, for rudos typically turn on a partner who makes a mistake and start fights with one another during and after the match. May Flowers, in contrast, told the reporter that he forgave his former partner. "I can't get angry," he said, "because I recognize that I was taking advantage by letting him intervene in the battle, and the sin brought its own punishment, and anyway, I am bound to [Pimpernela] in a friendship of many years, and I reiterate, the only thing he tried to do was help me" (Box y Lucha, 1996c: 13). In short, if one of the stereotypes of the maricón is disloyalty, then May Flowers made a point of playing against both rudo and joto stereotypes.

But the key challenge that the exoticos pose to the Mexican stereotype of the maricón lies in the fact that they can and do win their matches—not always, but about as often as any other rudo. Exoticos thus occupy a paradoxical space in the popular culture of Mexico. Like Annick Prieur's jota informants, the exoticos' identity as homosexuals is (at least ambivalently) bound to their appropriation of feminine signs and to the construction and presentation of an identity as neither men nor women. As Prieur points out, such self-construction comes at a price, since the relationship between masculinity and femininity is normatively "not only one of interdependence, but also one of domination" and thus "when the *jotas* appropriate for themselves feminine signs, they also expose themselves to domination and to social contempt, for not having defended their masculinity" (Prieur 1998). Exoticos, however, unsettle the equation by showing that they can appropriate feminine signs and still publicly dominate and vacate the masculinity of "real" men. Taking on an effeminate identity, they perform successfully in a contest of masculinity, and in so doing, I would argue, they also problematize the idea of the ring as masculine space. Entering the arena as (to paraphrase Kulick 1998) "not quite men," they appropriate and undermine the manhood of their opponents. They defend themselves, the one thing of which maricones are, by definition, thought to be incapable. As May Flowers put it, when asked how he and other exoticos cope with fighting big, strong male wrestlers: "Well, if you are talking about physical force, clearly it doesn't affect us, because even though we practice a different style, that is, even though we wrestle as exoticos, we are sufficiently prepared to face whoever is put in front of us, and even though we are exoticos, 'tenemos muchos pantalones' [we have a lot of 'pants'] with which to answer any physical or even verbal aggression" (*Superluchas* 1996: 13).

In the end, though, Los Exoticos are still rudos. Moreover, because they use fewer of the tactics that mark other rudos as bad guys, it is clear that their gender performance is enough to define their moral role.[19] The performance of Los Exoticos can be read in a variety of ways. It gives the audience a chance to abuse them and give delighted vent to their homophobia. They do nothing to challenge the notion that a maricón is a bad thing to be. On the other hand, by their very presence in the ring, they mock the system that they are supposed to ground. It is thus wholly possible for a gay teenager in a conservative small city to identify with them and feel proud instead of mocked when they come through on tour.

They nevertheless raise a question: Is it possible for a wrestler to be both exotico and a técnico?

DIVINO EXOTICO

> The Mexican venerates a bleeding and humiliated Christ, a Christ who has been beaten by soldiers and condemned by the judges because he sees in him a transfigured image of his own identity.
>
> OCTAVIO PAZ, *LABYRINTH OF SOLITUDE*

In a December 1997 issue of *Box y Lucha*, the arena schedule showed a wrestler called Bello Exotico listed in the técnico slot for the third match at an arena in the nearby city of Pachuca. Knowing that exoticos are always cast as rudos, I was intrigued—how might an exotico be cast as a good guy? Although I did not find an ethically affirmative representation of male homosexuality, what I did see astonished me. When the wrestler (whose name turned out to be Divino Exotico) entered the arena, I was dumbstruck—for I had never seen anything quite like him. A slim man, his lithe body was covered by a full bodysuit and a mask. His mask had fringe on the cheeks, red, heart-shaped lips, and teardrops sewn beneath the eyes. His multicolored bodysuit—pink below, black above, was also fringed, and when he moved, the fringes would accentuate his movements.

A clear crowd favorite, he used a very acrobatic movement vocabulary, incorporating a lot of somersaults and aerial moves. When he fell backward, he kept his back straight, which seemed to slow down the fall and give the impression that gravity itself had slowed. He was so graceful and expressive, I felt sure that he had trained as a mime. And in fine técnico fashion, he was made abject, beaten up and repeatedly fouled by the rudos. When the ruffians tore his mask off at the end of the match, two old women ran forward and tenderly covered his face with a blue acrylic sweater until he could remask himself.

After the match, I approached him with a friend. Women surrounded him, telling him that he was handsome (despite the bodysuit and mask that hid his features entirely). When I asked him for an interview, he responded in a soft tenor, "sí, son amores" (yes, you're a couple of sweethearts) touching my arm. His affect was startlingly feminine—not like a drag queen, but with the casual warmth of a Mexican woman. When I interviewed him a week later, I was somewhat surprised to meet the conventionally masculine (albeit soft-spoken) mustache-bearing factory worker who lived behind the mask.

Divino Exotico's project might be called transgender or gender-bending or androgynous. It is, however, quite a different project from that of May Flowers and the rest of Los Exoticos. Whereas Pimpernela Escarlata explained his exotico identity as the expression of an unmaskable inner self, Divino Exotico explains his androgyny as something that depends on the mask. Without the mask, he told me, people would say "you're no exotico," but with the mask he is transformed, "Because I put on the mask, I put on the little mouth, I cover myself completely, and I become an exotico."

The wrestler started his career in 1993. He started training after his older brother, fooling around, twisted his arm—and then invited him to learn lucha libre so he could twist other people's arms. He wrestled as several different characters after taking his license, originally as a rudo. He found that audiences would not accept him as a rudo but did accept him as a técnico. When I saw him in Pachuca, he had been wrestling as Divino Exotico for about a year.

Divino Exotico is not an exotico in the sense of Los Exoticos or their predecessors for two reasons. First, his performance of femininity is not parodic. Second, his character is not supposed to be a maricón. He decided to call himself exotico only when he learned that the word had another, nonsexual meaning. The idea came up when a friend told him that he had eaten some "exotic fruit":

> So I said, "What do you mean exotic?" I thought it was just something sexual, something to do with that whole thing. He said, "No, exotic is a tropical fruit, a flower, a perfume." I liked it. I liked the name exotico [so I said]—"I'm going to use 'Exotico,' but not like they do." He will have his own way of walking. Not like them, to be laughed at, for people to shout nasty things. So, I said, I'm going to make him for women, so that they see that there is someone who, despite being an exotico, wrestles like a man. So then they said to me, "Aren't you just divine in the ring?" and so I thought of Divino Exotico. (Interview with author, December 1997)

He created Divino Exotico as a male character with whom women could identify: androgynous and effeminate, but without conventional coded (or overt) references to male homosexuality. His graceful movements, which I thought were derived from mime, turned out to be his own expression of nonparodic drag. As he related, "I dedicated myself to see how women walk, how they move. I began to walk that way myself. I wanted to copy it, and I began to walk, even to make movements like a woman, like this."

By moving like a woman, he meant to appear vulnerable—like a child— to elicit feelings of protectiveness *from* women. Yet his performance would be enjoyable (for his hypothetical female audience) because he would demonstrate that for all his feminine vulnerability, he could defend himself like a man. His role is perhaps a transformation of another masculine archetype, one that has been less elaborated in the literature of national culture than the various transformations of the macho. Divino Exotico performs the role of the "bleeding and humiliated Christ" who suffers for his (female) public, which then rises to his defense. As the wrestler explained, "I like for them to hit him [Divino Exotico], so that the women say, 'Leave him alone.' I like it so much I feel like saying, 'Hit me more if you want to.' A little after I debuted, when I was entering the ring, the women would say, 'Come, we'll help you, but don't let yourself get hurt . . . if they hit you I'll defend you.'"

Divino Exotico is thus a very complex character. As the "bleeding and humiliated Christ," and through his denial of sexuality, he plays the role of the mujer abnegada. Indeed, through portraying himself as both suffering and impenetrable, he performs the role of the Virgin Mother. Women in the audience are invited to identify with him as a woman. But when he wrestles, when he wins, when he leaves the ring bloodied but victorious, he shows them that he defends himself (like a man). Divino Exotico makes the implicit structure of matches between men explicit: he is a decent woman, with the ability to triumph in the contest of masculinity.

Luchadoras

When I began to train in lucha libre, I was one of only two women in the class. The other was Alejandra, a small, fine-boned teenager, with a dark olive skin and long black hair. She had moved to Mexico City from Oaxaca with her family some time before and started training in lucha libre to learn self-defense. One of the first instructions Jaramillo gave me was to get a pair of shorts for practice—preferably lycra. He had given the same advice to Alejandra (as I later learned), but she preferred to train in nylon warm-up pants. Whenever she would tire or slow down during practice, Jaramillo would say she was overheated because of the pants.

That December, one of the students arranged for a reporter from a small weekly paper to do an article on our class. He came to the gym to take photos as we ran through warm-ups, rounds of amateur wrestling, and a series of professional routines. At one point, while I stood outside of the ring, alongside the reporter and Jaramillo, Alejandra worked through a series of moves with another student. She started to slow down toward the end of the routine, and Jaramillo started to chide her for wearing warm-up pants.[20]

"It's unprofessional," he told her. "If you want to be a professional, you're going to have to wear shorts, and you have to practice wearing shorts just like a masked wrestler has to practice with the mask on."

"That's right, you have to have an angle," added the reporter. "Everybody has to have an angle, even the guys."

"Look at Levi," said Jaramillo, turning to me. "She wears shorts. Have the others ever showed you a lack of respect?" (I wasn't happy to be used in their argument, but I admitted that they had not.)

"Lady Apache wears tights," countered Alejandra. But the profe and the reporter were unimpressed and continued. "Levi," they explained, is unembarrassed to wear shorts to class because *she* is civilized. "You are from *la provincia*, right?" said the reporter.

"That's right," continued Jaramillo. "Because here we are also *civilizing* you."

The interchange was as telling as it was uncomfortable (for me and, I assume, for Alejandra), but it brought out several points about the participation of women in lucha libre. First, it is a practice that is urban and therefore can be regarded by its practitioners as somewhat urbane. In Mexico City, *la provincia* means the rest of Mexico, and as the saying goes, "Outside of Mexico, it's all Cuauhtitlán."[21] But, as a friend observed when I recounted the incident later that evening, in Mexico City, *la provincia* is sometimes used as a euphemism for the impoverished and heavily indigenous state of Oaxaca (where, in fact, Alejandra was from), and so they also implicitly coded her as Indian. They were, thus, reminding her that her participation in lucha libre should be part of a process of personal modernization and embrace of sophisticated, urban mestizaje, in place of a provincial, ignorant Indian identity (and that urban mestizo sophistication should involve the wearing of shorts).

Second, it pointed up the apparently contradictory moral position of the luchadora. To enter the profession, women must train with men—they must dress in revealing clothing and touch and be touched by their fellow students. To continue in the profession, the luchadora must commit herself to a very public career. In the terms of the gender system outlined by Melhuus, Castillo, and others, they should find themselves positioned as indecent women, yet (as I will show below), they are treated in public and in private (as far as I could observe) as decent women.[22]

Women have worked as wrestlers in Mexico at least since the mid-1940s. At present, there are at least one hundred luchadoras in the country and probably many more (far fewer than there are luchadores, but a significant number nonetheless).[23] Women who wrestle have always had to overcome obstacles to their participation from audiences, coworkers, and the institutions that control and sustain lucha libre. In the 1950s, women entering the profession did not have access to regular trainers. Once working, they often suffered harassment from their male colleagues, who accused them of taking work that rightfully belonged to men. Veteran wrestler Irma Gonzalez recalls her male colleagues playing tricks on the luchadoras: "They nailed our shoes to the floor, they tied knots in our sleeves or pants legs. Sometimes I had to cut the knots out of my tights because I couldn't untie them" (interview with author, 1997). She and her fellow luchadoras also had to fend off more threatening and overtly sexual forms of harassment from promoters and luchadores.

Part of the luchadores' resentment may have been due to the luchadoras' success. On the national circuit, women could appear in the star position at the end of an event, and some promoters even organized all-women events. Because there were few of them, it was easier for individual luchadoras to find work then it was for most luchadores. Luchadoras were also connected to international circuits. By the late 1950s, U.S. wrestler Mildred Burke began to bring groups of North American and Mexican women to perform in Japan (where professional wrestling had recently been introduced). Lucha libre was and remains one of the few sports in which women could have a full-time, professional career.

But despite their popularity on the national and international circuits, luchadoras were prohibited from wrestling within the Federal District sometime in the early 1950s. This was a serious restriction, for Mexico is a highly centralized country and has become increasingly so over the past century. In 1950, the Federal District was home to over 12 percent of the

FIGURE 13 U.S. women wrestlers in Mexico City in 1948. HERMANOS MAYO
COLLECTION, ARCHIVO GENERAL DE LA NACIÓN

total population (Rowland and Gordon 2006). To be banned from Mexico
City was to be excluded from the center of industry, government, finance,
high culture, and mass culture. The ban was lifted in 1986. An interesting
thing about the ban, which lasted for about thirty years, is that no one took
responsibility for it. Rafael Barradas, the secretary of the commission of
lucha libre at the time, has said that it was beyond his control, and that he,
personally, never opposed the women's participation in lucha libre. On the
contrary, in interviews (with me and others) and in his book *Fuera Máscaras*, he maintains that he supported them, helping luchadoras get work
outside of the Federal District and insisting that they be treated with "respect" (that is, not be subjected to sexual harassment), instructing promoters to "forget that they are women, remember that they are athletes and
wrestlers and they are there to wrestle" (Barradas Osorio 1992: 10).

On the other hand, Juan Alanís, head of the Asociacion Nacional de
Luchadores, Referís and Retirados (National Association of Wrestlers, Referees, and Retirees), held Barradas personally responsible for maintaining
the ban. According to Alanís, the association took up the ban as a labor
issue in 1983. Every time he approached Barradas about the matter, however, he would be rebuffed: "I said, 'Mr. Barradas, help us. It's in your hands.
Give us permission for our comrade luchadoras to work in the Federal

District.' And he would say to me, 'Don't get involved in that problem—the ladies are good for nothing outside of the bedroom.'" (Interview with author, 1997)

In 1985, the year of Barradas's retirement, the association organized a series of closed-door matches between women in the state of Mexico, using a referee with a Federal District license to demonstrate that the women were qualified wrestlers. They then went to seek out the government office that had jurisdiction over the prohibition, but in the course of the process they discovered that officially there was no ban. It did not exist in written form. They discovered, moreover, that the commission itself had no legal authority over the spectacle. When I asked Alanís how he thought the prohibition against luchadoras originated, he speculated that it may have been a verbal instruction that accrued the force of custom:

> I think that the lack of participation of women in the sport had caused a certain veto. Because there was no regulation to prohibit them. After we went through all of those Departments, we realized that lucha libre wasn't [formally] regulated. So *someone*, an authority, [then mayor] Uruchurtu who was in the Departmento Federal, or someone else had given to understand that the luchadoras not wrestle. It was a veto, a veto by an authority that appeared one day and stayed on because of the mentality. (Interview with author, 1997)

The relevant office (Promocion Deportivo, part of the D.D.F.) granted official permission for luchadoras to wrestle within the Federal District the following year, but that did not usher in a golden era for luchadoras. In the 1950s and 1960s, women's lucha libre was marginalized from the center (from Mexico City), but in the provincial and international circuits luchadoras could have successful and relatively lucrative careers. By the time I arrived in Mexico, luchadoras had been working in the Federal District for ten years, yet they remained marginalized. I never saw luchadoras, regardless of their quality or popularity, appear in the more prestigious and more lucrative final or semifinal match. Instead, they were consigned to the second or third match, along with novices and minis. According to Irma Gonzalez, women were more likely to get star billing in the 1950s and 1960s, when they were exiled from the capital, than they are now. Television, thus far, reproduces the gender inequality of the live event.[24]

Nevertheless, lucha libre remains an activity performed by women as well as men. Although luchadoras were excluded from the formal training process in the 1950s, their successors were integrated into wrestling schools over the course of the 1960s and 1970s. In the empresas, men and women train together, at least during the preliminary exercises (afterward, wrestlers of both sexes practice with likely opponents). In short, trainers make little distinction between men and women during the training process. Most luchadoras I met trained almost exclusively with men until they became professionals. How intensely they were encouraged to train depended on the teacher. Although Jaramillo periodically claimed that he was being careful with me so that I wouldn't get hurt, he allowed me, and indeed expected me, to do everything the others did.[25] At some other gyms I saw women shown easier versions of the preparatory exercises; at others they keep up with the rest of the class.

According to Sharon Mazer, professional wrestling classes in Brooklyn are also co-ed. The few female students train together with the men, working the same techniques, the same material. She notes, however, that this parity does not extend to performance. Despite the equality of the training floor, she sees a fundamental difference between men's and women's wrestling in the United States, one that "is not to be located in the actual physical practices of the wrestlers, in the way they touch, understand and express the significance of touching each other[, but] in the way in which the act of wrestling is perceived from outside the ring, by promoters and spectators" (Mazer 1998: 124). Mazer argues that the public's reception of female wrestlers is markedly different from their reception of male wrestlers. In fact, women's presence in the ring tends to work against their presence at ringside. The entrance of the female wrestlers at a Brooklyn event she describes in detail, was accompanied by the exit of female spectators. The remaining spectators jeered the heel and cheered the baby face, but she argues that the nature of their participation changed radically with the entrance of the wrestling women. She observed:

> Whereas throughout the earlier matches the voices were balanced between those of male and female spectators, now the bulk of the responses were from the men. The women appeared to have disappeared, they had gone to the ladies room, were getting more beer for themselves or their husbands, or were talking to their children and amongst themselves. For their part, while the men carried on the call and response, they were no longer shouting the customary directives to kill or maim, but were instead yelling obscene sexual challenges at both women. (127)

The performance of the women, moreover, "seemed designed more to expose the women's bodies to the audience in a series of sexually provocative freeze-frames—the breasts pulled tight against Lycra, buttocks suspended through the ropes and so on—than as part of a progression toward victory" (126). In short, in the context of U.S. wrestling, the participation of women is marked as pornographic and parodic. Mazer argues that the difference between male and female performance is far from arbitrary but is rooted in the function of having women in the ring at all. Since wrestling is about masculinity, female wrestlers serve only to define the limits of masculinity for the men. Their role is not significantly different from that of ring girls and escorts—as objects of male heterosexual desire. In Mazer's analysis, "women, as they appear in the wrestling discourse, may necessarily be normatively and figuratively the target of the wrestler's sexual strutting and posturing . . . As 'real' women enter into the display as objects of desire, they authenticate the wrestlers' heterosexuality and as such provide the means of bridging the distance between men" (129).

Although luchadoras are marginalized in lucha libre, it is not because their performance is sexualized like that of their North American colleagues. When they enter the ring, women in the audience do not leave. The taunts aimed at the rudas closely parallel those aimed at rudos; if anything, the insults directed at luchadoras are usually *less* sexualized than those directed at luchadores. The few times I heard an audience member shout *puta* (whore), it was directed at the referee Esther Molina. Since puto is an invective that is hurled against male referees, it still paralleled the way the audience responds to men in the ring.[26]

The only event I attended at which audience members made unambiguous comments about the anatomy and sexuality of the luchadoras took place in a small arena in the city of Pachuca, Hidalgo, where I had gone to see Divino Exotico. When two luchadoras, Princesa Azteca and Pink Panther, fought the first match, two audience members began to harass them by shouting "up with the cunts!" and "I can see your donut!" One of them cheered on Princesa Azteca with "estas loca, pero buenota, mamazota" (roughly, "you're crazy, but you're hot, big mama"). The other addressed the Pink Panther: "I want you to meet my grandson. You like men, don't you?" and (when the ruda responded with a shrug) warned the técnica to "watch out, she's a maricona." Eventually the management announced, over the loudspeaker, that the two of them would have to pipe down or leave.

Unlike the event that Mazer attended in Brooklyn, the women in the audience had not left. Indeed, the two spectators engaged in "yelling obscene sexual challenges" and producing such rich ethnographic material for my benefit were both women who appeared to be in their sixties or seventies and had come with their extended families (including, presumably, the grandson one had offered to the ruda). They were the same women who, later that evening, would use their sweaters to protect Divino Exotico's anonymity and honor when the rudos tore his mask off. Moreover, there was nothing in the audience response to luchadoras to suggest that their role was to provide a pornographic contrast to the men's wrestling, since the luchadores who followed them were immediately treated to cries of "cortale el chile" (cut his dick off).

MARIANISMO REVISITED

Like their male counterparts, luchadoras are morally coded, some playing the role of técnica, others the role of ruda. Mazer writes of U.S. professional wrestling that the moral coding of female performance is clearly pegged to conformity with a passive femininity. A female wrestler's moral coding is determined in relation to a male wrestler with whom she is affiliated. Either she is "soft-spoken, accommodating to the man to whom she is attached, acting as a sign of the man's virtue" or unfeminine: the "loud, visible manifestation of the man's moral corruption" (Mazer 1998: 135). In this respect, the North American female heel is similar to the mala mujer of Mexican telenovelas and comic books.

However, that does not seem to be the case for Mexican rudas. First, the moral coding of luchadoras does not map on to the discourse of Marianismo in any unambiguous way. Rudas do not usually wear more revealing costumes than técnicas, and nothing I saw in their mannerisms alluded to the figure of the whore. They do not engage in suggestive wordplay or appear to flirt with spectators, male wrestlers, or one another. Until recently, they would not become implicated in conflicts with or between luchadores.[27] Instead, three things seen to define performance as a ruda or técnica. First, técnicas tend to conform more closely to urban Mexican standards of beauty. They are usually finer boned and more acrobatic than their ruda counterparts. Rudas tend to be heavier and clumsier, their movements less graceful and more forceful (which perhaps could be read as more masculine). This is, however, just a tendency—there are lightweight rudas and solidly built técnicas. Second, like their male counterparts, rudas are said to act out of passion and rage and are thought to be meaner than técnicas. In fact, some spectators told me that they thought that rudas showed more deliberate cruelty in their actions than did rudos. Finally, sequences that demonstrate the rudas' inability to cooperate with their allies occur more often than they do in matches between men. In other words, solidarity between and among women is a key indicator of moral position in lucha libre.

However, the moral positioning of luchadoras does not take place exclusively in the ring. In interviews and other articles that feature luchadoras, reporters often ask about their personal lives. The responses of both técnicas and rudas demonstrate a concern with how their behavior is perceived by others. While young luchadoras told me that they did not experience as much harassment from male colleagues as their predecessors, they are often reminded that many wrestlers and fans think that lucha libre is an inappropriate activity for women. Luchadoras and their supporters thus defend their participation on two grounds. First, luchadoras often stress that lucha libre is work. They take for granted that women work outside of the home and argue that since there are women cab drivers, women police officers, and so on—why not luchadoras, too? (This justification elides the fact that there have been luchadoras at least as long as there have been female cab drivers in Mexico.) Rudas and técnicas alike position themselves as working women—as do most of their female fans. As one male wrestler explained:

> The role of women, at least here in Mexico since lucha libre started, is . . . you're going to be part of, like, a representative symbol of feminine sport. And as for their presence in lucha libre, women practice and train just like men. Clearly, there are good luchadoras, luchadoras with ability who really train, because there are different levels of female wrestling, right? A woman has to put out a little more [se presta un poquito más] to reach star level than a man. When women go to another country, they have to arrive with the necessary skills, the ability, right? Because Mexican lucha libre is considered one of the best in the world. . . . Like Doña Irma Gonzalez says, there are [female] astronauts, chauffeurs, governors, deputies, senators—you can't keep women out of sports. (Hara Kiri, interview with author, 1997)

Second, luchadoras are careful to present themselves (and each other) as mothers (and, to a lesser degree, as wives). In interviews, luchadoras seldom talk about their marriages unless their husbands are also members of the "wrestling family." There is a perception among wrestlers that most luchadoras who marry marry luchadores. As several women explained, only a luchador would understand and tolerate the demands that lucha libre imposes on his wife. Regardless of their marital status, however, luchadoras often stress the fact that they are also mothers. It's not uncommon for them to be single mothers, or to have children from different marriages, and they are clearly proud to let that be known.

Luchadoras integrate a folklore of motherhood into their professional knowledge. One told me that, as a point of both honor and safety, they don't tell anyone they are pregnant until they can no longer hide it. It's thought to be healthy to keep wrestling, but it could be more dangerous if wrestlers are distracted or overly protective of each other. Children of luchadoras find themselves at ringside from infancy, and since many luchadoras' husbands are luchadores, the two take turns babysitting. When both have to wrestle, they either leave the young children with a relative or bring them to the arena, where other wrestlers greet them, play with them, or sit with them. For many luchadoras, the metaphor of the "wrestling family" can be taken quite literally.

They do not, however, draw a distinction between virtuous luchadora mothers and indecent luchadoras who are not mothers. Both técnicas and rudas present themselves as dedicated mothers, if not dedicated wives. As the ruda Tania explained in a 1993 interview: "Lucha libre takes up time, and a husband demands a lot of attention—when one is working it's hard to make room. . . . But a partner is not indispensable. My children fill all of my time. They are my three great treasures" (*Box y Lucha* 1993: 10).

But even luchadoras who are not mothers use the fact that other luchadoras are when they want to defend the participation of all women in lucha libre. In the words of Martha Villalobos (ruda, single, no children, national women's champion at the time): "I think we luchadoras get pregnant more easily because our bodies are healthier [than other women]; it's a lie that we lose our femininity" (quoted in Fascinetto 1995: 184). Luchadoras use motherhood as a moral claim, but not, apparently, in a way that excludes luchadoras who do not have children.

The representation of women in lucha libre is, therefore, complex. On the one hand, some luchadores and fans express discomfort with the idea or the image of women wrestling. I think this discomfort underlies the observation that several fans made, that rudas are "meaner" than rudos. I suspect that it is not so much that the rudas are meaner, but that those fans found physical aggression more disturbing in women than in men. However, fewer fans expressed discomfort or distaste when they talked about técnicas. Now, from the point of view of the discourse of Marianismo, luchadoras should figure as indecent women—committed to a public, money-earning, aggressive activity that may take them away from their husbands or children for months at a time. Yet neither the lucha libre public nor (for the most part) their colleagues generally respond to them as if they were indecent, or undeserving of respect. Moreover, their participation in a demanding career cannot be explained away as an activity of middle-class women, alienated (or protected) from a core Mexican culture. Like their male colleagues, luchadoras are drawn from the same class as their audience, the residents of areas like Ciudad Nezahualcoyotl. Instead, as athletes, performers, and mothers, luchadoras embody a visceral, grassroots, feminist argument that both alludes to and evades the dichotomy of decency and indecency that is said to structure the experience of lower-class Mexican women.

A STRUGGLE OF (ONLY) *TWO* MEN?

The activity of luchadoras and exoticos makes it difficult to sustain the claim that lucha libre is, in a simple sense, a dramatic endorsement of machista ideology. Lucha libre is a privileged space of gender experimentation where counterhegemonic constructions of masculinity and femininity can be performed in a public forum. Even in its most conventional form, when two masculine men face each other in the ring, it already problematizes conventional definitions of machismo.

To complicate matters further, the performance of lucha libre does not take place only in the ring. If luchadores could be said to perform conflict, the audience at lucha libre matches can be said to perform the public sphere. Wrestlers enter the ring as técnicos and rudos, but they can be successful only if the audience ratifies them in those roles—cheering the técnicos and taunting the rudos. The public voice is, to a great degree, a collective voice, but the public is also represented by a few especially enthusiastic fans in the front rows who engage directly with the wrestlers, haranguing the rudos and advising the técnicos. The rudos, true to their role, answer back. Thus the match between two wrestlers takes place on a second level as a verbal match between the rudos and the spectator-participants. These representatives of public opinion, these active fans, who represent the moral voice of the audience and evaluate the performance of the wrestlers, are almost always women over the age of fifty. The two women who harassed Princesa Azteca and Pink Panther in Pachucha are a case in point: as older women, the vulgarity of their commentary was atypical, but not their vociferousness.

One of the legendary figures of lucha libre was a fan named Virginia Aguilera. "Doña Vicky, the Granny of Lucha Libre," as she was known, attended her first match in 1934. After that, she became a regular, a fixture in Arena Mexico, coming every Friday night until a few years before her death in 1997. From her front-row seat, her support of the técnicos and verbal attacks on the rudos became part of the spectacle. She had a cameo in two wrestling movies and was played by the actress Sarah García in a third. Her successors can be seen in almost any arena—middle-aged or elderly women, sitting in a corner seat near the ring, with or without their staid husbands. As the rudos enter, they get up to scold them, sometimes following them to the ring. They stand up in front of their seats, letting out streams of invective, animated with fury. As soon as the last match ends, they leave with the grim dignity to catch the next bus home.

Lucha libre has always had a large female following, especially in contrast to other sports. As early as 1940, the literary figure and fan Salvador Novo observed that lucha libre was so popular among women that Arena Mexico had a ladies night, one Thursday a month. Even more women, he reported, attended the Sunday matches. "Sundays," he remarked, "without a doubt, are days in which the Arena appears more full of those of the fair sex who know how to pay for their treats. It is an important fact that the day after the night before (which is Saturday), the ladies favor the luchas libres more than on the neutral Thursday."

Novo further noted the vocal nature of their spectatorship:

Once again it is to be suspected that in the case of the screaming women of Sunday, dark, subconscious reasons explain their regular attendance—reasons as worthy and as Freudian as those that we noted above as the cause of masculine enjoyment of the encounter of locks and scissor legs; equally ancestral, profound and legitimate, because in them there flowers not only the satisfaction of the individual subconscious, but also the happy and probatory expression of the existence of the collective unconscious that Jung discovered, and that is able to remember words that haven't been used for centuries when confronted with an adequate stimulus. (1994: 603)

In this respect (as in many others) little has changed in lucha libre since the 1940s.

Wrestlers, journalists, and others have suggested to me that lucha libre attracts women of a certain age and class position because it functions as a catharsis. These, they argue, are the women who suffer all week through the unreasonable demands of their machista husbands, and lucha libre is their chance to blow off steam. Yet I find that explanation unsatisfying. No one would claim that working-class (or popular-class) men are not also repressed, do not also suffer daily humiliations and pressures that they would also like to relieve. Indeed, male fans of lucha libre do say that they go to blow off steam, but even more Mexican males blow off steam at soccer games. The catharsis hypothesis thus says nothing about the gendered specificity of lucha libre: why women, and why lucha libre?

I propose an alternative explanation that takes into account an element of gendered behaviors in Mexico City that is found in the literature of urban social movements, but not in descriptions of the discourse of machismo. The tremendous growth of the population of several Latin American cities in the 1960s and 1970s resulted in the unofficial settlement of tracts of land by *paracaidistas* (skydivers). Carlos Vélez-Ibañez (1983), Manuel Castells (1983), Matthew Gutmann (1996), and others have documented the social movements that arose as these urban settlers sought to legalize their claims and their right to infrastructural services. One thing that stands out in these accounts is that the day-to-day organization of the struggle was carried out primarily by the women. The adult men tended to spend the day working or looking for work, and defense of the community during the daytime, when confrontations with police or other authorities were most likely to occur, fell to the women. Vélez-Ibañez (1983: 263), writing about Ciudad Nezahualcoyotl, described one such confrontation between police sent to evict a family and the housewives who came to prevent the eviction:

During the first five minutes of activity, women continued to congregate close to the lot, until forty to fifty stood either on the lot and sidewalk or in front of other homes next to the lot. Meanwhile, they began to taunt the land developer's representative, the judge, and the policemen, calling them *cobardes* ("cowards") and *maricones* (sissies), after which they would be consumed by laughter. . . . One of the more vociferous of these *comadres* said *"Pero mira qué chingón contra las mujeres. Caras de papa y frijol. Que no tan machotes—no más que vengan los hombres"* . . . Of course, as soon as the women picked up the rocks, the policemen backed off. Threats of males entering the fray were unnecessary.

Matthew Gutmann argues that such activities by women during the struggles of the 1970s transformed local ideas about gender and authority. Chronicling a process similar to the one Vélez-Ibañez describes in Ciudad Nezahualcoyotl, he notes that circumstances of political organization in the southeastern colonía of Santo Domingo concentrated much authority into the hands of the neighborhood women.

With so many men working outside the *colonía* during the day, from its inception much of the daytime responsibility for constructing and defending Santo Domingo fell largely upon women. They were the ones in charge of communications during the early days when private and police connected goons roamed through the community trying to extort or evict less than vigilant squatters . . . Such exploits on the part of many women became emblematic of the invasion, not simply because of the courage and determination they evinced, but because women throughout the area were coming to be widely regarded as key decision makers and leaders. (1996: 000)

In the violent circumstances of urban settlement in the second half of the twentieth century, the working-class public sphere became, of necessity, a *female* public sphere. This phenomenon was not without historical precedent. For example, in 1922, working-class women of Veracruz (with prostitutes in the forefront) successfully organized a citywide rent strike, using the same tactics: organizing both communication and physical defense of their neighborhoods in what Andrew Wood (2001) calls "a kind of 'popular feminism' in which class and gender positions compliment each other."

Nor is moral authority held by women-as-public limited to situations of emergency. In situations of quotidian conflict, older women may play a role that sociologist Alfredo Mirande (1997) describes in an account of his brother's fight with another boy in his Mexico City neighborhood about thirty years ago. His brother's opponent was one of another group of brothers who threw a brick through their living-room window, challenging them to a fight. Their father insisted that they answer the challenge and appointed one brother, Hector, to fight one of the brothers from the other family. Although his opponent, a boy nicknamed "Chapulín" (Grasshopper), was the more experienced fighter, Mirande recalls:

> His biggest obstacle proved not to be my brother, but my family, and especially *las tías* [the aunts]. Every time that Héctor landed a punch, or even came close to landing a punch, *las tías* would go wild, screaming their approval, shouting: ¡Orale!, "Now you've got him!" "He's in trouble now!" or "Look, he's bleeding!" . . . Rather than concentrating on the fight at hand, Chapulín became distracted and looked down to see if there was actually blood and looked at *las tías* as they screamed. (1997: 82)

Mirande's brother's encounter with Chapulín sounds remarkably like a lucha libre match and helps to make sense of the actions of the older female public at the arena. Rather than (or in addition to) stealing a moment of expressiveness from their otherwise repressed lives, perhaps the older, female lucha fans are performing a role that is familiar to them: that of making moral judgments and expressing the will of the community around those judgments. It is their role to taunt the rudos or help Divino Exotico cover his face, as it was the role of the female settlers of Nezahualcoyotl to taunt the police. More than simple catharsis, this form of lucha libre spectatorship might be seen as a playful exercise of a real moral authority.

CONCLUSION

Marit Melhuus may be justified in her criticism of most ethnographic studies of women in Latin America, which, she says, attend little to the symbolic and moral dimensions of gender and suffer from an "economistic bias." Yet analyses like her own, which attend closely to the symbolic and moral dimensions of gender of Mexico in particular, suffer in turn from a structuralist bias. The problem with such analyses, as I see it, is that while such analysts might acknowledge (or even foreground) the notion of culture change, changes and inconsistencies in gendered behaviors are all too often glossed as effects of "modernization," which is itself understood as the inevitable diffusion of ideas as a byproduct of engagement with international capitalism (usually in its guise as the United States). The uniquely Mexican (or, for that matter, Iberian) elements of the lived experience of gender are described as if they constituted a balanced, stable system of domination and submission.

Yet there are many points at which the gendered ideas and practices of working-class Mexicans cannot be adequately described as part of the machista/marianista ethic. For example, most ethnographies describe Mexican postmarital residence as patrilocal, and such descriptions of patrilocality tend to connect the practice with a wider machista logic. Yet at least two ethnographers (Gutmann 1996 and Lomnitz 1987) have noted what has been my haphazard impression—that urban Mexican postmarital residence patterns have a strong matrilocal, even matrilineal bias. So, while the power of mothers has been analyzed in terms of its relationship to suffering, it has rarely been analyzed as a form of power. Except in the writing of Adelaida Del Castillo (1993) and Gutmann (1996), practices that seem to escape a totalizing "Mexican sex-gender system," even if they are seen as resistance (e.g., Behar 1993, Stern 1995) aren't described as having real power to challenge the political and psychic implications of the system. Thus Mexican feminism can be understood only in reference to other countries. The present situation, in which women have achieved considerable political power and authority in at least some aspects of Mexican society (for example, women have headed both major opposition parties, the PRD and the PRI—which, of course, was not an opposition party until recently), is left unexplained and inexplicable. This is not to say that women in Mexico have achieved anything near parity with men at the level of national politics. Mexico is far from a feminist utopia. However, the political system cannot, at this time, be described in simple terms as one based on the exclusion of women from positions of authority.

In this context, lucha libre provides a rich set of representations with which to interrogate structuralist descriptions of the limits of the machista/marianista complex in Mexico because, at one level, it epitomizes the system. In its most conventional version, lucha libre is a struggle for physical and psychological domination between two machos. But lucha libre performance also functions as a laboratory of gender experimentation that, even in its most conventional version, parodies and problematizes the standard description of machismo as hegemonic masculinity. The presence of gender nonnormative wrestlers in and of itself does not necessarily a counterhegemonic representation make. As Sharon Mazer has suggested, the presence of women in U.S. professional wrestling only underlines the masculinity of professional wrestling's men, including the Gorgeous Georges and Gold Dusts. But I don't think that that's all that is going on in lucha libre.

First, if Melhuus is right about the structure of gendered hierarchies in Mexico, then lucha libre divides men, like women, into decent and indecent, unifying the two. Second, where it divides women into decent and indecent, it does so in a way that is radically different from other genres of mass cultural entertainment, like the telenovela. Women's relative decency is, first of all, determined in relation to their treatment of other women, unmediated by their relationships to men (at least outside of televised lucha). While their relationships to men and to children are foregrounded in mass-mediated representations of the backstage of their lives, these are not relevant to their coding in the ring. Their identity as workers is noted and positively valued. Furthermore, indecency (insofar as rudismo is a form of indecency) is not inevitably punished. To summarize, there is a lack of fit between luchadoras' moral coding and any of the traditional measures thereof—técnicas, by definition decent, are public, are visible, and train with men. None of that affects their right to respect. Likewise, the role of exoticos challenges the place of effeminate gay men in Mexican society, even as it stereotypes them and positions them as rudos. Portraying exoticos as having the power to dominate masculine técnicos—even if only temporarily, and only some of the time—in itself undermines the stereotype of gay men as contemptible beings incapable of defending themselves (and thus their honor). Finally, the overall structure of live lucha libre provides a forum in which older women act out forms of authority that they may in fact have in their daily lives. In other words, it is a performance that displays many of the elements of machista discourse—male strength, male power, masculinity as an act of struggle—but places them in a context that disrupts the hegemony of machismo's terms.

6

MEDIATING THE MASK

Lucha Libre and Circulation

As I have shown in these chapters, as a signifying practice, lucha libre performance cannot be separated from its social context. Yet an important part of that context exists outside of the gym and the arena. This chapter addresses the issue of circulation in two senses: in the dissemination of lucha libre performance through the mass media and in the circulation of lucha libre imagery as a metonym for class identity and cultural authenticity in Mexico City.

Although film, comic books, and other media have been important to the mass circulation of lucha libre, this chapter will focus primarily on the association of lucha libre and television because the relationship between the two has been an important site of conflict in the world of lucha libre. I first became aware of the profound hostility that many wrestlers felt toward the televised version of the sport during my initial contact with Luis Jaramillo. When I approached him about accepting me as a student, he offered me a seat on one of the weight benches and gave me the following speech (which I was to hear several times in different versions over the subsequent year and a half):

> Lucha libre is not the clown show you see on television, with the ones from the AAA. If you want to learn the *real* lucha libre, you have to learn it step by step. First falling, tumbling, then Olympic wrestling, Greco-Roman wrestling, intercollegiate wrestling, locks from jiujitsu, strikes from karate. Only then can you learn *professional* wrestling. If you're willing to learn the real lucha libre, then I will teach you. I am a great teacher, many people know and respect me, but I had a greater teacher behind me and he had others behind him.

He was, I later learned, one of many in the wrestling family who believed this proud tradition was at risk—that televised broadcast had led lucha libre to a phase of decadence and vulgarization that threatened the sport with the loss of its audience and its identity. At the time I wondered what it could possibly mean for *professional wrestling to be vulgarized*, even by television (a question that eventually came to structure my research).

The resistance to televised broadcast of lucha libre had its origin in the fact that the sport was not televised in Mexico between 1954 and 1991 (unlike professional wrestling in the United States and Japan, the other two centers of professional wrestling). During the intervening years, lucha libre relied on a mix of other media to extend its reach beyond the arenas. Reports about lucha libre circulated in print. Some newspapers, notably *L'Afición* and *Ovaciones* covered lucha libre in the sports pages. Some biweekly (or less regular) magazines covered the sport in greater, more gossipy detail. The best established of these, *Box y Lucha*, began publication in 1954 as *Lucha Libre*. The name was changed to *Lucha Libre y Box* and finally to *Box y Lucha*. *Box y Lucha* presently functions as a kind of journal of record for lucha libre. In its first few issues, the magazine mixed reports on lucha libre matches, advertisements for upcoming events, and pieces about individual wrestlers with more eclectic features, like psychic predictions or fictional adventures of real wrestlers. In later issues, the magazine expanded its focus to include boxing news, and many of the peripheral features were dropped. In its current format, the first half of an issue is devoted to boxing, and the second half lucha libre. In the second half, a typical issue features descriptions of events (mostly EMLL and AAA, but often a few from other empresas as well), interviews with wrestlers, and gossip and opinion pieces about lucha libre's backstage politics.

In addition to *Box y Lucha*, a spectrum of magazines, ranging from the glossy pictorial *Colosos* to the typewritten, cut and pasted *Maskaras y Bikinis*, have gone in and out of print over the years. By the late 1990s, most had gone out of circulation, leaving only *Box y Lucha*, and a slick, full-color newsletter called *Superluchas*, which belonged to Antonio Peña, the owner of the empresa AAA/PAPSA. *Superluchas* usually contains less text than *Box y Lucha*, with fewer interviews and opinion pieces, and more photographs. Neither magazine depended on advertising revenues, relying instead on a combination of circulation and kickback from the empresas.[1]

Sold at newsstands and in the arenas between matches, the fanzines serve to connect the lucha libre public to the world of the familia luchistica. Most articles fall into one of three categories, each of which serves a different function in interpreting lucha libre for its audience. First, there are descriptions of events. These narrate and make sense of the text of lucha libre—the challenges, betrayals, triumphs, and defeats of lucha libre's characters. Second, there are interviews with wrestlers. These, in contrast, present the backstage (or at least something meant to be understood as the backstage) of lucha libre. Thus, although wrestlers sometimes appear in interviews in character, flinging challenges at their rivals, bragging about their prowess, or flaunting their *rudeza*, the interviews more often human- ize them and establish the existence of a regular person who lives behind the mask. Novices are portrayed as disciplined, ambitious youth, while older wrestlers, rudos and técnicos alike, are portrayed as devoted family men or women. One effect of the magazines, then, particularly *Box y Lucha*, is to draw a distinction between role and person, to remind the public that the rudos and técnicos are, in the end, all on the same side. A third function of the magazine's text is to provide a forum for gossip and criticism. During the mid-1990s, in particular, *Box y Lucha* became the main vehicle for the dissemination of the ongoing debate over the impact of television on the sport.

In addition to the lucha libre press, the sport and its imagery have cir- culated in other, more playful forms. Jose G. Cruz's *fotonovela* featuring El Santo appeared weekly, or more often over a period of thirty years (Ru- benstein 2003). Other comic-book treatments of wrestlers and wrestling- themed activity books for children are still available. Material objects— souvenir-quality wrestling masks, wrestling mask keychains, wrestler figurines, and so on—are produced in local workshops and sold in and outside the arenas as well as in public markets. During the 1970s, children collected and traded wrestling stamps, each one featuring a masked star.

LUCHA LIBRE AND TELEVISION

Although print media have been important to the circulation and interpretation of lucha libre, the two most important vehicles of its dissemination in terms of their impact on the sport have been television and film. Yet the relationship of the live performance to each of these media was radically different. During the period of fieldwork, lucha libre was broadcast twice weekly on television. That was not the case, however, for most of lucha libre's history.

Mexico's first televised broadcast took place in 1948. Soon afterward, the government issued the first two television broadcast licenses to Romulo O'Farrill and Emilio Azcarraga.[2] As in the United States and Japan, professional wrestling became one of Mexico's first televised offerings. Visually oriented, and likely to draw a larger, working-class audience to the new medium, the first televised wrestling matches were broadcast from the EMLL's Arena Coliseo on Romulo O'Farrill's Channel 4, in November 1950. Two years later, Emilio Azcárraga (O'Farrill's rival at the time) began to broadcast matches on his television network, Televicentro (the precursor of the media conglomerate Televisa). Rather than negotiate with the EMLL, the network put up a ring in the new Televicentro studios on Avenida Chapultepec (about two blocks north of Arena México) and recruited Jesús Garza Hernandez, the owner of Lucha Libre Internacional, to run an empresa owned by the television station. Using a mix of wrestlers from Lucha Libre Internacional and stars enticed away from the EMLL, Televicentro began to broadcast lucha libre directly from their studio. During 1953, broadcasts took place four times a week, as competition between the two networks intensified (Mejía Barquera 1999: 202–3, Barradas Osorio n.d.: 148).[3]

The broadcasts had a number of effects, some intended, others perhaps not. Even as lucha libre was supposed to draw a broader audience to the medium, television opened new spaces and practices of reception for the lucha libre. Few Mexicans could afford their own television set, but several of my informants recalled that, during the 1950s, in popular barrios, the owners of bars and *fondas* invested in the devices in order to attract clients. Those lower-class Mexicans who did manage to buy a set would charge

FIGURE 14 Marquee, Televicentro studios, circa 1953. HERMANOS MAYO COLLECTION, ARCHIVO GENERAL DE LA NACIÓN

FIGURE 15 El Santo and unidentified wrestler (possibly Eduardo Bonales) circa 1952. HERMANOS MAYO COLLECTION, ARCHIVO GENERAL DE LA NACIÓN

FIGURE 16 Apparently middle-class audience member, circa 1954. HERMANOS MAYO COLLECTION, ARCHIVO GENERAL DE LA NACIÓN

FIGURE 17 Children wrestling in ring, their class status indexed by their (then) fashionable Conejo Blas brand shoes. HERMANOS MAYO COLLECTION, ARCHIVO GENERAL DE LA NACIÓN

their neighbors to come watch, sometimes providing drinks and snacks with the price of admission. In the move to television, then, lucha libre spectatorship maintained its collective nature, even if the interaction between audience and performers was lost.

The audience for lucha libre in this era was not, moreover, limited to the popular classes. I interviewed several middle- and upper-class Mexicans who remembered watching lucha libre on television when they were children. Even though their families could afford their own set, they too remembered watching lucha libre as a collective experience, one that crossed generational and class lines, as it drew the extended household together, from the grandparents to the servants. One man described his upper-middle-class family's weekly television ritual: inviting their friends over to watch lucha libre one week and opera the next. Even the mother of Salvador Novo became an aficionado just as his passion for the sport had faded (Novo 1967: 684).[4] The live performance also drew a middle- or upper-class element, as photographs of the audience in the Televicentro studios (and perhaps the Fronton Metropolitano) attest. Photographs of the front rows show well-dressed, stylish men and women. The children, playing in the ring between matches, wear fashionable Conejo Blas brand shoes.[5] During the first, short period of televised lucha libre (and perhaps before), watching the wrestlers was an activity that transcended class divisions.

Within a few years of its first broadcast, however, lucha libre was taken off the air. Opposition to televised lucha libre seems to have begun with the Televicentro broadcasts. Before putting up the Televicentro ring, Azcárraga solicited authorization from the Secretary of Communications and Transportation (which was in charge of television), but he neglected to consult the Commission of Boxing and Lucha Libre. In response, Adolfo Fernandez Bustamante, the head of the Office of Public Spectacles, took Televicentro to court to block the broadcasts (Mejía Barquera 1999: 203). Once the case reached the courts, however, the argument against lucha libre broadcasts was reframed as matter of protecting underage viewers. Moreover, the subject of debate moved from the television studios to the live events, as the court decided to consider the question of whether minors should be permitted in the arenas.

The judge in charge of the case granted the Televisa empresa a stay and ruled that minors could continue to attend the luchas. But he also issued a strong condemnation of the behavior of the rudo wrestlers and ordered the commission to "clean up" the event. He charged the commission's secretary of lucha libre, Barradas Osorio, the EMLL, and the head of the wrestler's union with negotiating a list of rules for lucha libre performance that made it impossible to perform the rudo role at all (Seyde 1953a: 74, Barradas Osorio n.d.: 149). And of course, without the rudos, there is no lucha libre.

Meanwhile, the government's attention shifted from the issue of minors entering the arenas back to the question of televised matches. This time, the city's regent, Ernesto Uruchurtu, prohibited the transmissions by fiat because many parents had allegedly complained that their children had been injured while attempting to imitate the wrestlers.[6] Rafael Barradas later justified the ban in his memoirs: "It was said that even though little ones attended events, in those cases they were accompanied by adults who very probably explained to them what the wrestlers were doing, and that didn't happen in the intimacy of the homes where the wrestlers were seen by children to whom no one explained what was happening on the television screen, and from there came the danger that was involved with televising wrestling" (Barradas Osorio n.d.: 149).[7] Children were also barred from attending the live event on the grounds that they might try to approach their heroes during the match and accidentally be squashed by rudos fighting outside of the ring (in violation of commission directives).

Veterans of the era—wrestlers, officials, and journalists—do not challenge Barradas Osorio's account and agree that lucha libre was taken off the air to protect children. Yet, as José Agustín has suggested, the reasons behind the prohibition were likely more complex (Agustín 1990: 136–37). First, the ban on televised lucha libre should be seen in the overall context of the administrations of President Ruiz Cortines and Regent Ernesto Uruchurtu. The early 1950s were marked by attempts by both the national and the municipal government to exercise control over cultural expressions and social geography in Mexico City. For example, the boleros of Agustín Lara, which celebrated fallen women and the men who loved them, were banned from the radio, and independent vendors were pushed off the streets and into formal, state-constructed markets (Rubenstein 2000, Cross 1999: 160–87). In what could be seen as a brilliant containment of dissent, the government and the right-wing opposition worked together to tighten control over the content of comic books (Rubenstein 1998: 96–99). Seen in this context, the campaign to limit lucha libre's audience was both typical and atypical, since other campaigns (over comic books, music, film, and public education) were most often articulated in terms of protecting young women from *moral* dangers. The campaign to control lucha libre, however, sought to protect little boys from physical dangers.[8] And although there was no attempt to control adult female spectatorship of lucha libre, women were prohibited from working as wrestlers in the Federal District.

Second, there was already a certain ambivalence within the wrestling "family" over the effects of televised broadcast of their sport. Some were concerned that ticket sales at the arenas would drop. Others worried about the effect that increased government scrutiny would have on performance. One journalist viewed the court case and the judge's ruling as evidence of television's deleterious effect on lucha libre performance—allowing, as it did, for the interference of government officials who misunderstood the spectacle (Seyde 1953b: 73–74). Another journalist suggested that the entire epoch had been nothing more than an unfair move on the part of Jesús Garza Hernandez, whose Televicentro wrestlers were mere copies of the EMLL stars. Of Médico Asesino, a wrestler whose white mask resembled the silver one of El Santo, he wrote: "99 percent of the fans know that Médico Asesino was a product of the era of television, with an eye on the part of his promoter to compete with El Santo, when the reign of the Lutteroth family felt, more than ever, like it was trembling and about to go down. This was the main goal of the creation of Medico Asesino: to do away with the empresa of La Coliseo and start a new reign in which Chucho Garza Hernandez alone would rule" (*Lucha Libre* 1954:5).

Lucha libre's retreat from television reestablished the authority of the commission over the sport. Barradas Osorio discarded most of the rules controlling the performance but set up three "dispositions . . . of order, nothing more—not to wrestle below [the ring], to prevent accidents with the public; not to hit the referee, because he is an authority; and not to insult the public. They must be respected because their ticket makes the spectacle possible" (Barradas Osorio, interview with author, 1996). According to his own account and that of many veterans, he insisted that these rules be enforced. All lucha libre events in Mexico City were (and still are) attended by a representative of the commission, who would stop the match or levy fines if, in his opinion, the wrestlers were in violation of a commission directive.[9]

With the end of televised wrestling, Jesús Garza Hernandez thus lost the (semivirtual) space of the Televicentro studios and returned to the Cine Politeama and the Frontón Metropolitano. According to Barradas, he resisted the directive prohibiting the entrance of minors and so attracted the attentions of the commission. His wrestlers drew so many suspensions and fines (for various violations) that they became unwilling to work for him. Within a few years he was driven out of business. The EMLL, meanwhile, "voluntarily" stopped allowing children into their arenas and were able to continue unchallenged as the major empresa in Mexico City (Barradas Osorio 1990: 149).

THE CINEMA OF THE LUCHADOR

Without television, film became the main vehicle by which lucha libre was disseminated to a mass audience. The same year that lucha libre debuted on television, the sport also inspired a genre of low-budget action movies that featured the stars of the EMLL and Televicentro wrestling stables. Between 1952 and 1983, approximately three hundred such movies were produced. El Santo appeared in at least fifty during his twenty-five-year film career. El Santo's movies were among the most popular films in the history of Mexican cinema and gained an extremely wide audience, even among those who disparaged them. Although I have met very few middle-class Mexicans who have been to a wrestling match, I have yet to meet anyone who claims never to have seen an El Santo movie.

Wrestling movies began production in the aftermath of the golden age of Mexican cinema of the 1930s and 1940s. By the early 1950s, faced with a crisis of rising costs and collapsing foreign markets, Mexican producers began to dedicate themselves to the production of "churros." Named for a type of freshly made cruller, sold from a street cart, the movies were highly formulaic, low-budget films, produced (like their namesake) one after another, and fairly indistinguishable.[10] These repetitive films relied on a set of stock character types, some of which were developed during the golden age. Others borrowed heavily on the conventions of Hollywood imports, and a few, like the lady truck driver Lola Trailera, were unique products of the age of the churro. The luchador belonged to the latter category.

Wrestling movies themselves were not notable for their originality. In the words of Nelson Carro (1993: 47), the wrestling movie was "always a parasitic genre—of melodrama, of comedy, of horror and of science fiction. At no time did it look to be autonomous—on the contrary, in mixture, in pastiche, in anachronism, one finds much of its power." The first four films, all released in 1952, represented the range of the genre and neatly illustrate Carro's point. The most typical of those that were to follow, *El Enmascarado de Plata* (*The Man in the Silver Mask*) featured the white masked Médico Asesino, a star of the Televicentro/Garza stable.[11] The low-budget film pitted a mad scientist against the wrestler and hero El Enmascarado de Plata. The film paid little attention to dialogue, plot, or acting, thus setting in motion the conventions of the genre. *La Béstia Magnifica* (*The Magnificent Beast*) starred Wolf Ruvinskis, an Argentinean wrestler and stage actor, as one of two wrestler friends who have a falling out over a mala mujer. In the end, the two friends destroy each other in the ring—one lies crippled, the other dying—but their friendship triumphs as they forgive each other at the bitter end. Carro writes, "If the novelty of the film was that it had lucha libre, as far as the story was concerned it had very little that was original; it was a traditional, truculent melodrama, with friends separated and fighting each other because of a bad woman, with a tragic outcome, but that redeems the characters in the end" (25).

The third, *El Luchador Fenómena*, was a parody of wrestling movies (or perhaps of lucha libre itself), starring the comedian Resortes. The fourth (and most creative, in my view), *Huracán Ramirez*, is a deliciously hybrid film starring David Silva (best known for his roles in the boxing film *Campeón sin Corona* and as a bus driver in *Por Esquina Bajan*) as the eponymous Huracán Ramirez, a wrestler who wears a mask to hide his wrestling activities from his wrestler father, played by Garza Hernandez LLI star Tonina Jackson.

In the latter film the Tonina Jackson character is a professional wrestler whose career, as the movie opens, is undergoing an unexpected revival. A widower, he lives with his three children, whom he supports through his wrestling. He has defeated every wrestler he has recently faced, all but the masked Huracán Ramirez, who (to Jackson's outrage) refuses to accept his challenge. Unbeknownst to his father, David Silva is, secretly, Huracán Ramirez. And he has still more secrets: he works as a singer in a cabaret to earn money that he spends paying his father's opponents to take a fall. His teenage sister is courted by a goofy but sincere neighbor, but she is obsessed with the mysterious and muscular Huracán Ramirez. His younger sister has taken over their mother's role of caring for, disciplining, and generally holding sway over their large but gentle father. There are an evil woman and a good woman (who compete for Huracán's attentions), gangsters, a comedy of errors—eventually father and son are kidnapped and join forces. In other words, it is a family melodrama–*caberetera*––comedy–gangster movie with wrestlers: a hybrid of almost all of the conventions of Mexican cinema of the era.

None of the first four wrestling films featured El Santo, soon to be the genre's greatest star. His cinematic debut did not take place until 1958, when he starred in two movies, *El Cerebro del Mal* and *El Santo Contra los Hombres Infernales*. The movies were filmed in Cuba because the budget was too low to pay Mexican union wages. In *Cerebro del Mal*, El Santo, as "El Enmascarado" (the Masked Man), battled a mad scientist with the help of "El Incognito" (the Unknown Man). *El Santo Contra los Hombres Infernales* had him assist an undercover agent infiltrating a band of Cuban drug smugglers. The wrestler went on to star in over fifty movies, all of them pretty similar. The films usually featured one or more wrestling matches shoehorned into the plot like dance numbers (actually, most featured a dance number as well). Sometimes the match would provide the cover for the wrestler's secret mission. Other times, he would agree to a match simply because he was in town or to honor a previous commitment. Some matches appear to be filmed in a studio, while others appear to be cut with stock footage (including footage of the audience) from real matches.

El Santo was not the only star of the wrestling movies. Wolf Ruvinskis starred in a dozen wrestling films in the 1950s and 1960s.[12] Blue Demon, Mil Máscaras, and others advanced their careers on the screen as well as in the ring. Blue Demon's enormous hands became nearly as famous as his mask. Yet no other wrestler achieved the legendary status of El Santo. El Santo himself claimed that he didn't understand the attraction of his movies. In an interview with Elena Poniatowska (1990), he suggested that his fans came to his movies because they felt sorry for him. One informant of mine explained that the movies were an exercise in collective suspension of disbelief: "You'd see a cardboard box, and they said it was a cave, and you said, 'OK, if you say it's a cave, it's a cave' " (interview with author, 1997). Yet his movies had an extremely wide distribution, across both class and geographical borders. Along with other products of the Mexican film industry, they were distributed all over the Spanish-speaking world. They were also dubbed into English and distributed in the United States and subtitled for distribution in Europe.[13]

The masked wrestler became a stock figure whose significance might best be understood in relation to the range of such characters in Mexican cinema. The charro represented a vision of continuity and stability set in the world of the rural haciendas of Jalisco, removed from the urban present in both space and time.[14] Images of the city, on the other hand, tended to portray the urban world as the locus of instability. The caberetera genre, which flourished during the administration of Miguel Aleman, presented the cabaret as a microcosm of urban society, both seductive and tragic.[15] In the discourse of the treacherous city, the *fichera* (prostitute) represented its female victim. But its male victim was perhaps best represented by the figure of the boxer.

The figure of the boxer as tragic hero took its initial inspiration from the success of Mexican boxers in international competition. Kid Azteca held the welterweight championship from 1934 until 1949. Raton Macías won the world bantamweight title in 1955 (only to lose it two years later). The boxer was a figure of national pride. But the boxer also came to symbolize instability and the failure of social reproduction in the urban setting. As with the fichera, the stock narratives (in cinema and comic books) associated with the boxer portrayed the city as the locus of struggle, hard choices, betrayal, and defeat. Even in fanzines, boxers are often portrayed as tragic figures whose talent lifts them out of the desperate poverty that would have been their lot, but who, despite their talent and self-discipline, fall victim to rage or hubris and end their short lives in car accidents, violent altercations, or prison.

Cinema, comics, and journalism all presented a vision of the city as the site of social dislocation and broken hearts, where social reproduction was impossible—or if possible, uninteresting. In this context, the masked wrestler stood as a counterexample. El Santo's movies were set in a wide variety of locations—Haiti, New York, Dallas, Guanajuato—but the character himself was understood to live in Mexico City. Although he hobnobbed with Mexico's elite, he remained a man of the people. Unlike Cantínflas's peladito or Tin Tan's pachuco, he was not a figure of fun. In contrast to the boxer, he was not a figure of tragedy. Whether facing an international terrorist gang arming a race of electromagnetic men, a flock of buxom female vampires, or the mummies of Guanajuato, El Santo, Blue Demon, Mil Mascaras, and the rest fought for the common good and always won. As the years passed, because of the mask, the wrestlers of the big screen never appeared to age. In contrast to the narrative of the boxer—the meteoric rise, the personal turmoil, the crushing setbacks, and sudden fall from grace—the narrative of the luchador promised a vision of stability, an incorruptible hero immune to the ravages of time.

LIVE PERFORMANCE AND MOMENTS OF MEDIATION

Lucha libre's circulation in different kinds of mass media influenced the way the genre could signify for its audience. The early lucha libre broadcasts popularized the genre and may have, initially, broadened the audience to include middle- and upper-class sectors of Mexico City. But the broadcasts fell victim to rivalries between empresas and between branches of government, expressed as a moral panic over the safety of children. The ban on televised broadcast did not suppress lucha libre but it did reconfigure its public. The population of Mexico City increased by nearly 500 percent between 1920 and 1950 (Mitchell 1994: 43–44).[16] By the mid-1950s, as the center filled with growing numbers of the self-employed artisans and peddlers and underemployed or underpaid construction and service sector workers who made up (and continue to make up) the bulk of the population of Mexico City, the middle class began a migration to the south and west. By the time lucha libre was taken off the air, much of the city's middle class had moved to the suburbs of Narvarte, Coyoacan, and Pedregal (among others)—far away from neighborhoods like Doctores and Tepito, where the principal EMLL arenas were located. Apart from those neighborhoods, there were only two other ways to see lucha libre. Outside of Mexico City (and one or two other large cities, like Guadalajara), lucha libre came and went as a traveling show, like the circus. It played in temporary venues, which might not have been class-specific. In addition to the provincial circuit, lucha libre could be seen at the movies.

Cinema thus became the main vehicle for mass dissemination of the spectacle, crossing both class and geographic boundaries. As a result, the figure of the wrestler was constructed through a kind of collaboration between live performances and the fantastic narratives of the cinema. The live performance provided the model for the movies, but the movies elevated the flesh and blood wrestler to a mythic status. At the live event, the distance, both social and physical, between aficionados and wrestlers could be very small indeed. For the most part, both came from the same social environment. Those spectators who could pay for ringside seats could come into direct physical contact with their idols, on purpose or by accident. The mask, paradoxically, both increased and decreased the social distance between wrestlers and fans. On the one hand, it allowed a play of identification—the masked wrestler might be a stranger, yet he might be your next-door neighbor. At the same time, though, the mask increased the distance between the wrestler and the spectator, investing the wrestler with an aura of mystery. The aura of mystery was intensified by the relationship between the live event and the movies, which constructed the wrestler as larger than life, for the line between El Santo the wrestler and El Santo the scourge of evil was not strictly drawn. Both the live event and the movies were united by the fetishism of the mask.

But although the movies helped establish the image of the Wrestler, the live performance—wrestling as such—maintained its autonomy relative to the movies. In the movies, wrestling per se was unimportant to the plot, functioning as pretext or filler. The live practice, however, banished from both the airwaves and middle-class spaces of the city, became closely connected with the *colonias populares* where the arenas remained. The practice of professional wrestling flourished independent of mass mediation, becoming, a "semi-clandestine" ritual of the urban popular class (Marcos Ráscon, interview with author, 1997), distanced from the dominant discourse of modernity and urbanization.

The fact that lucha libre developed as a live, rather than mass-mediated genre, had several implications for both the institutional structure supporting lucha and the style of performance. In the United States, where television was a significant factor in the organization of professional wrestling, events took place in venues normally used for other events. In Mexico City, however, events regularly took place in spaces used solely or primarily for lucha libre. The power of individual promoters depended on their access to (preferably ownership of) an arena and their affiliations with wrestlers, the state (via the commission) and the wrestler's union rather than their connections with the mass media.

The separation of lucha libre from television also had an impact on the style of performance practiced in Mexico. The needs of the camera and the dispersed public did not condition the development of lucha libre as they did U.S. professional wrestling. In the United States, where professional wrestling evolved as a genre of television show, verbal displays came to supplement or even replace bodily performance. The pre- and postmatch interview and verbal interchanges between wrestlers became the central means through which rivalries were expressed and narrative lines developed.[17] Lucha libre, however, developed as a form of theater in the round that further emphasized the visual, gestural, three-dimensional aspects of performance. The matches themselves were lengthened from one fall to two falls out of three. Matches with a greater number of participants, notably the three-versus-three format of *relevos australianos*, became a regular feature. Displays of acrobatics and agility increased in importance, coming to define the specifically Mexican style of performance. The features of performance now considered specific to lucha libre (as opposed to both U.S. and Japanese styles), in other words, are those that would appeal to a physically present audience whose members, having paid for their tickets (and thus an evening's worth of entertainment), would be located at different angles and distances relative to the action in the ring. The Mexican style developed to play to the first row and the third balcony instead of to the camera or the microphone.

Moreover, as I have previously said, it developed as story that Mexicans (of a certain historically constituted class position) told themselves about themselves (and about the world they inhabited). In the interactions between abject técnicos and underhanded rudos, lucha libre dramatized and parodied popular understandings of the postrevolutionary system and the spectators' place within it. Its very name, lucha libre (which means not only "freestyle wrestling" but also "free struggle") resonated with the widespread perception that life is struggle. Wrestling performance itself (as I have explored in the previous chapters) paralleled a political system in which electioneering took place behind closed doors, elections ratified decisions that had already been made, and people who appeared to be opponents

FIGURE 18
Lucha libre
emphasizes
agility over size

were really working together. Ongoing dramas in the ring demonstrated that loyalty to kin and friends was more important than ideology, and that arbiters of authority could not be trusted by the honest and honorable.

LUCHA LIBRE AS HIGH AND LOW CULTURE

Lucha libre's expulsion from television amounted to a kind of ghettoization of its performance. Between 1956 and 1991, few members of Mexico City's middle class would be likely to see lucha libre outside of the context of the occasional El Santo movie. Yet in the 1970s, lucha libre began to figure in a project of reconceptualization of *lo mexicano* by a generation of avant-garde artists. The first such use of lucha libre imagery took place in 1973, when Felipe Ehrenberg produced a performance piece in which several men, dressed as (masked) wrestlers, walked around the Bellas Artes opera house with flashlights. The idea was to have them circle the building until the batteries ran out, but the police intervened first (Ehrenberg, interview with author, 1996). By the early 1980s, more artists began using lucha libre imagery in their work, among them Lourdes Grobet, Marisa Lara, Arturo Guerrero, and Sergio Arau. Writers like Carlos Monsiváis, Jose Joaquin Blanco, José Buil, Paco Ignacio Taibo II, and others wrote about lucha libre, celebrating it in essays or using it as a theme in works of drama or fiction. For a group of artists and writers engaged in a cultural project in opposition to both the official nationalism of the Mexican state and the elitism of the arts community in the aftermath of 1968, lucha libre came to play an important role.

The goal of participants in this movement (which I, following García Canclini 1995, will refer to as "neo-pop") was to reconsider the cultural categories implicit in both official state discourse of national culture and leftist critiques of that discourse. In the dominant discourse of postrevolutionary Mexico, the locus of authentic popular culture was (and is) imagined to be the Indian, campesino sphere.[18] The cultural and political apparatus of the postrevolutionary Mexican state took an ambivalent position vis-à-vis the category of the Indian and of "popular culture" in general. Indigenous Mexicans continued to be viewed as a problem to be solved: the most backward sector of the population, passively awaiting the civilizing efforts of the mestizo national subject. Yet identification with both the pre-Hispanic past and the Indian present was central in the discourse of national cultural identity (and remains so). A variety of forms of cultural production—the National Museum of Anthropology, the murals of Diego Rivera, history textbooks, and so on—identify the modern nation-state of Mexico with the monumental civilizations of the Aztec, Maya, and others that preceded the conquest. In addition, both nationalist intellectuals and a tourism industry heavily dependent on state investment have celebrated a romanticized vision of contemporary indigenous minorities as the repositories of Mexico's tradition.

But if in the dominant discourse of Mexican nationalism the sphere of the rural and Indian has stood for the realm of the authentic and popular (as well as figuring as a site for state intervention), the culture of the urban poor constituted a different problem in official (state) and unofficial discourse. The counterpart of the Indian was imagined to be the modern, civilized subject. But the residents of the perpetually growing colonias populares of the capital did not fit that image. On the one hand, they were not Indians, they were participants in urban modernity, consumers of mass-produced goods and mass-mediated cultural forms. But neither were they exemplars of orderly modernity, "the affable and reasonable member(s) of the middle classes" (Lomnitz Adler 2001: 74) that state and elite ideologies continued to promote as the national ideal. Moreover, in the 1960s and 1970s, at a time when left-wing analyses of mass-mediated culture depended heavily on the cultural imperialism thesis, their engagement with mass media (especially U.S. imports, but Mexican mass media too) was regarded (in both left- and right-wing circles) as evidence of alienation and false consciousness, rather than evidence of participation in a modernizing project.

In fact, the restriction of lucha libre spectatorship to the colonias populares appears to have coincided with a shift in the way that the urban popular classes would be perceived by the middle and upper classes and represented in the media. By the mid-1950s, the descendants of a proletariat and subproletariat who lived in the center of Mexico City for generations had been joined by ever-increasing numbers of immigrants from the countryside and the smaller cities. To the extent that these new urbanites constituted a social class, they were not explicitly accounted for by the ideology or institutional structure of the postrevolutionary state. As Martin Needler (1998) has pointed out, the Partido Revolucionario Mexicano (PRM), precursor of the Partido Revolucionario Institucional (PRI), was organized "explicitly as a class alliance" between labor, campesinos, and a popular sector, which "was to be the home of the Revolutionary elements of the middle class; its base was in the civil-service unions, which were probably kept out of the labor sector to limit its power" (1998: 14). The bulk of the population, then, most of whom were neither factory workers, civil servants, nor petite bourgeoisie, were not explicitly integrated into the institutional structure of the state.

Before the 1950s, they were, however, stereotyped and denigrated as *pelados*. The term *pelado*, which literally means "stripped," identifies the poor (man) with (his) lack: of possessions, of culture, of everything: "The dangerous shadow of poverty in the expanding city. The nameless and almost naked threat, the figure of riot, robbery and assault" (Monsiváis 1997: 96). In the 1930s, the figure of the pelado began to circulate in public discourse as a kind of every-Mexican in two very different incarnations. On the one hand, Samuel Ramos used the pelado as the emblem of the national inferiority complex that he theorized as the core of the Mexican condition. On the other, the comedian Cantínflas domesticated the pelado through his character, the *peladito*, a penniless urban "wise fool" who unintentionally ridicules the pretensions of the Mexican elite as he struggles through his misadventures.

In the 1950s, however, the term *pelado* began to be replaced by the term *naco*. When it first came into use, "it was used as a slur against Indians or, more generally, against peasants or anyone who stood for the provincial backwardness that Mexico was trying so hard to dispel . . . the uncultured and uncouth Indian who could only be redeemed through an international culture" (Lomnitz 1996: 56). Both Lomnitz and Monsiváis claim that the term originated as a contraction of *Totonaco* (the name of an indigenous ethnic group), although others have told me that it is a contraction of *Chinaco*, which they explained as a term for the soldiers of Zapata's peasant army during their occupation of Mexico City. Either way, the initial point of reference for the naco, like the Andean chola (Weismantel 2001) is the Indian inappropriately situated in urban space. Thus, one could say that whereas the pelado was defined by his lack—of resources, of culture—the naco was defined by an excess of culture, by the inability to shed Indian tastes despite engagement with the urban world. As Monsiváis writes: "The term goes beyond socioeconomic identification (before it was said, 'he may have a lot of money, but he's basically a peasant'; now it has become 'he may have millions, but he'll always be a naco.') . . . It eventually becomes one of the many vehicles through which the cultural contempt for Indians is articulated" (1997: 102).

But, as Lomnitz Adler notes, around the 1970s the term underwent a transformation in meaning. It has since come to refer to a specifically urban social class and aesthetic, "a very particular form of 'kitsch' that is considered vulgar because it incorporates aspirations toward progress and material culture of modernity in an imperfect and partial way" (Lomnitz Adler 1996: 57). The way *naco* is used now, it might be applied to someone of any social class, any degree of mestizaje. Its primary frame of reference for the past thirty years, however, has been the same class that used to be referred to as *pelado*. In other words, while rural, indigenous Mexicans were seen as the impoverished, alienated guardians of Mexico's cultural traditions, lucha libre's fanship was made up of people who both left and right regarded as simultaneously urban and provincial, modern and backward, unpretentiously inauthentic—in short, naco.[19]

In this context, the project of the Neo-pop movement could be seen as a reformulation of the system of distinctions implicit in both state-endorsed and critical leftist versions of national culture and cultural authenticity. In a sense, its goals were very close to those of postrevolutionary intellectuals like Samuel Ramos, Frida Kahlo, Diego Rivera, or Octavio Paz: to construct an autonomous Mexican cultural scene and to create "different links within the art world that will allow [Mexicans] to be as proud as the Frenchman about their art instead of trying to be like the Frenchman" (Ehrenberg, interview with author, 1996). But several things distinguished the Neo-pop project from the cultural nationalism of the 1930s. One was an attitude of extreme suspicion of the Mexican state, particularly in the wake of the Tlaltelolco massacre. Another, related to the first, was a deliberate turning away from the trope of the rural and Indian as master symbols of the nation. The photographer Lourdes Grobet, for example, made an explicit decision not to use photographs of rural poverty. In her words, "I swore never to take folkloric photos. I never wanted to, because, some do it very well, but I feel that it is a safe and easy way to get images, taking photos of these poor people, the poverty, to move people" (interview with author, 1997).

Instead, like-minded artists and writers looked to the cultural practices of Mexico City's neighborhoods for imagery and inspiration. As Eric Zolov writes of the period (1999: 258), "The larger theoretical paradigm of what now constituted 'popular culture' was itself being challenged by a new level of critique that questioned the validity of a narrowly defined notion of cultural imperialism. The very term *cultura popular* underwent a transformation from its exclusively rural orientation into one that embraced all levels of urban cultural expression." They sought to validate cultural practices and images that had evaded the networks of both official and commercialized culture and exploded the contradiction between modernity and the indigenous sphere, celebrating forms left out of the discourse of the postrevolutionary state and disparaged by the middle and upper classes. In short, they celebrated *lo naco* as the essence of *lo mexicano*.

Lucha libre came to hold a privileged place in this movement for several reasons. First, it was perceived as uncorrupted. Once it was off the air, lucha libre could not attract the moneyed interests that other sports (and other kinds of performance) did. Stars like El Santo did very well, financially, but very, very few people got rich by wrestling. More important, no one else (except the EMLL) stood to make much money off of it either. As many in the lucha libre world stressed, in contrast to other sports, there is no gambling on lucha libre. In the words of Apolo Dantes:

> I think it's one of the most honest spectacles that there is in Mexico, because the people who go to the arenas don't bet. There's no gambling, no betting in lucha libre. It's very honest. The mafias that buy boxing matches, horse races, cockfights . . . if there's money in it, they'll be in football, wherever there's betting. In lucha, there's no betting. You have the whole family, the grandmother, grandchildren, brother-in-law, everybody comes to see the lucha, and they don't bet. The mafias that bet tried to insinuate themselves into the arena to buy matches before, but there is no response from the public. There's no money in the arena, and so there's no reason to do it. For that reason it's the cleanest sport. The people come to entertain themselves, to drink a soda, a sandwich, a beer, they yell, and they go home. If they see it at home on television, eating a snack, that's it. But they don't bet. In the lucha, the most anyone bets is a beer, a supper between friends. Not even a shirt or a watch. Not like other sports that come with the checkbook in hand. (Interview with author, 1997)[20]

Furthermore, lucha libre attracted no endorsements—no Nikes, no Reeboks, no sports drinks. It could thus be seen as a cultural practice that had escaped cooptation. Lucha libre could thus figure as an organic expression of urban popular culture.

Second, the Neo-pop movement's attention to home altars, salon dancing, and other cultural performances was rooted in a theory of *lo mexicano*: that the central, distinguishing value of transhistorical, transregional Mexican culture is a love of ritual and form. In this context, lucha libre could figure as an exemplary practice, because, with its emphasis on the visual and gestural, the cult of the body, the fetishism of the mask, it exploded the distinction between the ritual world of indigenous Mexico and the modern, urban, proletarian public sphere.[21] Lucha libre became valorized as a space where specifically Mexican cultural practices were renewed in performance rather than preserved as folklore. As Lourdes Grobet recounts:

> I went in [to the arenas] with the idea of taking a few pictures, but I discovered something fantastic. So I stuck with it. I got into it because one thing that interested me in my photographic work was culture . . . not art, but culture. . . . And it really struck me. And there I discovered the urban Mexico . . . in the lucha, I discovered pre-Hispanic Mexico, indigenous Mexico, but urbanized. The aesthetic is the same, and the same people, with very little material resources, take hold of the urban space. It's a very basic cultural manifestation, and then there's the whole representation—the use of the mask in a masked culture, the modernity in the ritual mask, in the costume, in the characters, the theater . . . that is . . . all that the Mexican culture carries, all of the values of Mexican culture are found there. (Interview with author, 1997)

Some, like Grobet, Ehrenberg, and the painters Marisa Lara and Arturo Guerrero immersed themselves in the lucha libre world, developing friendships with individual luchadores, and have remained (to a greater or lesser degree) in contact with the cultural environment. Other artists took up the wrestling motif without identifying with the neo-pop movement or pursuing any further connection with the lucha libre world. The wrestlers, in general, welcomed the exotic and legitimating attentions of the artists and intellectuals. This collaboration reached its climax in 1992, when the Museo de Culturas Populares in Coyoacan featured an exhibition on lucha libre titled "La Lucha (Libre) La Hacemos Todos."[22]

Although the neo-pop movement (if that's what it should be called) consisted of a handful of artists and intellectuals, their impact on the ways that lucha libre would circulate as a symbol had far-reaching effects. Their interest in the sport was rooted in its separation from conventional mass-mediated networks of circulation, from its status as a "semi-clandestine rite." The fact that it was unredeemably naco was the very thing that drew them to it. Artistic appropriation of lucha libre carried it to spaces outside of the arena and the movie theater, and into circulation in the sphere of high culture as a symbol of the urban popular culture of which it was a part. This focus on lucha libre's capacity to signify as a master symbol of the popular subject was, in turn, important to the capacity of Superbarrio to signify himself as the representative of "the people" (see chapter 4).

In 1991, the media giant Televisa announced that it would bring lucha libre back to the small screen for the first time in thirty-five years. Felipe Ehrenberg has suggested that one reason for Televisa's decision was that the attention that artists and journalists (because of the social wrestlers) paid to lucha libre made it seem more respectable (interview with author, 1996). The embrace of lucha libre by the neo-pop movement coincided, however, with a boom in professional wrestling in the United States when Vince McMahon's reorganized World Wrestling Federation succeeded in bringing professional wrestling from regional networks to national networks and cable.[23] Televisa may have seen a lucrative model in the revamped WWF.

Many wrestlers and promoters saw televised lucha libre as an opportunity to increase their profits and expand their audience. But other members of the world of wrestlers, promoters, journalists, and dedicated fans that make up lucha libre's subculture saw the revival of televised lucha libre as a disaster. The broadcasts were not accepted passively by the wrestling community. Instead, televised broadcast of lucha libre became a battleground over labor rights, aesthetics, and cultural integrity.[24]

Televisa's interest in lucha libre came after a decade of reorganization as well as resignification of the genre. In the mid-1980s, the Commission of Boxing and Lucha Libre began to loosen its control over the sport. In 1985, the EMLL was granted permission to allow children into the arenas.[25] Later that year Luis Spota, president of the commission since 1957, died, and in 1986 Rafael Barradas retired. The commission itself was reorganized. Lucha libre and boxing were administratively separated, and the administration of the former was placed in the hands of a string of retired luchadores. In 1985, in the course of working for the repeal of the prohibition against luchadoras working in the Federal District, the CROC-affiliated Association of Luchadores, Referees, and Retirees discovered that the commission had never been granted legal authority and that lucha libre had no binding regulation (see chapter 5). Thus by 1990, when Televisa began to reconsider lucha libre, the commission's authority over the spectacle had diminished.

In the spring of 1991, Televisa signed a contract with the "serious and stable" EMLL to tape performances in Arenas Mexico and Coliseo and broadcast them on Saturday afternoons. They later switched to Sundays.

The EMLL had been able to maintain its hegemony in the Federal District over the years. It was (and remains) the largest, oldest, and (arguably) most prestigious empresa in Mexico. The second largest, Carlos Maynez's *Lucha Libre Internacional*, promoted shows at the Toreo Cuatro Caminos, a bullfight ring just over the border from the Federal District, in the state of Mexico.[26]

From the start, many wrestlers and promoters expressed concern over the economic impact of television. Some veterans of the 1950s remembered that arena attendance dropped sharply when it was broadcast by Televicentro. One journalist (echoing accusations leveled against the Garza Hernandez Lucha Libre Internacional forty years before) called televised wrestling an underhanded attack on Carlos Maynez's Lucha Libre Internacional by the EMLL.[27] Other wrestlers did not oppose televised broadcast as such but were worried about its terms, especially the scheduling of the broadcasts. The two biggest shows at the arena are Friday nights and Sunday afternoons, and many feared that Sunday broadcasts would compete directly with the arenas. Hence televised broadcasts immediately raised a host of concerns.[28] Manny Guzmán, president of the Sindicato Nacional de Luchadores (SNL), was in charge of representing the wrestlers' interests in the EMLL's negotiations with Televisa, but in the spring of 1992 several disgruntled wrestlers broke with the Sindicato, publicly accusing Guzmán of selling out the membership. They were immediately blackballed by the union (*L'Afición* 1992b).

Unveiling the AAA

The deal between the EMLL and Televisa was brokered by the former's director of programming and public relations, Antonio Peña. Peña (whose duties included scouting new talent and developing new characters) was known for making changes to the live event. He had added several foreign wrestlers to the EMLL stable who had never trained as wrestlers before their recruitment.[29] Notable among these were Conan el Bárbaro, a Cuban American recruited from the streets of Miami, and Vampiro Canadiense, a tall, muscular rock 'n' roller from Canada.[30] In addition, Peña added a number of new elements to lucha libre performance (musical themes and scantily clad female escorts for the wrestlers, and special lighting for the arena) that some thought innovative but others thought degrading.

As the controversy over the broadcasts continued, rumors began to circulate that Peña was leaving the EMLL to start his own empresa. The rumors proved to be true, and on June 7 he left, taking a group of about thirty wrestlers (among them some of the Empresa's biggest stars), to whom he promised higher pay and more exposure. He gave the empresa the rather dry name of Asistencia, Asesoria y Administracion (Assistance, Accounting, and Administration, but better known as the AAA, and pronounced triple-A). In the weeks following the announcement, journalists wondered aloud how he was going to support an empresa with no reliable access to arenas. He wouldn't have use of the EMLL arenas, and it was unlikely that smaller arena owners would want to antagonize the empresa by letting him use theirs.

Peña retorted that his empresa would bring stars of lucha libre to the provinces and "internationalize" lucha libre through his connections with the World Wrestling Federation in the United States. His goal, he said, was to "bring innovation to the spectacle by creating new characters, and to elevate the dissemination of this rough discipline not only at the national level, but in places like South America, Europe and the United States. We will make it so that the public of the provinces has access to the great stars" (*L'Afición* 1992a: 28).

But it soon came out that the owner of the new empresa was not Antonio Peña but Televisa itself. The stable, dependable space of the AAA would not be in any arena, but in the virtual space of channel 9. Like its precursor Televicentro in 1952, Televisa seized control of the spectacle by going around the EMLL and sponsoring a network empresa. AAA stars would appear in independent arenas outside of the Federal District (and thus outside of the jurisdiction of the Federal District commission), where their performances would be taped for broadcast.[31]

From the point of view of the EMLL, this was an act of base treachery on the parts of both Televisa and (especially) Antonio Peña. They closed ranks with Lucha Libre Internacional and the Sindicato against the AAA, and warned that their wrestlers were free to go with Peña but might not be free to come back if things didn't work out (*L'Afición* 1992c: 25). Guzmán announced that the Sindicato, as "the only legitimate holder of the national collective contract for wrestlers," could legitimately demand the suspension of all AAA functions but would graciously refrain from doing so. Any union member who participated in a AAA function, however, would be expelled from the Sindicato (*L'Afición* 1992e: 25). In addition, he negotiated an agreement in the state of Mexico with the Commission of Lucha Libre and the owners of the major arenas, to prohibit the entrance of new empresas, allegedly to protect the public from fraudulent advertising by fly-by-night promoters (*L'Afición* 1992e: 25).

Some wrestlers followed Peña. The wrestler Justiciero took over as head of a new AAA-affiliated union to represent the now blackballed wrestlers (*L'Afición* 1992d: 25).[32] Meanwhile, the Sindicato, still led by Guzmán, suddenly changed its position to oppose televised broadcast. The movement against televised lucha libre climaxed in June of 1993, when the Sindicato went on strike. The strike culminated in a march on the presidential residence of Los Pinos by a group of about three hundred wrestlers, many wearing their masks. The strikers hoped to get an audience with President Salinas de Gortari to ask for his intervention in the matter, but the president was unavailable and the strike fell apart (*L'Afición* 1992f: 9). As a result, the Sindicato lost much of its influence. One group of wrestlers left to join Juan Alanis's union, while others reached an accord with the EMLL to form an in-house union. Televisa agreed to continue to broadcast EMLL events (one of the demands of the strikers), but the strike failed to stop the televised transmission of lucha libre, or to wrest its control from the media conglomerate.

The victory of Televisa and the AAA had a number of consequences for the practice and reception of lucha libre. First, television changed the rhythm of the wrestling event. Rather than show a series of five matches in one arena, the broadcasts show a number of events from different arenas around the republic.[33] The action, moreover, is not confined to the ring (and the space surrounding it) but includes areas separated in space and time from the arena (the locker rooms, the parking lot, the promoter's office before the event, and so on). The broadcast audience is separated from the wrestlers, and even spectators in the arena are separated from the ring and the wrestlers by movable barricades. Where live (not broadcast) lucha libre problematizes the difference between participants and observers, televised lucha libre reinforces it. In the words of Ecologista Universal, "television kills the relationship between the wrestlers and the audience" (interview with author, 1996).

Perhaps more significant, the AAA and televised wrestling in general promoted a shift in the composition of the wrestling audience, for once again, the broadcast of lucha libre brought the sport-spectacle to a new audience of middle-class children and youth. During the golden era, when lucha libre was enmeshed in a particular class culture, the class composition of the live audience was secured not only by middle-class disdain of the genre, but by the actual and perceived risks of going to an arena. In addition to the real and imagined dangers associated with entering neighborhoods in the center, or settlements like Ciudad Nezahualcoyotl, many middle-class Mexicans were (and are) wary of the behavior of the lucha audience (which they imagine to be far more unruly than it is). For example, several middle-class Mexicans told me that they didn't want to go to the arenas, because people in the balcony throw cups of urine onto the ringside seats—an apparently widespread (and erroneous) belief.[34] Broadcast of lucha libre meant that an emerging middle-class fanship could watch from their homes, where many developed a taste for the AAA version of the sport. In general, middle-class Mexicans with whom I spoke identified lucha libre with its mass-mediated manifestations: television during the 1950s and the movies from the 1950s through the 1970s. As far as they were concerned, lucha had been dormant since the decline of the wrestling movie (or even since it was taken off the air in the 1950s), and the new televised version represented its revival.

Television thus took the place of cinema as the main means of dissemination of lucha libre to middle-class and provincial audiences. But unlike cinema, which had relatively little impact on the form of the live event, televised wrestling generated changes in the genre itself. There has always been a tension in lucha libre between spectacularity and the display of wrestling skill. Retirees whose careers spanned the 1950s and 1960s told me that even then there were those who disparaged the more acrobatic wrestlers for being "maromeros" (tumblers). In the late 1960s, when lucha libre started to include more aerial moves than before, sportswriters and veterans complained that the changes would degrade the sport to mere circus (Juanito Diaz, interview with author, 1996). However, in those years (at least according to nostalgic veterans), wrestlers in the Federal District first had to be conversant in standard wrestling techniques and be able to display that knowledge in the ring. Thus lucha maintained its character of being, first and foremost, an exhibition of skill in a specific physical discipline, that of wrestling.

Televised events, on the other hand, make more use of the broad pantomime that already typified pro wrestling in the United States. There is less exchange of locks, and more hitting. Elements of action that used to be used sparingly (bloodletting, obvious use of props as illegal weapons, and so on) are used liberally in lucha's televised incarnation. That, in turn, changed the expectations that spectators have of the live event, and wrestlers now must accommodate those expectations to be successful. AAA-affiliated wresters and their fans portrayed the empresa's innovations as progress: both aesthetic (asserting that "lucha libre is always evolving") and in terms of expanding lucha libre's audience. Fans from lucha libre's traditional public, and many veterans of the lucha world, rejected the discourse of progress for one of decadence. When Vampiro Canadiense would appear in the ring his young fans cheered wildly, but more committed aficionados taunted him with cries of "El Vampiro doesn't know how to wrestle."[35] They said that it might be libre, but it wasn't really lucha.

Third Round: PromoAzteca

From the 1970s to the 1990s, Televisa, formed when the Azcárraga family's Televicentro absorbed other private networks into a media conglomerate, held a monopoly on commercial television. In 1993, in line with the neoliberal policies of the Salinas administration, the state-owned Corporación Mexicana de Radio y Television, which ran television stations 7 and 13, was privatized, ending Televisa's monopoly on commercial broadcast television in Mexico. It was sold to Ricardo Salinas Pliego, owner of the appliance chain Elektra, despite his lack of experience in mass media. Although they had not submitted a bid, the Azcárraga family, who had long been active supporters of the PRI, vigorously protested the sale. They, along with companies that had submitted bids (all of them with experience in radio broadcasting), accused the president's brother Raul Salinas de Gortari of selling the station at a loss to a relative. The government denied the charges, insisting that Salinas Pliego was not related to the Salinas de Gortari.[36] Salinas Pliego named the new station TV Azteca.

In 1995, Pedro Ortega, then secretary of the Commission of Lucha Libre, and Raul Reyes, a promoter who owned a few arenas on the outskirts of the Federal District, approached Salinas Pliego with the idea of starting a wrestling empresa, sponsored and broadcast by the new network. He agreed, but Reyes was forced out of the organization before the contract was signed.[37] Shortly thereafter, in the fall of 1996, a group of wrestlers from the AAA, led by Conan, Peña's director of international relations, and including stars like Vampiro Canadiense and Máscara Sagrada, left to join the new empresa.

In a televised interview, thirteen of the errant wrestlers accused Peña of corruption and unfair labor practices (*En Caliente*, 1996). Conan accused Peña of breaking (unspecified) promises and of docking his pay when he was working in the United States. Juventud Guerrera charged Peña with having his U.S. visa canceled when he left to join PromoAzteca (the new empresa). Máscara Sagrada complained that Peña was promoting droves of spurious Máscara Sagrada spin-offs (juniors, IIs, etc.) without his consent.[38] Using language that was often used to criticize the PRI, they described the AAA as a corrupt monopoly, a "dinosaur."[39] In response, Peña and his allies portrayed the PromoAzteca wrestlers as a group of disloyal stooges, led astray by perfidious foreigners (Conan and Vampiro). Peña accused the fleeing wrestlers of "lack of gratitude toward the house which saw their birth," and Perro Aguayo, speaking for the wrestlers staying with the AAA, avowed that it was "a shame that a foreigner could offend and fool the public and that a television station that carried the name of an ancient Mexican culture, the Aztec, could be used for this" (*La Jornada* 1996b: 52).

All of the parties in the dispute positioned themselves in ways that reflected the current political discourse and paralleled the conflict between the two networks. In 1991, Peña portrayed AAA as an innovative, internationalizing enterprise that would maximize employees' earnings—in other words, an enterprise in line with Salinas de Gortari's program of neoliberal modernization. When the Promo-Azteca wrestlers broke away, they echoed the terms that people used to condemn the president of the republic and the PRI, claimed the discourse of modernization for themselves, and condemned Peña's corruption and monopoly of power. The PromoAzteca wrestlers' accusations of corruption were met with countercharges of *malinchismo*.

The New Traditionalists

This time, however, there were no strikes and no organized opposition to the saturation of the airwaves with even more lucha libre. During 1997 and much of 1998, lucha libre was broadcast twice a week: once by TVAzteca and once by Televisa, which broadcast four hours of AAA and EMLL wrestling on Sundays. The relationship between the broadcasts and arena attendance is not well documented, but there was general agreement that attendance fell. Most luchadores, trainers, and administrators outside of PromoAzteca and the AAA agreed that it was the fault of the televised broadcasts coupled with the economic crisis that followed the 1994 crash of the peso.

During the period of my research, there was a great deal of free-floating discontent in the wrestling world over the decline of live lucha libre. There was, however, one novel response to the perceived crisis: the formation of a wrestling empresa dedicated to the reformation and renovation of Mexican lucha libre. The new empresa, called Renovación 2000, began as an alliance between associates of Juan Alanís's union (the Association), Raul Reyes (the disenfranchised cofounder of PromoAzteca), and a number of other promoters and wrestlers who were left out of televised lucha libre. Reyes was named president of the new empresa, which also had the support of the EMLL.[40] Renovación 2000 was, like the AAA and PromoAzteca, critical of both the labor and aesthetic practices of their competitors. Their critique, however, differed radically from those of the other two. When Peña and his followers left the EMLL, they criticized the empresa's failure to maximize the exposure and income of their wrestlers. PromoAzteca condemned the AAA for failure to deliver on its promises. Renovación 2000, however, contended that the problem was that too few wrestlers could earn a living wage. They repeated criticisms that already circulated at the time of the first 1991 broadcasts: that lucha libre was suffering from *estrellitis* (star-itis), and that television limited the number of opportunities for wrestlers so that only a few carefully managed stars could find enough work to support themselves. Television, they argued, not only took work away from wrestlers, but from the cleaners, ushers, and concessionaires who worked in the arenas. Empresas, they implied, like the government, have a social obligation to provide jobs for the people—an obligation that the major empresas ignored.

Many of the associates of Renovación 2000 participated in the protests of 1993, and their economic analysis of television was much like the one in circulation at that time. But they linked their criticisms to an aesthetic vision that recast lucha libre as a traditional practice. In other words, the leadership (and some of the rank and file) embraced the discourse of the neo-pop movement to claim lucha libre as a popular art form. As such, they argued, it was part of Mexico's national patrimony and therefore deserved the protection of the state. (This posture was very distinct from that of the neo-pop movement, which looked to lucha libre as a cultural performance that had evaded state cooptation.) Their position (which was by no means limited to wrestlers working with Renovación) was that the AAA had not only disrupted the economic base of lucha libre but also was bringing about its aesthetic degradation. The Renovación project thus was one of cultural renovation: to define and promote the real, traditional lucha libre Mexicana. Naturally, defining traditional lucha entailed defining what it was not.

The Real Mexican Lucha Libre

Renovación 2000 members (and those who shared their point of view) complained about a number of practices of the televised empresas, especially the AAA. Their most frequently voiced objection was the same one that outsiders often make about professional wrestling in general: it is not really wrestling. They complained that televised wrestling involved too much indiscriminate use of props and novelties, and that "ya no hay llaveo" (nobody uses locks anymore). But their critique of televised wrestling went further, to define an aesthetic and ethical vision of lucha libre that they were ready to defend on several grounds.

One site where the traditionalists criticized the AAA and PromoAzteca was in relation to gender and performance. The luchador, they insisted, should embody virility. Yet they did not consider the presence of luchadoras problematic (although there are many individual luchadores who disapprove of women wrestlers). Renovación's traditionalists accepted luchadoras as part of the Mexican lucha libre tradition. Indeed, women have wrestled in Mexico since the late 1940s. In many conversations with wrestlers and others in the wrestling world (both inside and outside of Renovación), I was told that the participation of women in lucha libre was just another example of their participation in the workforce: there are women cabdrivers, women police officers, so why not luchadoras? No one challenged the right of women to engage in paid employment, and only some questioned the appropriateness of wrestling as woman's occupation (see chapter 5).

Renovación 2000 militants disapproved of mixed (male-versus-female) matches and were critical of the relationship between the rudo Killer and his escort Miss Janeth (who sometimes comes to his aid in the ring or helps him to cheat against an opponent). They found both examples disturbing because they believed mixed wrestling to endanger and degrade the luchadora and elicit dishonorable and inappropriate behavior from the male luchadores. But (unsurprisingly, given its affiliation with the Association) they did support women in wrestling, as long as luchadoras wrestled only each other. Renovación thus did not regard the AAA's support of women in the ring (which was not notable) as problematic. They were, however, outraged by the AAA's promotion of the Exoticos, which they regarded as a prime example of the sport's degeneration at the hands of the television industry.[41]

The complaint that I heard most frequently from associates of Renovación 2000, however, had to do with bodies. The wrestler, they said, was supposed to represent something. If a wrestler walked down the street, people were supposed to know it. Even if he fought incognito, they should be able to say, "Ah, there goes a wrestler." Thus the physical development of the (male) wrestler was supposed to be directed to the formation of a thick, muscular physique. Even though the Mexican style emphasizes agility over size, the wrestler was not supposed to look like a soccer player or a bicyclist. His physique was supposed to be on display in the arena, and thus certain types of costume were preferable to others.

In the early days of lucha libre, most wrestlers wore a pair of boots, a pair of trunks and, in some cases, a mask. The typical wrestling mask was a smooth piece of fabric that completely covered the face and head with trim around the eye, nose, and mouth holes, and perhaps some discreet insignia. To this basic costume might be added tights, knee pads, and a tank top. The overall effect called attention to the wrestler's musculature, especially his bare (or nearly bare) torso and arms.[42] Traditionalists were thus critical of a style of costume promoted by Antonio Peña that featured ever more elaborate covering of the body. The costumes, worn by some of the AAA wrestlers, consisted of boots, tights, briefs, a jersey that completely covered the arms, and elaborate masks with horns, beaks, or other extensions. The physique of the wrestler was obscured by the costume, a physique, traditionalists complained, that was not meaty enough to be convincing as a wrestler's body.[43]

Behind their aesthetic critique (which I also heard from aspiring wrestlers planning their costumes) lay questions about labor conditions and copyright, for the fully covered body has the power to disrupt the ambiguous relationship between the wrestler and the character. That disruption lay at the root of Máscara Sagrada's conflict with the AAA (or at least according to his televised interviews). Before the current round of televised wrestling, ownership of the wrestler's character was assumed to reside with the wrestler. Antonio Peña, however, made a point of copyrighting the characters that he promoted (and claims to have developed).[44] In promoting the Máscara Sagrada spin-offs, Peña asserted ownership of the character: a character fully alienable from the wrestler who embodies it. When the original Máscara Sagrada left, he simply put another wrestler into the costume. Thus in 1997 there were two Máscara Sagradas in circulation, one belonging to the AAA and the other (the "original") still with Promo-Azteca. Even more disturbing to my informants was the case of the wrestler Pentagón, who was permanently disabled by a neck injury sustained in the ring in 1994. Many wrestlers were unnerved when Peña hired a another wrestler to wear the Pentagón costume without consulting the original or explicitly marking (with Jr., II, or another indicator) the fact that it was a different man.[45]

The question of costume, therefore, was enmeshed in discourses about tradition, embodiment, and labor rights. A traditionally masked wrestler hides the face better to display the body. In concealing his or her identity, he or she heightens the identification between wrestler and character. A fully covered, elaborately masked wrestler, on the other hand, cannot embody the physical ideal and becomes interchangeable with others in the same costume. For wrestlers and others in the world of lucha libre, the idiosyncrasies of performance (the fixed ending, the right of the rudos to cheat) do not constitute fraud, but the interchangeability of wrestlers does. The shift in costume style, in their analysis, spoke directly to questions of authenticity.

But beyond such aesthetic matters, the main concern of the Renovación 2000 militants was the decline in attendance at lucha libre functions with the advent of televised wrestling. As predicted in 1991, arena revenues fell. Many neighborhood arenas closed down (Raul Reyes, for example, shut down three of his four arenas), and in July 1997, even the EMLL closed the smallest of its three arenas in the Federal District, the Pista Arena Revolución (which operated three days a week when I started fieldwork in 1996). Some wrestlers outside of the televised empresas complained to me that they had gone from working several days a week to a few days a month.

In the eyes of the Renovación 2000 group, this decline was due not to televised broadcast per se, but to the fact that the televised empresas had abandoned their public. The problem, some argued, was not that potential spectators wanted to see more blood or more acrobatics, but that the true aficionados of real lucha libre did not want to have to leave their neighborhoods and could no longer afford ticket prices at the remaining arenas.[46] Others blamed the decline in attendance to generalized malaise, resulting from overuse of novelties (blood, props, disrespect to referees and audience), and a subsequent decline in the quality of wrestling available to spectators. The Renovación traditionalists tried to address both of these issues. They held events in gyms, dancehalls, and other spaces in marginal neighborhoods, charging "popular prices" (5 or 10 pesos). The functions would feature several matches between novices recruited by Alanís and end with a match between stars of the EMLL. Reyes would attend the events and stop the matches if the wrestlers did something (like hitting another wrestler with a chair) that violated the empresa's directives. He acted, in other words, like commissioners were said to have done during lucha libre's golden age. But the Renovacionistas did not believe that their efforts would save lucha libre. Its recovery, in their analysis, depended on re-establishing the control of the Commission of Lucha Libre over the content of the spectacle.

During 1997, when the term of Acting Secretary Luis Gonzalez was about to end, various discontented parties (including Renovación 2000, the Association, independents like my teacher, and some members of the wrestling press) began to demand increased intervention in lucha libre by the state, in the form of a strengthened commission. As noted before, in the 1980s, Association militants discovered that lucha libre had no formal regulation. The commission had no legally binding authority and thus no formal power to authorize or prohibit functions in the Federal District. That authority lay, instead, with the political delegation of the neighborhood where the match was to take place.[47] In the eyes of the traditionalists, that meant that wrestlers had no recourse against those who would degrade their art. As Hara Kiri complained:

Even if the secretary or president of the commission were to put forward a very complete plan to regulate the spectacle, if the promoter already complied with his documentation, it would mean nothing. That's why lucha libre has degenerated. Because if the gentleman has complied with the requisites of the corresponding state, municipality, and delegation, and they authorized the function, the gentleman could put a person in to wrestle with a lion. . . . And if the gentleman says to a wrestler, "You're going to dress like a monkey and swing from the lights," that's it. (Hara Kiri, interview with author, 1997)

The Renovación wrestlers with whom I worked lived in areas of the city that were, by then, strongholds of support for the PRD, the leftist opposition party that won the municipal elections that July.[48] Some had worked with the Asemblea de Barrios and with Superbarrio since the late 1980s. They hoped to use those connections to ask the new government to return lucha libre to the control of the commission by granting it the legal authority to regulate the spectacle—not only to oversee work conditions, but to determine what could or could not count as real, Mexican lucha libre.

CONCLUSION

Professional wrestling may not seem a likely site to play out conflicts over neoliberal economics or cultural authenticity, yet lucha libre has been the locus of just such struggles, particularly in relation to questions of mass mediation. Both times that the sport was televised, it precipitated a crisis that reconfigured relationships among participants in the sport and between the sport and the state.

Lucha libre underwent a complex series of resignifications after its arrival in 1933. It started as ritual of modernization, linked to processes of migration and urbanization centered in the Federal District. This set of associations might have been reinforced or changed in other ways in the 1950s, had its run on television lasted longer. Instead, the exposure that television gave it brought it under greater scrutiny by the state. That scrutiny strengthened the hand of the commission and reinforced the links between state institutions and the occupational subculture of the wrestlers. As a further result, lucha performance was confined to spaces that, in that moment, were strongly marked as popular, or even naco. The ban on broadcast guaranteed that it would continue as a class-specific, neighborhood-centered performance. This eventually made the genre reconfigurable by the artistic and political avant-garde as a quasi-artisanal practice. Artists and organizers came to view it both as a source of imagery and as an exemplary nonalienated ritual of lived urban reality. Thus resignified, it gained a measure of respectability that carried it out of its niche.

Its return to television in the 1990s precipitated another crisis. In many ways it paralleled the conflicts of the 1950s: Televicentro/Televisa challenged the hegemony of the EMLL in their attempts to control the spectacle; the competition, conflicts, and alliances between rival empresas became enmeshed in competition among rival broadcasters. In the 1950s, the conflict between empresas and networks was resolved by the actions of the state in ways that seem to have benefited the EMLL (at the expense of their biggest rival) and kept lucha libre independent of the exigencies of television.

The conflicts of the 1990s echoed those of the 1950s. First, the decision to televise lucha libre proved controversial in both cases. Second, the broadcasts led to a complex set of alliances and enmities between and among wrestling impresarios, broadcasters, and politicians. The antagonism between Televisa and TVAzteca, for example, went well beyond "competition" and was part of a larger set of conflicts playing out between different factions of the PRI. The rivalries between and among the EMLL, the AAA, and PromoAzteca reflected those of their sponsoring networks.

In the 1990s, the success of televised broadcast imposed a different structure on the event and a different relationship between performers and spectators. A conflation of labor and aesthetic issues then led wrestlers, fans, and reporters to ask what constituted lucha libre. Are promoters, as the name implies, free (libre) to make of it whatever the market demands? Can or should the conventions of its performance be regulated by the state? The response of Renovación 2000 made sense within this context and clarified stakes of the EMLL/AAA conflict. Lucha libre's transition to a televised genre paralleled the more general shift from an economic and ideological complex based on import substitution to one based on neoliberal globalization.[49]

The traditionalists saw television alienate lucha libre from the space of the arenas and the communities in which the arenas were located. Lucha's traditional audience, now less able to afford the ticket, is more likely to bypass the arenas and watch at home, while a new, young, middle-class audience has learned to enjoy the imagery without the gestalt of the arena. Many luchadores welcomed the return to television, eager for the level of celebrity it could offer those lucky enough to succeed (even as the broadcasts made fewer jobs available). But those displaced by televised lucha libre embraced and resignified the assessment of the artists who celebrated the genre in the 1970s and 1980s. In what is, in effect, a critique of the neoliberal stance of the large empresas, they made the claim that lucha libre, a practice which many believe to be intrinsically vulgar, intrinsically corrupt, was instead a popular tradition, part of the national patrimony, and worthy of the state's protection from corruption and vulgarization.

EPILOGUE 2001

Renovación 2000's candidates for president and secretary of the commission were passed over in 1998. Rafael Barradas was reappointed to the commission as secretary, the wrestler Fantasma was appointed as president, and Renovación 2000 fell apart. TVAzteca decided not to renew its contract with PromoAzteca. As of 2001, the latter still functioned as an empresa, but there were rumors that it had been secretly co-owned by Antonio Peña all along. Yet another empresa, the Grupo Revolucionario Internacional de Lucha Libre (based in Naucalpan in the state of Mexico), broadcast matches on Friday nights on ESPN2. Televisa continued to offer four hours of lucha libre a week. Although the arenas were often half-empty, the live event continued to attract its public. They came week after week to cheer on the técnicos and curse out the rudos (or vice versa).

If Antonio Peña was really a partner in PromoAzteca, perhaps the entire episode was just a lucha libre metamatch where, despite the appearance of implacable hostility, rudos and técnicos are always working together behind the scenes to create the spectacle. So perhaps the last word belongs to the wrestler Canek. At least I think it was Canek.

Canek is a star, one of the few wrestlers affiliated with Lucha Libre Internacional who can always get work. I spoke to him one day when I was in a wrestling gym, interviewing the patrons. When I asked other wrestlers there what they thought of the changes of the last decade, all responded eagerly, bemoaning the damage that had been done to the sport and the community of professional wrestlers by the AAA and Televisa. Finally, I went to talk to a dark, muscular, and taciturn wrestler that the owner insinuated was the famous Canek. He declined to give me his name or nombre de batalla but reluctantly agreed to the interview just before starting his daily weight routine. I asked him what he thought of the changes lucha libre had undergone since his debut in 1972. Turning to the weight bench, he growled laconically, "There haven't been any changes. It's like Mexican history, it never changes."

CONCLUSION

But (like his nineteenth-century namesake) Canek cannot have the last word . . .

His axiomatic statement—nothing ever changes—is really a statement about the priority of structure over event. The basic structure of lucha libre has not changed since the 1930s. Rudos and técnicos still face each other in their violent tango. As Novo described in the 1940s, "each rheumatic and bald master of a two peso ticket at ringside [still] loses the kilos and years necessary to transform himself [(or herself)] into [Rayo de Jalisco Jr.], and with equal ease, find in [Dr. Wagner Jr.] or in [SuperElektra] his enemies scattered about the world . . . and contributes from his seat to exterminate them, to kick them, to throw them out of the ring" (Novo 1994: 600).

As always, the fate of the wrestlers depends on the loyalties, preferences, and backstage maneuvers of the promoters who organize the sport, the commission that regulates it, and the various media through which their battles and news of their battles circulate. Like lucha libre, Canek implies, the structure of political power in Mexico never changes. Despite the appearance of change, the same people are always in charge—or if not the same people, the same corrupt forms of domination. The problem with Canek's analysis of the situation is that, at the level of event, both lucha libre and Mexican history *do* change, and those changes do transform both structures.

In his often-cited article on the Balinese cockfight, Clifford Geertz described cockfighting as "a story the Balinese tell themselves about themselves." Specifically, he argued that the frenzied encounter of the fighting cocks held such fascination for Balinese men because it expressed an essential, hidden element of the Balinese conception of the self: the violent, passionate animal that each man kept concealed beneath his public mask of composure. The cockfight article came under criticism from two directions. Alan Dundes (1994) pointed out that the cockfight is by no means unique to Bali. Since it is an extremely widespread form of entertainment, its popularity could not be accounted for by a Balinese theory of self. Instead he advanced a psychoanalytic explanation for the ubiquity of the cockfight—cocks, in short, are cocks wherever they are found, and the cockfight is therefore, always and everywhere, a form of public, ritual, male masturbation. William Roseberry (1989), on the other hand, criticized Geertz for paying insufficient attention to the political and material context of the cockfight. He asserted that a proper analysis of the cockfight would need to consider the broader conditions in which the cockfight took place (Balinese subordination to Javanese hegemony, the configuration of gender in Bali and the predominance of women in the marketplaces where the cockfights would take place, and so on).

Any engagement with professional wrestling runs into a similar problem. Professional wrestling is performed in many different countries. The conventions in settings as diverse as the United States, Mexico, Australia, and Japan are similar enough that wrestlers from any country can work in any other. But the significance that professional wrestling will have depends on the cultural context in which it takes place. Scholars of U.S.-style professional wrestling have interpreted it in a multiplicity of ways—as a radical critique of capitalism, as a conservative celebration of U.S. militarism, as a ritual confrontation of ethnic and national types, or as presentation of different modes of masculinity. All of those readings make sense because each is an aspect of the exercise of power in the United States. In a very general sense, then, professional wrestling does have a universal meaning. Wherever it is performed, professional wrestling is *fundamentally* about the exercise of power, *where physical power stands in for other modes*. The kinds of social actors and modes of domination that professional wrestling portrays will necessarily vary depending on local configurations of power.

I have argued here that, in Mexico, lucha libre developed as a way for people to think about different aspects of the postrevolutionary political system. It communicates complex and contradictory ideas: about gender, about national and regional identity, about moral and immoral modes of conflict. But the central statement that lucha libre makes about power in twentieth-century Mexico is made through its basic structure. The ambiguity of the genre that places it between sport and theater, fact and fiction, conflict and collaboration, coupled with the discourse of the mask, highlights the importance of secrecy to the operation of power. It portrays the secret as something that is both intelligible and worth staging. As I have shown in chapters 4 and 6, for most of its history, lucha libre could signify as an implicit, critical parody of the postrevolutionary political system.

My research on lucha libre has been organized around two problems. First, there is the question of Superbarrio—how did it make sense for serious political organizations like the Asemblea de Barrios and the PRD to use a masked wrestler not only as their mascot, but also as their spokesman? Second, why did so many in the wrestling community complain that lucha libre—a form of professional wrestling after all—was being vulgarized and should be subjected to greater control by the state? The answer to both questions is that lucha libre's relationship to processes of mass mediation had a direct impact on how it signified in Mexico. Its long exile from television affected the aesthetics of performance, the reception practices of audience, and the balance of power between wrestlers, empresa, and the media. Wrestlers' participation in the film industry added a mythic dimension to their performance, but lucha libre itself developed to please physically present, local, class-specific audiences. Lucha libre existed as a mass spectacle but maintained a certain autonomy from processes of mass mediation.

This is one reason that neo-pop invoked lucha libre as an example of nonalienated, authentic urban culture: popular, rather than mass. But by circulating lucha libre imagery in forms and contexts usually associated with high culture—painting, theater, museums—where it was celebrated as a counterhegemonic practice, the neo-pop group also began to resignify it. With its masks and its melodrama, lucha libre symbolized a rethinking of national identity. The emergence of Superbarrio thus made sense for two reasons. First, through the interventions of the neo-pop group, lucha libre had come to be interpreted as a master symbol of urban Mexican cultural authenticity. Second, wrestling performance was full of elements that could be read as a parody of the postrevolutionary political system. Superbarrio was implicitly present in every lucha libre match.

If lucha libre's exile from television had unintended consequences, so too did its return to television. Many in the wrestling world blamed television for a steady decline in arena attendance since the early 1990s. Some wrestlers understood the decline as the result of a simple, economic decision: given the choice of watching the luchas for free at home or paying for a ticket, lucha fans preferred the former.[1] Others, like the wrestlers of Revolución 2000, traced the decline in lucha libre spectatorship to the changes in costume and movement vocabulary that televised broadcast apparently demanded. They saw nothing wrong with televised wrestling as such but insisted that real fans wanted to see real, traditional lucha libre and would abandon the arenas as long as the promoters ignored them. But I would argue that even if television did not generate changes in the aesthetics of performance, it would have changed the semiotics of performance. The interaction between the wrestlers and the audience is a crucial element of lucha libre, and television, as Ecologista Universal proclaimed, "kills the relationship between the wrestlers and the audience."

There are thus at least two possible explanations for the decline in arena attendance during the 1990s. Television let people watch without buying a ticket, and it modified the performance in ways that some fans might have found distasteful. But I would like to propose a third explanation for lucha libre's decline. The transition from live (and cinematic) lucha libre to televised lucha libre took place in a broader social and political context. The controversial election of 1988 resulted in a gradual erosion of the PRI's hegemony in Mexico. Subsequent events—the post-NAFTA crash of the peso, the Zapatista rebellion, the assassination of presidential candidate Donaldo Colosio, the loss of several governorships to the PAN and (in the case of Mexico City) the PRD—constituted a crisis in the system. The last presidential election, in which the PAN candidate, former Coca-Cola executive Vicente Fox won a decisive victory over the PRI candidate Francisco Labastida, consummated a process that began at the end of the 1980s. In short, lucha libre imagery began to circulate in the discourse of the left opposition just as the system that it reflected began its long collapse. For better or worse, the political landscape of Mexico has changed.

Perhaps, then, its manifestation as explicit political theater and the decline of its audience are traceable to the same thing: lucha libre represented the workings of a political system that was in decline. In a sense, lucha libre's "secret" was that it was a parody of the postrevolutionary state. By appropriating lucha libre imagery and applying it directly to political discourse, Superbarrio and his allies unmasked lucha libre performance. Once a secret is revealed, once the implicit becomes the explicit, it loses some of its power. Moreover, if a system that is parodied loses its hegemony, the parody loses its power. It could be, then, that by the end of the 1990s lucha libre was in a necessary state of transition. Pace Canek, Mexico has changed, and the old forms of corruption and domination are being replaced. Lucha libre may need to adapt, to reflect the structuring principles of the new forms.

EPILOGUE 2007

It has been over ten years since I first stepped into an arena (and over a year since I last did). Since then, Mexico has been through enormous changes. Lucha libre has changed in some ways as well. First, many of the people who helped make this book what it is are gone. When I returned in 2001 to do follow-up interviews, I learned that both Juan Alanís and Pedro Bolanis/Caballero Tigre (founder and main organizer of the Agrupacion Nacional de Luchadores Retirados) had passed away. I couldn't find Luis Jaramillo, or either of the two Irmas. Since then, many of the old-time stars have died: Blue Demon, Diablo Velasco, Daniel Garcia/Huracán Ramirez, and the masterful referee Güero Rangel, to name a few. Hara Kiri, who had retired from wrestling to work as a police officer, was killed in the line of duty in August 2006. One day this past October (back in Mexico City), I turned on the television to see scenes of lucha libre: a cage match, followed by a match with exoticos, minis . . . an octagonal ring . . . male-female tag teams. The scene changed, and various wrestlers came on camera to talk about

Antonio Peña, founder of the AAA and the center of so much controversy at the time of my fieldwork. As they talked about how important he was both to the sport and to them personally, I realized that he must be dead. Indeed, on October 6, Peña died of a heart attack at the age of fifty-five.

Ten or even five years ago, lucha libre was unfamiliar in the United States except among a relatively small number of fans and hipsters. Lucha libre has, of course, been familiar to Mexican American and Chicano communities in the United States for a long time. Some cities with large Latino communities (Chicago, Los Angeles, Houston, and others) have their own, local lucha libre circuits. Lucha libre has also had a certain hip cachet in particular circles in Anglo U.S. subcultures. The Straitjackets, a band that plays refritos (Mexican cover versions of early rock and roll hits), and whose members perform in lucha masks, brought lucha libre to the attention of their underground following. In cities like New York and San Francisco, lucha libre–themed items could be found in some of the stores selling Mexican handicrafts or punk paraphernalia. But in general, if I spoke to people about lucha libre, I first had to explain to them what it was. That is no longer true (or at least not as true as it once was). The cartoon *Mucha Lucha*, and (especially) the film *Nacho Libre* (whose eponymous character is loosely based on Fray Tormenta), as well as the increased visibility of luchadores working in WWF, WCW, and other U.S wrestling leagues, has made lucha libre familiar to U.S. audiences.[2] But ripped from its historical and social context, these representations of lucha libre tend to emphasize its "wacky" qualities. One has only to think of serapes, sombreros, and Speedy Gonzales to place this in a longer history in which elements of Mexican popular culture(s) cross the border, only to be resignified as kitsch.

In its home context, in Mexico, there have been other changes. According to Sandra Granados, the CMLL's director of public relations, ticket sales are up this year. She credits lucha libre's revival in part to the empresa's newest star: Místico. Místico is a técnico's técnico. Young, charismatic, acrobatic, he claims Fray Tormenta as his trainer and spends his spare time (or at least some of it) visiting the orphanage in Teotihuacan. The luchador Dr. Wagner Jr., who seemed to me so perfectly suited to his role as rudo, switched over to fight as a técnico after the death of his father in 2005. His brother, Silver King, has fought as a masked wrestler (Black Tiger) in

Japan and Mexico. He appeared in *Nacho Libre* as the luchador Ramses and is credited as the Bronco. As for televised wrestling, it continues, and continues to include all of the innovations (from octagonal rings to male-female tag teams) that were so opposed by my friends in Renovación 2000.

Wrestling imagery seems more ubiquitous than ever. Pay phones on many street corners show a masked wrestler boasting: "Tres pesos sin limite de tiempo!" (three pesos with no time limit!), a parody of the way matches are usually announced: "En dos de tres caidas [in two out of three falls] sin limite de tiempo!" On television, a public service announcement encouraging people to get their voter identification cards shows a masked wrestler trying to prove his identity by performing his signature move in front of an attractive and apologetic but unmovable bank teller. The advertising campaign of the chain store Bodega Aurrera uses the cartoon figure Mama Lucha, who battles against high prices. I have seen, for the first time, lucha libre masks for sale inside the folk art stands of the handicraft market of La Ciudadela. Lourdes Grobet finally published a book of her gorgeous lucha libre photos (2005), edited by Televisa's lucha libre commentator Alfonso Morales. As of this writing, blow-ups of the photos, roughly three square feet in size, are on display in four metro stations.

Perhaps strangest of all, Hijo del Santo has opened a combination café and El Santo paraphernalia store in the fashionable neighborhood of Condesa. In a continuation of the trend that I noticed ten years ago, lucha libre has reentered the middle-class spaces of the city. It has gotten to the point where a twenty-three-year-old student at the private Universidad Iberoamericana informed me that she hadn't really been interested in going to the luchas, not because it was déclassé or (as middle-class informants used to tell me) she was nervous about entering such a chaotic social space, but because it was "so trendy."

What does lucha libre's new visibility mean? I am not sure, but I would like to point out that this visibility is either taking lucha libre into new social spaces (chic cafés, public service announcements), or inserting it in strange new ways into its old spaces. While Hijo del Santo now inhabits Condesa, his father has returned to Tepito, this time cast in bronze. On May 9, 2006, in the middle of the presidential campaign season, the city put up a statue of the legendary wrestler in a small park in the Peralvillo section of the *barrio bravo*. The unveiling was attended by a number of celebrities (actors and singers as well as wrestlers), and the statue was unveiled by Hijo del Santo and by outgoing president Vicente Fox.

This shifting circulation is taking place in a particularly contentious political climate. The hotly contested election of 2006 took place against a background of diffuse civil unrest.[3] Two months after El Santo was unveiled in Tepito, PAN candidate Felipe Calderón (who had been chosen by his party and thus, unlike El Santo, had not been unveiled by Vicente Fox) won the presidential election by a margin of just over half of one percent. The PRD candidate, Mexico City's former mayor Andres Manuel Lopez Obrador, immediately challenged the result on two grounds: first, that Fox, a business consortium called the CCE, and other organizations had interfered illegally in the election, and second, that the votes had been fraudulently tallied.[4] He demanded a recount, citing alleged irregularities in roughly half of the precincts. The Instituto Federal Electoral (IFE) agreed to a recount in approximately nine percent of the polling stations.

Accusing Calderón and the IFE itself of cronyism and corruption, Lopez Obrador and thousands of his supporters (from all over the country) occupied the Zocalo and a long section of the (normally busy) Paseo de la Reforma, demanding a full recount of all precincts and refusing to recognize Calderón as president elect of Mexico.[5] The limited recount changed the final numbers for both candidates, but not the result. At the end of August, in what was, by then, a foregone conclusion, the IFE declared Felipe Calderón the president elect of the republic. Lopez Obrador and his supporters refused to accept the result.

Although they were not able to change the official outcome, they were able to prevent or disrupt three of the crucial political rituals associated with the transition from one president to another: the president's final address to congress on September 1, his last delivery of the Grito de Dolores on September 15, and the incoming president's swearing-in ceremony in front of the Senate on December 1. In the first event, PRD representatives took over the floor of the legislature just as Fox was due to enter and make his final address. Fox entered the Palacio San Lazaro (Mexico's congressional building) but left shortly afterward, delivering the address in written form. In the month leading up to Independence Day, both Lopez Obrador (whose supporters continued to occupy the Zocalo) and Fox each claimed for themselves the right to deliver the Grito from the Palacio Nacional.[6] In the end, both compromised. Fox delivered the Grito from the palacio municipal in Dolores Hidalgo, and the acting mayor of Mexico City delivered it from the Palacio Nacional (the site of the original Grito). The following afternoon, a convention of Lopez Obrador's supporters declared the ex-candidate the legitimate president of Mexico, agreed to set up a parallel government, and dispersed. All that was left was the inauguration of the official winner.

On November 29, a rumor spread in the Senate that the PRD planned to occupy San Lazaro to prevent the presidential inauguration from taking place in its traditional location. In response, senators of the PAN attempted to drive out the PRD representatives. The brawl that followed was broadcast on television, and photographs of the mass fistfight appeared in the major newspapers. The next day, members of both parties, bringing their own pillows and blankets, set up camp in the chairs on the Senate floor.[7] On November 30, a cartoon by El Fisgón, titled "Hacía el 1° Diciembre" ("Toward December First"), appeared in the newspaper La Jornada. The cartoon shows two bulky men, one dressed in a windbreaker and carrying a gym bag, the other wearing a sweater under a blazer and a scarf around his neck. Their features are rough, their hair short; one sports a mustache. They walk past posters advertising "Lucha by two out of three . . . Kid Acuña vs. Human Rights" and "The Monstrous Monopoly vs. Minimum Wage."[8] One says: "There are rumors that they are looking for an alternative site for December first." The other answers: "How about Arena Coliseo?"

I wish I could end here, on a note that reasserts lucha libre's value as a source of political metaphor, but I can't. After all, despite the textual references to lucha libre, the cartoon implicitly references Arena Coliseo's other function: as a boxing venue. Indeed, at least this year, Mexican political culture has borne more resemblance to a boxing match than it has to lucha libre. The civic rituals that once served to produce the appearance of consensus in Mexico aren't working, and new ones do not seem to have taken their place. The political theater that was so central to the maintenance of hegemony seems to have been emptied of its power. As for lucha libre, it seems to me that its capture as a tool of commerce empties its use as political countertheater. What meaning is it to have when it is consumed by the Mexican middle class (whether as mexicanidad or as kitsch)? How does it change as a signifying practice when it travels to the United States to be consumed as yet more Mexican kitsch, and then is shipped back to Mexico as Spanish-language versions of *Mucha Lucha* and *Nacho Libre*? Yet despite all the apparent change, the core culture of lucha libre remains. The wrestling schools still abound in the barrios populares, and Arena Coliseo (still a little risky to get to if you look like you have money) still runs shows twice a week. So perhaps Canek will turn out to be right after all.

NOTES

PREFACE

1. I thank Henry Goldschmidt for this wonderfully apt phrase.
2. *Profe,*" a contraction of *profesor*, is a common respectful but relatively informal form of address from students to teachers in Mexico and other Spanish-speaking countries.
3. Tepito is a neighborhood just a bit north of the Zocalo. Known as the "barrio bravo" (rough or fierce neighborhood), it has long been famous as the cradle of some of Mexico's greatest boxers and notorious as a center of illegal activities of various sorts. It is also well known as a neighborhood with its own traditions, and as a site of legal and semilegal street commerce. El Santo's family lived there when they first moved to Mexico City, as did the "Sanchez" family of Oscar Lewis's *Children of Sanchez* (1961).
4. When I returned in 2001 to follow up on old contacts, I learned that the Association had disbanded in 2000 amid accusations of embezzlement, and that Juan Alanís died of a heart attack early the following year.

CHAPTER 1: STAGING CONTRADICTION

1. Luchadores tended to distinguish between lucha libre and U.S. professional wrestling, which they described (in English) as "all show."

2. Doc. 6/2.2/1, AGN Archivo Abelardo Rodríguez. The translation in the section epigraph and all subsequent translations are by the author unless otherwise indicated.

3. The Cristero War (1926–29) was an armed uprising based in western Mexico against the enforcement of the anticlerical provisions of the 1917 Mexican Constitution.

4. This argument had its precedent even before the Porfiriato. In 1868, Representative Jesús López proposed the prohibition of the bullfight, arguing: "Since it is not possible to establish schools everywhere where this class can be well taught, remove at least those other [schools] where they learn evil, where the sight of blood easily fosters the savage instincts to which they have, by nature, a propensity. If we want good citizens, if we want brave soldiers who are animated in combat and humane in triumph, prohibit spectacles that inflame the sentiments and dull [*embrutecen*] reason" (quoted in Lomnitz 2001: 66).

5. The placement of the bullfight into the category of sport is by no means inevitable. In Spain, in fact, it is subsumed under the category of culture and appears in newspapers and other media alongside dance and painting.

6. Mexico also boasts a number of "autochthonous sports," competitive physical activities that may have a long history in diverse indigenous communities. It is tempting, of course, to draw parallels between modern ball sports and the famed (or infamous) ballgame of the precontact Mesoamerican civilizations. Any arguments about historical continuity are, however, difficult to sustain and ignore the distinction that various scholars have made regarding the distinction between sports and games.

7. Admittedly, there are other sports (for example, ice skating) in which the transition from amateur to professional brings a loss of prestige.

8. The crowd identifies with the wrestler coded most closely to its collective ethnic self-image. An exciting match, she asserts, "allows the crowd to participate in a ritualized confrontation between good and evil, a participation made more intense by the possibility of identifying with the characters of the wrestlers" (Webley 1986: 73). But since "fair and foul play are both available to all wrestlers, whatever their roles" (77), and wrestlers can thus change their moral identification in the course of the match, the subtext of a battle between self and other outweighs the importance of the moral text.

9. An inversion ritual (or ritual of inversion) is a ritual in which the social order is temporarily turned "upside down." The term was coined by Max Gluckman in the 1930s to describe Zulu rituals in which women would dress and act like men, or commoners like royalty. The purpose of such rituals, according to Gluckman, was to make the social order explicit through the display of social disorder—in other words, to show how the world should be by showing how it must not be.

10. I refer here to Sedgwick's formulation of the relationship of gender and performativity, in which she describes gender as "kind of real, kind of not."

11. Salvador Novo (1904–74) is a key figure in the cultural history of twentieth-century Mexico. Often compared to Oscar Wilde, Novo, who was openly, flamboyantly gay, was known as a poet, playwright, dramaturg, entrepreneur (he owned a theater and a restaurant), television commentator, bureaucrat, docent, official chronicler of the city, and general man about town.

CHAPTER 2: TRADE SECRETS AND REVELATIONS

1. In a *lucha de apuesta* (betting match), wrestlers make a public bet on the outcome of the match. The most common forms are the mask-against-mask, hair-against-hair, or mask-against-hair matches. A wrestler who loses his or her mask has to remove the mask after the match. A wrestler who loses his or her hair has his or her head shaved immediately afterward. For an extended discussion, see chapter 4.

2. The practice of blading has been reported elsewhere (Rugos 1994). Two people in the business, who asked to remain anonymous, told me about the practice in Mexico. Blading explains the number of short, vertical scars, or little band-aids that line many wrestlers' foreheads just below the hairline.

3. The term *habitus*, as it was used first by Marcel Mauss and later by Pierre Bourdieu, refers to the totality of skills, preferences, tastes, dispositions, and so on that, while essentially cultural (and thus learned), are anchored in the body. One's social identity is the product of essentially physical acts and experiences. Most of the ways in which habitus is formed and experienced lie beyond the level of consciousness for most people. There are, however, practices in which the cultivation of habitus is conscious and explicit, as in sports, dance, or other explicitly physical disciplines.

4. For an important exception, see De Garis 2005.

5. The gym moved from this location to a smaller space down the block late in 1999 (Greg Gransden, personal communication, 2000). When I looked for it in 2001, it had moved to about ten blocks away. My profe no longer taught there and was said to be giving classes somewhere in the neighborhood of La Merced.

6. The *plancha*, which literally means iron or press, is called a "flying crossbody" in English. It's a move where one wrestler belly flops onto a supine opponent.

7. "Julio" identified his character (Alex Dinamite) as a técnico in an interview with *Box y Lucha* in 1996, but when I last saw him (in 1998) he was wrestling as a masked rudo. I have used the real first names of most of my classmates in this chapter with the exceptions of Julio and Marcos.

8. One way in which my gender negatively affected my fieldwork was that I lacked access to the men's locker room, where further teasing (of students like Mario), gossip, or other kinds of discourse probably took place. Since the staircase

leading to the wrestling ring was inside the locker room, I would pass through it before and after class, escorted by one or more classmates, once they had assured that all the men present had at least wrapped towels around their waists. I usually crossed as quickly and discreetly as I could. It was clear, however, that the men's locker room was a social space. The women's locker room, by contrast, was not a social space. Roughly a fifth of the size of the men's, it had very little seating, a single, seldom used shower, and a toilet that tended to back up. Not even women who arrived, trained, and left together exchanged more than a few pleasantries as they changed their clothes.

9. At least some professionals, however, hire drama coaches or work with a drama coach hired by the EMLL (see chapter 3). That, however, is a secret.

CHAPTER 3: OF *CHARROS* AND JAGUARS

1. There are, in fact, two more dimensions to lucha libre performance—the performance and the lifeworld of the lucha libre audience. This chapter will address issues of audience and reception only indirectly, but as I will make clear, the audience takes an active part in lucha libre performance.

2. If a wrestler bets his or her mask in a match, he or she is publicly unmasked, and his or her identity is published in the wrestling press (see chapter 4).

3. The bias toward a Federal District or Guadalajaran origin is to be expected, since I was in Mexico City, and the EMLL often hires former students of Diablo Velasco, a trainer who ran a school in Guadalajara until his death in 2000. The association of Guadalajara with the Velasco school is one reason that a wrestler may wish to claim to be from Guadalajara, even if he or she is not. The association of Jalisco (the state of which Guadalajara is the capital) with such symbols of Mexican national culture as the charro, the mariachi, and tequila may be another.

4. The Basilica is on the site of the apparition of the Virgin of Guadalupe to "the Indian Juan Diego." The apparition at the site (which had been the site of a temple of the pre-Columbian goddess Tonantzin) has been a central symbol in Mexican nationalist discourse since the late colonial period. It is the most important pilgrimage site in Mexico (and perhaps Latin America). Every year on December 12, millions of people converge on the site, many walking for days to get there. Many come as a corporate group with other members of their profession, displaying the tools of their trade. For wrestlers, this means coming in full costume, including the mask (if applicable). *Box y Lucha* still reported on the pilgrimage during the early 1990s, but I saw no mention of the pilgrimage in 1996 or 1997, and nor did any wrestler mention it to me.

5. Since the EMLL management and some of its wrestlers (including the empresa's trainer El Faisán) had been affiliated with the PRI, the empresa did not participate in the 1998 parade (which took place after the PRD won control of the

Federal District, and thus the parade). I was later informed that that since the EMLL stayed away, the AAA sent wrestlers to participate in the PRD-organized parade. The parade is just one instance of the intersection of lucha libre and the political system.

6. Of the wrestlers I interviewed, ten had a family member in the business: five had parents or uncles, the rest had a a spouse, one or more siblings or children. In a column in *Box y Lucha* called "Mirada con Ojos Azules" (which consists of brief interviews with wrestlers in a "fifty-questions" format), a much higher proportion of wrestlers claimed to come from wrestling families. Approximately half of the wrestlers interviewed during 1997 said that they had a parent, aunt, or uncle in the business. Yet only a few of those named the senior wrestler. Their reluctance to give the wrestler's name could reflect one of three things. First, the parent might not have been a star and thus wouldn't be familiar to the magazine's audience. Second, if one of the wrestlers in question is masked, the interviewee might be protecting his or her secret identity. But it might also be that wrestlers want to appear to have family in the business whether they do or not.

The overlapping nature of professional affiliation and kinship ties may be stronger in the EMLL, and weaker in newer empresas. Nevertheless, many of the wrestlers affiliated with other empresas came from wrestling families or were married to a wrestler.

7. Irma Gonzalez was partly serious, partly joking when she used the phrase "puro valor Méxicano." While the phrase does imply a feeling of national pride, in her usage it also had implications of jumping into something blindly, with the courage that comes from ignoring the consequences.

8. Los Villanos sometimes fight in teams of two or three, and sometimes solo. Los Brazos usually fight solo but have teamed up in the past.

9. Other second jobs of wrestlers I met included union administrator, ambulant ice cream vendor, retail store employee, data processor, bookkeeper, secretary, or owner of a restaurant or other small business.

10. Professional wrestling in the United States used to be organized into territories: regions under the control of a particular promoter. The current hegemony of the WWF and the WCW is widely understood to have undercut the importance of wrestling territories in the United States.

11. Both women wished to make it clear that Irma Gonzalez maintained as much contact with her daughter as possible, calling and writing letters, to maintain the bond between them.

12. Chabela Romero was a ruda who many consider to have been the greatest luchadora of all time. She died of cancer when she was in her mid-thirties.

13. The formalization of training over the past thirty years appears to have taken place in the United States as well (De Garis 2005).

14. As of 2001, the EMLL was no longer offering classes to outsiders (Greg Grand-sen, personal communication, May 2001).

15. The schedule of classes allowed his students to train after work. Some other trainers started classes in the early afternoon instead—sometimes around Mexico's 2:00 or 3:00 lunchtime, sometimes in the middle of the workday.

16. "De que lloren en tu casa . . ." is a proverbial expression, one of Jaramillo's "philosophy of sayings" that he integrated into our training, such as "lo cortes no quita lo valiente" (having manners doesn't make one less brave/valiant/fierce) and "el valiente vive hasta el cobarde quiera" (the brave man lives as long as the coward wants/allows him to). Jaramillo often told us about close calls he had had in bar fights in his youth, and about wrestlers who died because they thought they could outfight an opponent who turned out to be armed. He was particularly concerned that his students understood the need to control their aggression outside of the ring.

17. When he said "someone is envious of me," my impression was that he was not referring to Mastín, but to a third party, another worker in the gym, implying that the person was, in fact, using some form of sorcery against him.

18. Themes of race and racism, which have also been central to the production of U.S. national culture, were not dealt with explicitly in professional wrestling at the time it was imported to Mexico.

19. *Mestizaje* literally means mixture. In Latin America (and writings about Latin America) it refers to the racial and cultural mixture of Indian, Spanish, and African "blood" and culture that typifies most inhabitants of most of the region.

20. Ray and Ringo Mendoza are not related. Ray Mendoza was a star of the golden age of lucha libre, whose indigenous features and frequent dislocations earned him the nickname Chief Crooked Fingers. According to wrestling writer Rio Lorenzo, Ringo Mendoza entered the world of lucha libre as a teenager, when he sold concessions in the EMLL arena in Guadalajara. Many people noticed the striking resemblance between the two men and began to joke that he was Ray's illegitimate son. The rumor became so widespread that when Ringo was ready to become a wrestler, he had to meet with Ray's wife to assure her that he knew his father, and he was not her husband. Once that was established, he took Ringo Mendoza as his nombre de batalla, as if the rumors had been true (personal communication, Rio Lorenzo, 1997).

21. For example, in 1997–98, a Canadian wrestler called Steel fought a series of matches with different Mexicans in which he boasted that he would destroy all the Mexicans. His attack on the nation (or at least its wrestlers) was eventually channeled into a pique with Rayo de Jalisco Jr. In the weeks before their final match, he attacked the retired Rayo de Jalisco Sr. (who had come to assist his son), reportedly breaking the older man's arm. By the end of the pique, Rayo de Jalisco Jr. was positioned to stand for Mexico, and for such family values as respect for elders, against the nefarious Canadian.

22. In fact, Charro Aguayo, one of the four Texans that Salvador Lutteroth brought to Mexico City in 1933, was a Mexican immigrant to the United States.

23. In Mexico, *Caló* refers to Mexico City street slang (in Spain, it is the dialect spoken by Gypsies). La Merced is a neighborhood in the city center that contains the central market.

24. See Saunders 1988 for a discussion of the significance of jaguars and jaguar symbolism in Mesoamerican cultures.

25. This is the title of a documentary on lucha libre released in 1997, dir. Janina Möbius.

26. Ordinal numbers in a wrestler's name may also mean that he or she is one of a set of brothers or sisters (for example, the sons of Ray Mendoza, a well-known veteran wrestler, fight as the Villanos I–V), or they may be unrelated but work as a team.

27. Ciclón Ramirez was originally a masked character, a Huracán Ramirez spinoff, but he lost his mask to Felino sometime before the interview.

28. I make this argument in greater detail in Levi 1999.

29. For an example of sport in the mode of tragedy, a Peruvian friend described the central dramatic tension in the Peruvian national soccer team's games as not "Who will win?" but "How will victory be torn from our grasp this time?" (Eduardo Bryce, personal communication, September 1996).

30. Eduardo Bonadas performed as Huracan Ramirez from 1952 to 1959, after which he chose to fight unmasked under his real name. Later that year, the movie studio (which owned the rights to the character and costume design) chose Daniel Garcia to continue to wrestle as Huracan Ramirez mask. Garcia is, generally, considered to be "the" Huracan Ramirez, although he was not the first (nor the last).

31. The actual distinction between these two sides was not so clear in practice. Lomnitz and Adler (1993) have argued that, at the federal level, the distinction between the personal following of the president and those party members who constitute the "system" was far more important in terms of the way that positions were distributed and policies developed. Both groups might contain both técnicos and politicians.

32. Although my interviews with wrestlers support a view of role as naturalized and freely chosen, the frequency with which wrestlers do change roles for longer or shorter periods and during particular narrative cycles suggests that the empresas have quite a bit to say about role as well as character.

33. For example, Luis Jaramillo's wife once threatened him with divorce after she saw him give two young female fans the kisses they requested and autograph their blouses. She wouldn't speak to him until their *compadre*, with whom they shared a house, pulled her aside to remind her that their income depended on his popularity, and as técnico, his popularity depended on his making himself available to his fans (personal communication, 1997).

34. *Limpio* (clean) is another, less commonly used term for the "good" wrestler.

35. Rafael Barradas Osorio (1992: 191–93) recounts two such incidents, each of which resulted in the rudo's suspension.

36. In contrast with rudo wrestlers, I found that wrestling reporters really did express contempt for the audience. Several commented to me that the public didn't understand lucha libre, did not appreciate what they were watching, or were insufficiently objective (!) as observers.

37. Most people in the industry agreed that wrestling used to take place *al ras de la lona* (on the surface of the canvas), and that it entailed more exchanges of locks and less jumping off of the cords. A number of wrestlers said that old-style wrestling led to a high rate of relatively minor injuries—dislocated fingers, the occasional dislocated shoulder or sprained ankle. The currently popular aerial style has a lower rate of minor injuries but a higher possibility of life-threatening or disabling injuries to the back or neck.

38. It is difficult for an observer to tell if a wrestler has really been injured or is acting, or is injured slightly and is acting. The one time I definitely saw a wrestler fall badly (I was close enough to see him hit his head on the floor of the arena after a misjudged salto mortal), the empresa doctors came over and examined him for a concussion before carrying him out on a stretcher. They would have done the same if it had been an act. There were only two differences between this and other incidents that (I thought) were staged. First, the doctors loosened the wrestler's mask as they examined him. Second, instead of calling attention to the injured wrestler when they carried him out, the other wrestlers and the referee shifted the audience's focus away from him. While the doctors examined the fallen wrestler (a técnico), the two rudos ganged up on his partner, kicking him and dragging him around the other side of the arena while the referee followed, scolding hysterically. Meanwhile, the medics exited discreetly with the stretcher.

39. The story also appears in his autobiography, *Fuera Máscaras*.

40. In contrast, according to Bruce Lincoln (1989), the wrestler slated to win the match in U.S. televised wrestling enters last.

CHAPTER 4: THE WRESTLING MASK

1. Jacobo Zabludovsky was the nighttime anchor for Televisa's national news show *24 Hours* from 1971 to 1998. As the network was closely tied to the PRI, Zabludovsky's reporting was generally uncritical of the ruling party and highly critical of the opposition.

2. I will address the implications of this idea for discourses of gender in Mexico in chapter 5.

3. According to Carlos Alfonso Sanchez Hernandez (1997), in the most traditional version, the play begins with the Three Kings, who are guided by an angel but

beset by a number of devils who try to keep them from their goal. More angels defend them. Finally, the angels defeat the devils and the Three Kings arrive at the manger to adore the Christ Child.

4. For an example of this claim in the Mexican context, see Cordry 1980.

5. Lucien Levy-Bruhl (1837–1939) posited the existence of a qualitative difference in the psychological orientation in "primitive" and "Western" man. In *How Natives Think* (1910) he argued that primitive thought processes were characterized not by logic but by an inability to recognize contradiction or to differentiate between the supernatural and natural worlds, and by an attempt to control the world through what he labeled "mystical participation." In a masked ritual, for example, it would be possible for the masked figure to be taken for the literal incarnation of a supernatural being, even as the ritual's participants are aware of the identity of the masker.

6. Stephen Lutes (1983) writes that commitment to the role of p'askola clown facilitates the acquisition of spiritual power for the masker. The mask is considered to have a kind of life of its own, but the p'askola spirits do not possess the initiate during performance. Instead, through contact with them, the masker gains (healing and other) powers that can be used outside of performance. In this case, the masks themselves empower performance by facilitating the spiritual powers of the performer. I have not found anyone who addresses this issue regarding the danza de tigre.

7. As I learned in practicing lucha libre, the acrobatic moves place an enormous strain on the feet and ankles. When the feet land at the end of a lucha libre–style forward roll, there is a shock, and the foot absorbing the impact slides toward the inside. To protect the wrestler, the boot needs to provide a lot of shock absorption, a lot of ankle support, and extra reinforcement on the arch side of the toe box. The elder Martinez designed a boot, still used by wrestlers, that is nearly knee high, with a heavy rubber sole, built-in arch support, and a reinforced toe box.

8. At the time, the Ku Klux Klan was famous in Mexico as a menace to Mexicans in the United States (Anne Rubenstein, personal communication, 2001). His use of the hood may, therefore, have marked him as a rudo.

9. Andy Coe (1992), in fact, attributes the craze for masked wrestlers to the popularity of *The Phantom*.

10. The same television executive also recalled watching, to his eight-year-old confusion, as the cameras began to roll. El Santo (now recognizable in his mask) stood facing the other actors, but when it came time for his lines, he would gesticulate and intone only, "One, two, three, four . . ."

11. The importance of verbal interactions in U.S. professional wrestling has increased since the 1980s and with the consolidation of Vince McMahon's WWF. However, the use of verbal interchanges, particularly pre- and postmatch inter-

views, became a significant means of narrative development when the genre was first televised (Mortensen 1999).

12. When wrestlers go on tour outside of Mexico, the problems of border crossings can be literalized. Several people told me that El Santo had an agreement with U.S. customs that he would be taken to an office to remove his mask, so that only one or two customs agents would see his face or his passport.

13. The very biggest stars, like Hijo del Santo or Mil Máscaras, are independent agents. Their mask collection reflects not only their position within whatever empresas they have worked in, but also their position in lucha libre as a whole.

14. The thing inherited is not the physical object but the design and the character. Masks can get torn, wear out, and at minimum get very sweaty, so a masked wrestler actually owns several copies of the same mask. Sometimes the mask can come in different colors, or in different materials. The design, however, is usually stable and is passed on.

15. As far as I can tell, the series fell through. I never saw it listed or otherwise mentioned again.

16. This was, incidentally, in violation of a commission regulation that prohibits bringing national or religious symbols into the ring.

17. Most working professionals do not buy their masks from Martinez. They go instead to one of two other mask makers who work out of their homes. Martinez currently sells professional-quality or near-professional-quality masks over the Internet to wrestlers and nonwrestlers alike.

18. The recent conflicts of copyright of character may reflect a greater interest in formal copyright in Mexico in general under the Salinas de Gortari administration and NAFTA (Anne Rubenstein, personal communication, 1999).

19. Since the photograph is in black and white, I can't tell if it is Blue Demon or Black Shadow, but it is clearly one of those two.

20. For analyses of the political system under the PRI, see Needler 1998, Smith 1979, Camp 1999, and Lomnitz and Adler 1993. For a historical account of the PRI's electoral tactics (among other things), see Agustín 1990 and 1992. The remarkably resilient system faced its first serious challenge in 1988. The "classical" system appears to have collapsed with the victory of the PAN candidate Vicente Fox in July 2000.

21. In Mexico the word "vecindad" refers to buildings in the city center that were once elite houses but were subdivided to provide cheap housing for the very poor. In a typical vecindad a large number of small apartments are organized around a central courtyard used by the residents for shared facilities (such as bathrooms and laundry sinks). There is usually more than one entrance onto the central courtyard, allowing residents and their friends quick passage between different streets.

22. Actually, El Santo retired in 1983 but did not die until February of 1984.

23. The "key," in Goffman's terms (1974: 43–44), is "the set of conventions by which a given activity, one already meaningful in terms of primary framework, is transformed into something patterned on this activity, but seen by the participants to be something quite else."

24. For examples of how such cooptation is carried out with ambulant vendors, squatter settlements, and right-wing cultural activists, see Cross 1998, Vélez-Ibañez 1983, and Rubenstein 1998 respectively.

CHAPTER 5: A STRUGGLE BETWEEN TWO STRONG MEN?

1. See www.demographia.com/db-mxcsector.htm.

2. In contemporary usage, at least, the word *chingón* has very positive connotations. It is usually used as a colloquialism meaning "great" or "terrific."

3. I find it interesting that, while Lewis identifies matrifocality and an absence of fathers and father figures as typical of cultures of poverty, Jesús Sanchez's various children all seem to suffer an absence of mothers and mother figures.

4. The definition: "If someone shouts, you've got to shout louder. If any so-and-so comes to me and says, 'Fuck your mother,' I answer 'Fuck your mother a thousand times.' And if he gives one step forward and I take one step back, I lose prestige. But if I go forward too, and pile on and make a fool out of him, then the others will treat me with respect. In a fight, I would never give up or say 'Enough,' even though the other was killing me. I would try to go to my death, smiling. That is what we mean by being '*macho*,' by being manly" (Lewis 1963: 38). As Gutmann demonstrates, many ethnographers (and not only of Latin America) have used this quote as a ready-made definition of *machismo*, which has helped to reify the term.

5. The term *marianismo* was coined by Evelyn Stevens to describe the set of ideal female behaviors (self-abnegation, denial of sexuality, focus on motherhood) in Latin American societies. Whereas machismo is (or at least has become) an emic term in Mexico and elsewhere in Latin America, the use of the term *marianismo* seems limited to social scientists.

6. The word *joto* can be gendered either masculine or feminine to refer to male-bodied people. According to Annick Prieur, at least for her informants, *joto* is used to refer to male homosexuals in general, whereas *jota* is only used for vestidas—male-bodied people who cultivate a feminine image and subjectivity. In this chapter, I will use whichever spelling or pronunciation was used by the informant or writer in question.

7. Although women do not in general initiate interchanges, they are not excluded from the game of albures. Men will use albures in a game of deniable flirtation or harassment with individual women. Some women pride themselves on being able to recognize an albur when it is directed to or against them, and (better still) to answer it in a way that un-mans the original speaker.

8. The rana invertida is the hold that Black Warrior applied on Silver King in the match described in chapter 3.

9. The ideal man, one who is dominant and potent, who supports his family, whose kinswomen are chaste, who seduces the kinswomen of other men and who might also penetrate other men would be considered to have more of masculinity than a man who does not seduce other men's kinswomen, one who does so but can't support his family, or one who does both but has a wife who cheats on him.

10. The maricón, however, is not necessary to the construction of the feminine hierarchy of virtue. The relationship between the male hierarchy of masculinity and the female hierarchy of virtue is itself thus asymmetrical. Moreover, while men, as well as women, label women as whores (or cause them to be so labeled), only men are concerned with labeling other men as maricones or as impotent. Thus both men and women judge, indeed determine, the decency of women, but women do not actively evaluate the masculinity of men.

11. Telenovelas are television serials, similar to North American soap operas, that run for periods of six months to a year. For detailed analysis of Mexican telenovelas, see Lopez 1995. For analyses of the telenovela form in Columbia that makes reference to Mexico, see Martín-Barbero 1987.

12. See Rubenstein 1998 for a detailed history of the portrayal of women and women's roles in historietas at midcentury.

13. Castillo, in effect, also reprises Paz, who writes: "The image of the mala mujer is almost always accompanied by the idea of aggressive activity. Activity and immodesty unite to petrify her soul. The mala is hard and impious like the macho" (Paz 1985: 39).

14. I found, in contrast, evidence of a relative tolerance toward lesbians (as long as they maintain a certain discretion). As one male wrestler explained, relations between women are seen as less degrading than relations between men: "A relationship between two women is nicer because . . . as I see it, a relationship between two women, I imagine, is a nice, exquisite relationship because there's a similarity of tastes. A woman knows what a woman likes, and that's how she treats her. And a man, no, a man is vulgar, it's about something awful. A woman puts on perfume, and she treats the other woman with delicacy . . . I say this because in our environment there are many relations of this type and, sometimes they are a matter of, 'Aw, how are you?' There's a sweetness in the relations between ladies." Relationships between men, however, were condemned by the same wrestler as being based in exploitation, inherently brutal and animalistic.

15. Lancaster translates cabrón, which literally means "big goat," as "cuckold," but in Mexico the connotation is closer to the English "son of a bitch"—mean, dangerous, and exploitative.

16. The only information I have about this person came from a story told to me by Irma Gonzalez. When she was seven months away from marriage, her fiancé ordered her to stop wrestling. She told him that she would, but then decided that since he traveled a lot, she could get away with wrestling until the marriage, as long as she wore a mask and used another name. She asked her friend El Santo if she could copy his mask and wrestle as "Novia del Santo" (El Santo's girlfriend/fiancé) until her marriage and retirement.

Seven months later, she got married and retired (she returned to wrestling and divorced the husband sometime after the birth of her daughter), but just before then she was approached by "un jotito," who asked if he could use the character, now that she was giving it up. There was, she says, a terrific demand for luchadoras, but there were only a few women in the business. Because of the shortage of luchadoras, he was able to work as a woman.

She told him to ask El Santo for permission, but he said he would be too embarrassed (and perhaps assumed that the wrestler would have refused). After Gonzalez retired, he began touring as Novia del Santo, until word got back to El Santo. They met when they were both scheduled for an event in Acapulco. "And so they wound up at the same time in Acapulco in the same arena," she recounted, "and he was just waiting for him to arrive. Afterward he told me about it. El Santo . . . he says, as soon as he arrives, 'Hey, come here. Why are you going around as Novia del Santo? This is the last time you're going to do it, OK? Because if I find out that you're going into the ring again, I'll get in and I'll strip you right there! I'll take off your clothes so they see what you are . . . um . . . you're not Irma.' " That was the end of Novia del Santo, but it may not have been the end of the wrestler's career. S/he might have retired after El Santo's threat or s/he may have just changed masks and continued. What I find interesting is that lucha libre provided a venue for him (her?) to pass as a woman and make a living as a woman in a stereotypically masculine profession.

17. I know of only one exotico who wears a mask, and he (Divino Exotico—see below) claims to perform something other than homosexuality. In fact, in marked contrast to masked wrestlers, exotico performance is grounded in the constant, ostentatious revelation of a sexuality that is supposed to be kept secret.

18. A suicide match is a variation of the lucha de apuesta. In a suicide match, several duos or trios challenge each other until one team is declared the winner. Then the members of the team have to fight each other in a lucha de apuesta.

19. At the time that I interviewed May Flowers, Televisa had barred the Exoticos from performing on television, so May Flowers had joined a group of *roqueros* (gangstas, literally rockers) called Los Vatos Locos. When I asked him if he missed being an exotico, he said that he did, mostly for "el relajo que hago con la gente" (the craziness/disorder that I stir up in people). In other words,

what he missed about being an exotico was the hostile audience response that he got as a rudo.

20. It was impossible to tape-record while I participated in classes, so this dialogue was reconstructed from memory later that evening.

21. Cuauhtitlán (now part of the Mexico City metropolitan sprawl), used to be a small town. The meaning of the saying is that outside of Mexico City it's just one irrelevant little backwater after another.

22. The actress and model Leelee Sobieski seems, in contrast, to have been treated as an "indecent woman." In 1999, she appeared in a photo spread with luchadores from the EMLL at Arena México. She is quoted in the article saying, "It's bad enough they're so big, and spent the whole time pinching me. . . . but those masks are so weird. You have no idea what's going on behind them. Scary" (*New York Times Magazine*, 31 October 1999).

23. In the late 1980s, Rafael Barradas Osorio (the recently retired secretary of the commission of boxing and lucha libre) estimated that there were approximately one hundred luchadoras in Mexico (Barradas Osorio 1990: 10). More recently, a reporter for *Box y Lucha* in 1997 named one hundred women as his selection of the best luchadoras in Mexico.

24. During my fieldwork, I very seldom saw luchadoras on television. The AAA (see chapter 6) now runs women's matches on television, but as in the arenas, they are usually the first or second match of the show; warm-ups for the more elaborate and longer star matches. The CMLL does not seem to televise matches between women at all.

25. There was, however, one sense in which I probably was being protected. One of the most important skills of a professional wrestler is the ability to *medir sus fuerzas*, measure and control one's strength. Everything a wrestler does has to look "real," so a wrestler has to know how far he or she can push a joint lock before he or she would actually injure his or her opponent, depending on the other wrestler's size and strength. This can also be true for throws—a much larger wrestler needs to exercise a caution when throwing a smaller opponent. In practice that means that men have to control their techniques when working with women, but women don't have to control their force when working with men—especially the larger men. When luchadoras finally do reach the professional level, it can be difficult to adjust to working with other women, with whom they do have to measure their force.

26. The meaning and valence of *puta* and *puto* differ somewhat. The former primarily implies prostitution (although it can, like *whore*, be applied to a woman who is considered to be inappropriately sexually available to men). The latter, like *maricón* or *joto*, primarily means any anally receptive male, although it does have the connotation of male prostitute.

27. An exception to this is a wrestler called Miss Janeth. At the time of my field-

work, her character is allied with a rudo called Killer, and she helps him to cheat in his matches against other male wrestlers. She dresses provocatively and sometimes flirts with other wrestlers, which gets Killer into fights outside of the ring. It is interesting that she has no técnica counterpart. Alliance with a male figure is represented as a sign of bad character.

CHAPTER 6: MEDIATING THE MASK

1. In the late 1990s *Box y Lucha* and *SuperLuchas* had two different categories of writers on staff. A few independent reporters would be paid the equivalent of five or ten dollars a page by the magazine. Others would be paid a salary and expenses by a specific empresa, which would also buy a certain number of pages in the magazine. Until 1998, the only advertisement I saw in *Box y Lucha* was for Deportes Martinez, or the occasional gym. In 1998, the magazine started running ads for small businesses—restaurants, clothing stores, and so on. *Super-luchas*, owned by PAPSA, was basically an advertisement for the empresa.

2. The Azcárraga and O'Farrill families were, at the time, competitors in the media industry. Luis and Raul Azcárraga founded the first radio station in Mexico in 1923. In 1930, Emilio Azcárraga Vidaureta founded XEW, then the most powerful station in the Western hemisphere. He and Romulo O'Farrill, the main investor in the Packard assembly plant in Puebla, both invested in movie theaters in the 1940s. Azcárraga was driven out of the movie theater business in 1944 but continued to invest in film production, beginning construction of the Churubusco Studios that same year. Theirs were the first two television broadcast licenses in Mexico.

3. For some reason, none of the veterans that I interviewed (including Rafael Barradas) ever mentioned the O'Farrill–EMLL broadcasts. The 1950s is remembered as the era of Televicentro, when there was no competition between television stations or empresas (in contrast with the conflict-ridden present).

4. In February 1952, Novo wrote: "While I was reading, I looked over once in a while at the television, where my mother was getting excited over the luchas. The Bulldog and Rubinsky were falling out of the ring, getting back in, throwing themselves around. Is it possible that twelve years ago the luchas so interested and entertained me? For now, I would rather read *El Vendedor de Muñecas* while listening to the radio, as background music, the jokes of Régulo and Madaleno. I couldn't answer. It's not even worth the trouble" (Novo 1967: 746).

5. I thank an anonymous informant for identifying the children's shoes, as well as for her reminiscences of family lucha libre nights in front of the television. She and other informants suggest that these evenings carried a certain sense of formality, when their father, in his role as patriarch, would gather the family together with their guests.

6. Until 1997, the regency (mayoralty) of Mexico City was a presidential appointment and was considered an important post on a national level.

7. It is interesting that Barradas imagined viewing to take place in an isolated, individualized context, which is quite different from the context that my informants remembered.

8. Anne Rubenstein points out, however, that these concerns were not unique to the moral panic surrounding lucha libre. Radio, for example, was promoted as a boon not only because it kept the family members at home, but also because its use would protect the family from the eyestrain resulting from overconsumption of comic books (personal communication, 2005).

9. An interesting thing about the three dispositions is that they are about maintaining the boundaries between performers, the public, and the representative of (state) authority. At present the three dispositions are not generally enforced and were probably enforced unevenly in the past. Moreover, they are not really the only rules of performance. There are, for example, rules defining the parameters of the event—the size of the ring and so on, not to mention the rules of the sport itself.

10. About the churros, Carl Mora writes (1998: 102), "the films turned out . . . were ostensibly serials designed for television, however, their marketability on that medium was so restricted that the producers turned to combining the separate serials into one or more full length features that were released to neighborhood theaters."

11. The film was originally supposed to star El Santo, who was already a star of the ring and television screen, but he turned the project down, saying that he didn't think the film would make any money (Carro 1993: 27)

12. Ruvinskis was a professional actor as well as wrestler and starred in other film genres and "legitimate" theater as well as wrestling movies. During most of my research period, Ruvinskis was president of the Commission of Lucha Libre.

13. El Santo movies currently have a certain hipster cachet, and dubbed versions are sold and traded over the Internet. The dubbed versions seem to have originally been distributed in Texas. Spanish versions were also distributed in areas of heavy hispanophone immigration, such as New York (Isabel Pinedo, personal communication, 1995). There are rumors that different versions were produced for the domestic and export markets. For example, it is said that the impossible-to-locate export version of *Tesoro de Dracula* (*The Treasure of Dracula*) includes nude scenes. They were also distributed in France, where they were considered the epitomic expression of André Breton's contention that Mexico is the land of surrealism.

14. The Ranchera film genre and its charro hero can be compared to the Hollywood Western and the cowboy. However, Mora (1995) notes that the charro was not quite the equivalent of the cowboy. The cowboy "embodied Turner's thesis of

the expansion and conquest of the frontier—the rugged individualist confronting a hostile and primitive environment and overcoming it through sheer willpower. The hero confronts the local tyrant on behalf of the 'little people.'" The charro, on the other hand, "came to represent the traditional and Catholic values in defiance of the leftist, modernizing tendencies emanating from the cities . . . exalting the traditional *patrón-peon* and male-female relationships, and by so doing . . . struck a responsive chord in the Mexican middle class" (46).

15. Mora writes, "The comedia ranchera symbolized traditional values, the cabaretera symbolized the breakdown of those values . . . The urban night spot, in its surrogate role as the city in microcosm, was also a conduit for foreign influences. The music especially symbolized this. Most of it was Afro-Cuban . . . musical forms with a high level of erotic suggestiveness, which in turn highlighted the freer sexual standards of post war urban life" (1995: 47).

16. Between 1960 and 1990, the population of the Federal District grew from 4,870,876 to 8,235,744. In addition, the metropolitan area began to absorb several areas of Hidalgo and the State of Mexico. The current population of the Mexico City metropolitan area is now over 19 million, although some claim that the figure should be higher (for data, see www.demographia.com/db-mxcsector.htm).

17. Although professional wrestling was always televised in the United States, it too has undergone shifts in the way it has been televised. In the early 1950s, it was featured on network television. Soon after, however, it was replaced by programming oriented to a more middle-class audience and relegated to local television channels. In the 1980s, the WWF brought a revamped professional wrestling back to national television, with even more emphasis on verbal performance and long-term narrative conflicts (Jenkins 2005, De Garis 2005).

18. The term *popular culture* has come to mean different things in Anglo and Latin contexts. In Great Britain and the United States, it usually refers to television, rock music, fan magazines, and other products of the culture industry. In this usage, popular culture (whether reviled or celebrated) is basically equated with mass-mediated culture. In Italian, French, and Latin American usage, however, popular culture is the culture of the subaltern classes. It may be imagined as a site of authenticity and resistance, in contrast to inauthentic and/or hegemonic mass (-mediated) culture. Popular culture in the anglophone sense may also be turned to counterhegemonic uses but is usually produced or distributed by the dominant cultural and financial apparatus.

19. Around the same period, the slang terminology used to refer to the city's middle classes also changed. The children of the first few generations of the old and new postrevolutionary wealth were called, and called themselves, "juniors." By the 1980s, they were referred to and self-identified as *fresas* (strawberries). The term *naco* (unlike *fresa*) is never used as a term of self-identification (except

ironically). Instead, members (especially youth) of the urban popular classes are more likely to self-identify as *banda* (band, in the sense of group) if they identify as anything at all.

20. That lucha libre is uncorrupted because there is no serious betting is a statement I heard from a number of people (wrestlers and others) and that is interesting for two reasons. First, since the outcome is normally fixed, it would make little sense to bet on it. It would make even less sense to try to fix it illegally. The fact that no one bets on lucha libre suggests that spectators are aware that the endings are predetermined. What is more interesting still is Apolo Dantes's suggestion that friends will make small bets on lucha libre matches, since this would suggest either ignorance of the fixed ending, or a kind of complicity on the part of the friends really to suspend disbelief.

21. One could draw a connection between lucha libre's updated use of the mask with the engraver José Guadalupe Posada's use of the skull motif in the early twentieth century. Posada's satirical engravings of skeletons dressed as members of Mexican society have been considered emblematic of *lo mexicano*, utilizing, as they do, the "traditionally Mexican" motif of the skull, transposed to an urban environment. An interesting coincidence, in this regard, is that the grandson of Posada's printer Arzacio Vanegas (a central figure in the culture of the penny-press movement that played a crucial role in the development of the prerevolutionary proletariat public sphere) became a wrestler. The grandson, Arzacio "Kid" Vanegas, is remembered today as the wrestler who trained Fidel Castro and Che Guevara in wrestling and physical fitness just before they sailed on the Gramma.

22. The title is a pun on the adage "la lucha le hacemos todos" (roughly, "everyone fights the battle" or, in effect, "life is a struggle"). The exhibit was curated with the collaboration of sociologists Jorge Cano and Sonia Iglesias.

23. During the mid-1980s, the World Wrestling Federation, under the direction of Vince MacMahon Jr., began to emphasize the theatrical, verbal aspects of the spectacle. It proved a successful strategy that brought professional wrestling back to mainstream television. Jeffery Mondak has argued that pro wrestling in the United States peaks in popularity during cyclical waves of nationalist, xenophobic sentiment, and that its revival in the 1980s can be attributed to the political culture of the Reagan years.

24. Description of the following events relies primarily on articles that appeared in the newspaper *L'Afición* and wrestling magazine *Box y Lucha* (from 1992 to 1993 and from 1996 to 1998) and interviews, conversations, and gossip with members of Renovación 2000, the Asociación Nacional de Luchadores, Referís y Retirados, and unaffiliated wrestlers. Many thanks to all, and my special and affectionate thanks to Irma Gonzalez, Irma Aguilar, and the late Hara Kiri for their generous assistance.

25. The change in policy came about after the secretary of tourism polled children in a number of schools about what sporting event they would like to see in honor of the UN Year of the Child. Unsurprisingly, 75 percent wanted to see the forbidden lucha libre. The commission, together with the EMLL, organized a special, "clean" event in Arena Coliseo, and since nothing bad happened, the empresa was given permission to continue to allow minors into the arena (Barradas Osorio 1992: 153).

26. As far as I know, there is no connection between the Maynez LLI and the Garza Hernandez empresa of the 1950s.

27. "The EMLL wants to do away with their antagonists from El Toreo [Cuatro Caminos], or, the same thing, they want to liquidate (promotorily) [sic] Don Carlos Maynez and all of the small empresas, so that they are left with nothing more than to accept the servitude of the EMLL" (Suplemento de Lucha Libre 1991, 2). Lucha Libre Internacional matches were broadcast on the public television station Imevision for a few months, but the quality of the broadcasts was very low, and they did not develop an audience (Box y Lucha 1992b: 29; 1992c: 26).

28. According to some of my informants, the return to television happened at a moment when the Sindicato was particularly unstable. Around 1990, under the leadership of union president Manny Guzmán, the Sindicato began to charge arena owners a fifty peso–per-wrestler insurance fee. This represented a significant expense for smaller arena owners, compromising their ability to hire more than a few wrestlers per night. During the same period, wrestlers who approached the union to collect their pensions or other compensation were told that the organization was bankrupt (Irma Gonzalez and Hara Kiri, interview with author, 1997).

29. Peña's job included acting as promoter for individual wrestlers. Promoters are not only responsible for managing their clients' appearances but often design their characters. A wrestler thus owes his or her promoter not only their support in getting into the arenas, but his or her professional identity.

30. Rafael Barradas, interview with author. For the interview with Conan, see Fascinetto (1995: 29).

31. Despite the blows to the commission's legitimacy in the mid-1980s, wrestlers still regard the Federal District commission as a more active and authoritative body than other, regional commissions.

32. Justiciero had already been blackballed from the Sindicato Nacional in April.

33. One implication of televised wrestling is that the most prestigious matches may take place outside of the jurisdiction of the Federal District commission.

34. Wrestling audiences can be very aggressive toward the wrestlers, but I've never seen (or heard of) audience members becoming seriously aggressive toward one another. While it could happen, and probably has happened at some time, it is not a regular feature of lucha libre spectatorship.

35. Insulting wrestlers is an important part of fan participation, but the case of Vampiro Canadiense in particular was unusual. First, his detractors didn't break down along rudo/técnico lines. Second, insults are usually not about technical skill. More common are cries of *matonero* (gang-up-er), *metiche* (busybody), *maricón* (faggot), and so on. The closest thing to "X doesn't know how to wrestle" that one usually hears in the arena is "No puede" ("X can't do it") or "Solo así puede" ("X can only do it that [dishonest or cowardly] way"), which is quite different.

36. In fact, Raúl Salinas de Gortari and Ricardo Salinas Pliego were not related, but the former had loaned the latter 30 million dollars through a Swiss bank toward the purchase of the television station. The Televisa conglomerate did not bid on channels 7 and 13, but were later granted a no bid contract to run sixty-two concessions of channel 14 (de la Selva 2003). TVAzteca summarized and responded to Televisa's charges against them in a two-page advertisement in La Jornada (1996a: 26).

37. This was, at least, the version recounted to me by wrestlers from Renovación 2000.

38. Juniors, IIs, and sons-of are ideally sons or nephews of veterans, but the relationship is sometimes spurious. But even when the junior (or whatever) is not related to the original, the connection is normally worked out with the cooperation and sometimes remuneration of the original.

39. Interview with group of thirteen wrestlers from PromoAzteca, October 1996. The use of the term *dinosaur* resonates particularly with a then current derogatory term for old-style PRI militants who had come up through party ranks and were associated with corruption and stagnation.

40. Although the EMLL participated fully in the televised broadcast of lucha libre, the empresa allied itself with Renovación 2000 partly to make common cause against Peña and the AAA, and partly because it promoted itself as the "serious and stable" empresa, defenders of "real" lucha libre (as opposed to the AAA).

41. Their objection to the AAA's use of the Exoticos was odd for two reasons. First, there is nothing novel about effeminate male luchadores. In fact, exoticos have participated in lucha libre almost as long as have women and thus could have been understood as part of lucha libre's tradition. Second, at the time, Televisa had banned the Exoticos from performing in drag on the air. Instead, the three wrestlers appeared on television as members of the Vatos Locos made up to look like members of the rock band Kiss. They wrestled as exoticos only in live performances that were not taped for broadcast (May Flowers, interview with author, 1997).

42. The discourse of the wrestling costume seemed only to apply to male wrestlers. At no time did anyone express an opinion about costume trends among luchadoras.

43. Despite the criticisms of full-body costumes that I often heard expressed by Renovación associates, many of their younger wrestlers wore the very costume styles that their spokespeople regarded with suspicion.

44. At the time of my research, several wrestlers contested Peña's claim to have created their characters. Other wrestlers do credit Peña with having developed their characters, but I do not know whether he created all of the ones he copyrighted.

45. Some of the wrestlers who objected to the use of Pentagón's costume further accused the AAA of having failed to make expected disability payments to the injured wrestler.

46. The remaining venues included centrally located arenas like the EMLL arenas, and irregular, relatively expensive venues like the Toreo Cuatro Caminos. Ticket prices at Arena México usually ranged from about US$2–7 and tickets at the Toreo cost from about US$7–15 at the time of research (prices varied according to the event, and according to the seat). A movie, by comparison, cost US$1–3. There were, in fact, still a number of small arenas where Renovación and other minor empresas would charge less (US$1.50–2.00)

47. Mexico City is divided into delegations, each one consisting of several colonies (neighborhoods). A political delegation is an administrative body in charge of a given delegation, and has the power to give out or deny permits, levy fines, and so on.

48. The person behind Superbarrio's mask was elected to the Camera de Deputados in the same election.

49. It is this shift that Claudio Lomnitz Adler argues is at the root of the phenomenon of *lo naco* (Lomnitz Adler 1996).

CONCLUSION

1. Another possible factor in the decline of live lucha libre is a change in patterns of cultural consumption in Mexico that Nestor García Canclini and his associates documented at the beginning of the 1990s. In a survey of 1500 homes in Mexico City in 1993, they found a trend toward domesticization of cultural consumption. Over 40 percent of their sample had not been to see a movie in over a year, and almost a quarter reported that their major leisure activity was watching television. Presumably, attendance at lucha libre events would have been affected by this trend, whether it was televised or not.

2. For an analysis of the positioning of Mexican and other Latino wrestlers in U.S. wrestling leagues, see Serrato 2005.

3. In April, federal police broke up a miner's strike action by firing on the demonstrators from helicopters. Later that month, a sit-down strike by ambulant flower vendors in the town of Atenco, Mexico, led to an occupation of the town by 2,000 police, 200 arrests, and several deaths. Many of those arrested (some of

them bystanders) have since accused the police of torture and (in the case of over twenty female detainees) sexual assault. In Oaxaca City, a teacher's strike turned into an occupation of the Historic Center (and, for a time, of the city offices, as well as its media outlets) by supporters of the strikers (a group calling itself the Asamblea Popular de Pueblos Oaxaqueños, or APPO) demanding the resignation of the PRI-affiliated governor, Ulises Ruiz. The standoff lasted for several months until paramilitary police fired into a crowd of demonstrators, killing three people, among them an independent journalist from New York. Fox responded by sending 3,000 members of the federal police force (PFP) and 3,500 military police (with the support of 5,000 regular army troops) to forcibly evict APPO from the occupied sections of the city, effectively using federal power to support Ruiz. A few days later, eight bombs went off in Mexico City, damaging offices of the PRI, the IFE, and branches of Scotiabank. As of this writing, Ulises Ruiz is still governor, and the PFP is still in Oaxaca.

4. Lopez Obrador had his own troubled history, including a bribery scandal and an attempted impeachment. The entire story is far too complicated and colorful to recount here. Suffice it to say that by the time of the elections, the mayor had recovered from the scandal and enjoyed a solid and enthusiastic base of support in the capital.

5. In August, the tribunal of the IFE decided that although Fox and the CCE had interfered illegally with the election (by paying for and running ads implicitly and explicitly favoring Calderón), there was no way to quantify the effects of said interference. I was in Mexico City during the campaign and was, in fact, struck not only by the number of direct campaign ads on television supporting Calderón (as opposed to his main two opponents), but by the number of ads indirectly supporting him. For months before the election, there was a virtual barrage of public service announcements extolling the accomplishments of the government under Vicente Fox and the PAN (announcements that continued to run after the election, while Lopez Obrador's supporters demanded a recount). In the two months following the election, in the midst of Lopez Obrador's accusations and the occupation of the Zocalo and Reforma, these were supplemented by advertisements asserting the irreproachable credibility of the IFE and its representatives.

6. The Grito de Dolores is a speech that commemorates Miguel de Hidalgo's 1810 call to arms in the town of Dolores that set off the popular phase of the Mexican War of Independence. Although it can have variations, it always ends with the speaker and the crowd shouting three times: "¡Viva México!" The mayor of each town in Mexico is supposed to deliver the Grito from the balcony of the municipal building at midnight on September 15. In Mexico City, however, the president of the republic delivers it from the balcony of the Palacio Nacional.

7. Calderón's inaugural took place under conditions unique in postrevolutionary

Mexican history. Vicente Fox formally turned over his power as president to Calderón in a ceremony in the presidential residence of Los Pinos (instead of San Lazaro), one minute before midnight on November 30. A disembodied voice, offstage and off camera, delivered the words of the ceremony. The next morning, following a second fistfight in the Senate, Calderón entered the Palacio de San Lazaro, took the oath of office, and left five minutes later.

8. "Kid Acuña" is a reference to Francisco Ramírez Acuña, the incoming secretary of the interior.

BIBLIOGRAPHY

Afición, L'. 1992a. "Inicia Actividades la Nueva Empresa Luchistica." March 1, 28.

———. 1992b. "Manny Guzmán es un Líder Nefasto: Justiciero." April 3, 25.

———. 1992c. "La EMLL Da a Conocer su Postura ante la Nueva Competencia." May 7, 25.

———. 1992d. "Nace un Nuevo Sindicato Pancratista, Afiliado a la C.O.M." May 8, 29.

———. 1992e. "No Habrá Oposición a las Funciones de la 'AAA.'" May 15, 25.

———. 1992f. "Pugnarán Promotores del Edomex por Evitar Funciones de Intrusos." May 15, 25.

Agustín, José. 1990. *Tragicomedia Mexicana*, vol. 1. Mexico City: Editorial Planeta.

———. 1992. *Tragicomedia Mexicana*, vol. 2. Mexico City: Editorial Planeta.

Alipi, Dario. 1994. "Entrevista con Sergio Arau: La Lucha en el Art-Naco." *Colosos de la Lucha Libre*, no. 41.

Arbena, Joseph L. 1992. "Sport and the Promotion of Nationalism in Latin America: A Preliminary Interpretation." *Studies in Latin American Popular Culture* 11: 143–55.

———. 1991. "Sport, Development and Mexican Nationalism, 1920–1970." *Journal of Sport History* 18: 350–64.

Archivo General de la Nacion. Document 612.2/1, Archivo Abelardo Rodriguez.

———. Document 432/222, Archivo Avila Camacho.

Ball, Michael. 1990. *Professional Wrestling as Ritual Drama in American Popular Culture.* Lewiston, N.Y.: Edwin Mellen.

Barradas Osorio, Rafael. 1990. *Fuera mascaras: La realidad de la lucha libre Mexicana.* Mexico City: Mi Lucha Para Limpios y Rudos.

———. 1992. *Fuera Máscaras.* Mexico City: Mi Lucha para Limpios y Rudos.

Barthes, Roland. 1972. *Mythologies.* New York: Hill and Wang.

Bartra, Armando. 1994. "The Seduction of the Innocents: The First Tumultuous Moments of Mass Literacy in Postrevolutionary Mexico." *Everyday Forms of State Formation: Revolution and the Negotiation of Rule in Modern Mexico,* ed. Gilbert M. Joseph and Daniel Nugent, 301–25. Durham: Duke University Press.

Bartra, Roger. 1992. *The Cage of Melancholy: Identity and Metamorphosis in the Mexican Character,* trans. Christopher J. Hall. New Brunswick: Rutgers University Press.

Beezly, William. 1987. *Judas at the Jockey Club and Other Episodes of Porfirian Mexico.* Lincoln: University of Nebraska Press.

Behar, Ruth. 1993. *Translated Woman: Crossing the Border with Esperanza's Story.* Boston: Beacon.

Beidelman, Thomas O. 1993 "Secrecy and Society: The Paradox of Knowing and the Knowing of Paradox." *Passages* 5: 6–7.

Bellman, Beryl L. 1981. "The Paradox of Secrecy." *Human Studies* 4: 1–27.

Birrell, Susan, and Allan Turowetz. 1981. "Character Workup and Display: Collegiate Gymnastics and Professional Wrestling." *Sport in the Sociocultural Process,* ed. Marie Hart and Susan Birrell. Dubuque, Ill.: Wm. C. Brown.

Bourdieu, Pierre. [1978] 1991. "Sport and Social Class." *Rethinking Popular Culture,* ed. Chandra Mukerji and Michael Schudson, 357–73. Berkeley: University of California Press.

———. 1990. "Programme for a Sociology of Sport." *In Other Words: Essays towards a Reflexive Sociology.* Stanford: Stanford University Press.

Box y Lucha. 1992a. "Espaldas Claras." March 15, 29.

———. 1992b. "Yo Mejoraría las Transmisiones de los Independientes Cambinado de Canal y Locutores: Dr. Wagner Jr." May 1, 26.

———. 1992c. "Rudy Reyna, Maná de los Exoticos del Ring." July 10.

———. 1993. "El S.N.L. Realizó Marcha en Contra de las Transmisiones de Luchas Por TV." June 25, 9.

———. 1996a. "Alex Dinamo." November 6, 21.

———. 1996b. "Ecos del Cuadrilatero." November 13, 16.

———. 1996c. "Yo Perdí la Cabellera y Comprendí Que en la Lucha Libre Hay Jerarquias." November 27, 13.

———. 1997a. "Rifarrafe en el Ring." May 9, 22.

Bricker, Victoria. 1973. *Ritual Humor in Highland Chiapas*. Austin: University of Texas Press.

Brownell, Susan. 1995. *Training the Body for China: Sports in the Moral Order of the People's Republic*. Chicago: University of Chicago Press.

Camp, Roderic Ai. 1999. *Politics in Mexico: The Decline of Authoritarianism*. New York: Oxford University Press.

Carrier, Joseph. 1995. *De Los Otros: Intimacy and Homosexuality among Mexican Men*. New York: Columbia University Press.

Carro, Nelson. 1993. *El Cine de los Luchadores*. Mexico City: Filmoteca de UNAM.

Castells, Manuel. 1983. *The City and the Grassroots: A Cross-Cultural Theory of Urban Social Movements*. Berkeley: University of California Press.

Castillo, Debra A. 1998. *Easy Women: Sex and Gender in Modern Mexican Fiction*. Minneapolis: University of Minnesota Press.

Coe, Andrew. 1992. "La Mascara! La Mascara!" *Icarus* 8: 157–70.

Colegio de México. 1996. *Diccionario del Español Usual en México*. Mexico City: Colegio de México.

Cordry, Donald. 1980. *Mexican Masks*. Austin: University of Texas Press.

Cross, John. 1998. *Informal Politics*. Stanford: Stanford University Press.

Crumrine, N. Ross. 1983. "Mask Use and Meaning in Easter Ceremonialism: The Mayo Parisero." *The Power of Symbols: Masks and Masquerade in the Americas*, ed. N. Ross Crumrine and Marjorie M. Halpin, 93–101. Vancouver: University of British Columbia Press.

Cuéllar Vasquez, Angélica. 1993. *La Noche es de Ustedes, el Amanecer es Nuestro: Asemblea de Barrios y Superbarrio Gomez.* Mexico City: Universidad Nacional Autonoma de Mexico.

Da Matta, Roberto. 1991. *Carnivals, Rogues, and Heroes: An Interpretation of the Brazilian Dilemma*, trans. John Drury. Notre Dame: University of Notre Dame Press.

De la Selva, Alma Rosa Alva. 2003. "De la expansión a la cúpula del poder: Quince años de televisión en Mèxico." *Revista Mexicana de Comunicacion*, no. 83, www.mexicanadecomunicacion.com.mx.

Del Castillo, Adelaida R. 1993. "Covert Cultural Norms and Sex/Gender Meaning: A Mexico City Case." *Urban Anthropology* 22: 237–58.

De Garis, Laurence. 2005. "The 'Logic' of Professional Wrestling." *Steel Chair to the Head*, ed. Nicolas Sammond, 192–212. Durham: Duke University Press.

Dundes, Alan. 1994. "Gallus as Phallus: A Cross-Cultural Psychoanalytic Consideration of the Cockfight as Fowl Play." *The Cockfight: A Casebook*, 241–84. Madison: University of Wisconsin Press.

Edgar, Andrew. 2002. *Cultural Theory: The Key Thinkers*. New York: Routledge.

Emigh, John. 1996. *Masked Performance: The Play of Self and Other in Ritual and Theater*. Philadelphia: University of Pennsylvania Press.

En Caliente. 1996. Interview with six wrestlers from PromoAzteca, October 29 [television broadcast].

Fascinetto, Lola Miranda. 1992. *Sin Máscara ni Cabellera: La Lucha Libre en México Hoy*. Mexico City: Marc Ediciones.

Foucault, Michel. 1978. *History of Sexuality*, vol. 1. New York: Random House.

Freedman, Jim. 1983. "Will the Sheik Use His Blinding Fireball? The Ideology of Professional Wrestling." *The Celebration of Society: Perspectives on Contemporary Cultural Performance*, ed. Frank E. Manning. Bowling Green: Bowling Green University Press.

García Canclini, Néstor. 1995. *Hybrid Cultures*. Minneapolis: University of Minnesota Press.

García Canclini, Néstor, et al. 1995. "Mexico: Cultural Globalization in a Disintegrating City." *American Ethnologist* 22: 743–55.

Geertz, Clifford. 1973. "Deep Play: Notes on the Balinese Cockfight." *The Interpretation of Cultures*, 412–54. New York: Basic Books, 1973.

Gilmore, Frances. 1983. "Symbolic Representation in Mexican Combat Plays." *The Power of Symbols: Masks and Masquerade in the Americas*, ed. N. Ross Crumrine and Marjorie Halpin, 102–10. Vancouver: University of British Columbia Press.

Goffman, Erving. 1974. *Frame Analysis*. Cambridge: Harvard University Press.

Golden, Tim. 1995. "Mexico's New Offensive: Erasing Rebel's Mystique." *New York Times*, February 11.

Grobet, Lourdes. 2005. *Masked Superstars of Mexican Wrestling*, ed. Alfonso Morales. Mexico: D.A.P. Trilce.

Guillermoprieto, Alma. 1995. "The Unmasking." *New Yorker*, March 13, 40–47.

Gutmann, Matthew C. 1996. *The Meanings of Macho: Being a Man in Mexico City*. Berkeley: University of California Press.

Guttmann, Allen. 1978. *From Ritual to Record: The Nature of Modern Sports*. New York: Columbia University Press.

Halpin, Marjorie M. 1983. "The Mask of Tradition." *The Power of Symbols: Masks and Masquerade in the Americas*, ed. N. Ross Crumrine and Marjorie M. Halpin, 219–26. Vancouver: University of British Columbia Press.

Jares, Joe. 1974. *What Ever Happened to Gorgeous George?* Englewood, N.J.: Prentice Hall.

Jenkins, Henry III. 2005. "'Never Trust a Snake': wwf Wrestling as Masculine Melodrama." *Steel Chair to the Head*, ed. Nicholas Sammond, 33–66. Durham: Duke University Press.

Joseph, Gilbert M., and Allen Wells. 1987. "The Rough and Tumble Career of Pedro Crespo." *The Human Tradition in Latin America: The Twentieth Century*, 27–40. Wilmington, Del.: Scholarly Resources.

La Jornada. 1996a. "Las 20 Mentiras de Emilio Azcarraga y Ricardo Rocha." November 4.

——. 1996b. "Konnan Engaña al Público, Afirma Perro Aguayo." November 7.

Joyrich, Lynne. 1992. "All That Television Allows: TV Melodrama Postmodernism and Consumer Culture." *Private Screenings: Television and the Female Consumer*, ed. Lynn Spigel and Denise Mann. Minneapolis: University of Minnesota Press.

Knight, Alan. 1994. "Popular Culture and the Revolutionary State in Mexico, 1910–1940." *Hispanic American Historical Review*, August.

Kulick, Don. 1998. *Travesti: Sex, Gender and Culture among Brazilian Transgendered Prostitutes*. Chicago: University of Chicago Press.

Lancaster, Roger. 1992. *Life Is Hard: Machismo, Danger, Intimacy and Power in Nicaragua*. Berkeley: University of California Press.

Levi, Heather. 1999. "On Mexican Pro Wrestling: Sport as Melodrama." *Sport/Cult*, ed. Randy Martin and Toby Miller, 173–90. Minneapolis: University of Minnesota Press.

Lewis, J. Lowell. 1995. "Genre and Embodiment: From Brazilian Capoeira to the Ethnology of Human Movement." *Cultural Anthropology* 2: 221–43.

Lewis, Oscar. 1961. *The Children of Sanchez: Autobiography of a Mexican Family*. New York: Random House.

Lincoln, Bruce. 1989. *Discourse and the Construction of Society: Comparative Studies of Myth, Ritual, and Classification*. New York: Oxford University Press.

Lomnitz Adler, Claudio. 1992. *Exits from the Labyrinth: Culture and Ideology in Mexican National Space*. Berkeley: University of California Press.

——. 1996. "Fissures in Contemporary Mexican Nationalism." *Public Culture*: 55–68.

——. 2001. *Deep Mexico, Silent Mexico: An Anthropology of Nationalism*. Minneapolis: University of Minnesota Press.

Lomnitz, Claudio, and Ilya Adler. 1993. "The Function of the Form." *Constructing Culture and Power in Latin America*, ed. Daniel Levine, 357–402. Ann Arbor: University of Michigan Press.

Lomnitz, Larissa Adler, and Perez-Lizuar, Marisol. 1987. *A Mexican Elite Family, 1820–1980*. Princeton: Princeton University Press.

Lopez, Ana. 1995. "Our Welcomed Guests: Telenovelas in Latin America." *To Be Continued . . . : Soap Operas around the World*, ed. Robert C. Allen, 256–70. New York: Routledge.

Lucha Libre. 1954. April 1, 5.

——. 1955a. "Máscara Mania I." March 1–15, 17–18.

——. 1955b. "Máscara Mania II." March 16–30, 18–19.

Lutes, Steven V. 1983. "The Mask and Magic of Yaqui Paskola Clowns." *The Power of Symbols: Masks and Masquerade in the Americas*, ed. N. Ross Crumrine and Marjorie Halpin, 81–92. Vancouver: University of British Columbia Press.

Martín-Barbero, Jesús. 1987. *De los medios a las mediaciones: Comunicacion, cultura y hegemonia*. Barcelona: Gustavo Gili.

Mazer, Sharon. 1998. *Professional Wrestling: Sport and Spectacle*. Jackson: University Press of Mississippi.

McDonald, James H. 1993. "Whose History, Whose Voice? Myth and Resistance in the Rise of the New Left in Mexico." *Cultural Anthropology* 8: 96–116.

Mejía Barquera, Fernando. 1999. "Televisión y Deporte." *Apuntes para una historia de la Televisión Mexicana*, vol. 2. Mexico City: Revista Mexicana de Comunicacion.

Melhuus, Marit. 1998. "Configuring Gender: Male and Female in Mexican Heterosexual and Homosexual Relations." *Ethnos* 63: 353–82.

Meyer, Jean A. 1976. *The Cristero Rebellion: The Mexican People between Church and State, 1926–1929*. Cambridge: Cambridge University Press.

Migliore, Sam. 1993. "Professional Wrestling: Moral Commentary through Ritual Metaphor." *Journal of Ritual Studies* 7: 65–84.

Mirande, Alfredo. 1997. *Hombres and Machos: Masculinity and Latino Culture*. Boulder: Westview.

Mitchell, B. R. 1994. *International Historical Statistics: The Americas, 1759–1993*. New York: Stockton.

Möbius, Janina. 1997. *Dioses de Carne y Hueso* [film].

Mondak, Jeffery J. 1989. "The Politics of Professional Wrestling." *Journal of Popular Culture* 23: 139–50.

Monsiváis, Carlos. 1978. "Notas Sobre Cultura Popular en Mexico." *Historia General de Mexico* 4: 305–476. Mexico City: El Colegio de Mexico.

———. 1981. "Mexicanerias: Pero Hubo una Vez Once Mil Machos?" *Escenas de Pudor y Liviandad*, 103–18. Mexico City: Grijalbo.

———. 1997. *Mexican Postcards*, trans. John Kraniauskas. New York: Verso.

Mora, Carl J. 1995. *Mexican Cinema: Reflections on a Society*. Berkeley: University of California Press.

Morales, Alfonso. 1998. "La Máscara Rota." *Luna Córnea* 14: 88–97.

Mortensen, Chris. *Unreal Story of Professional Wrestling*. New York: A&E, 1999 [video].

Nájera-Ramirez, Olga. 1997. *La Fiesta de los Tastoanes*. Albuquerque: University of New Mexico Press.

Needler, M. C. 1998. *Mexican Politics: The Containment of Conflict*. Westport, Conn.: Praeger.

New York Times Magazine. 1999. "Interview with Leelee Sobieski." October 31.

Nonini, Donald M., and Arlene Akiko Teraoka. 1992. "Class Struggle in the Squared Circle: Professional Wrestling as Working Class Sport." *The Politics of Culture and Creativity: A Critique of Civilization—Essays in Honor of Stanley Diamond*, ed. Christine Ward Gailey. Gainesville: University Press of Florida.

Novo, Salvador. 1964 [1940]. "Mi Lucha (Libre)." *La Vida en Mexico en el Periodo Presidencial de Lázaro Cárdenas*. Mexico City: Empresas.

———. 1967. *La Vida en Mexico en el Periodo Presidencial de Miguel Alemán*. Mexico City: Empresas.

———. 1965. *La Vida en Mexico en el Periodo Presidencial de Manuel Avila Camacho*. Mexico City: Empresas.

Oakley, Sir Atholl. 1971. *Blue Blood on the Mat: The All-in Wrestling Story*. London: Paul.

O'Malley, Ilene V. 1986. The Myth of Revolution: Hero Cults and the Institutionalization of the Mexican State, 1920–1940. Westport, Conn.: Greenwood.

Pacheco, Cristina. 1990. *Los Dueños de la Noche*. Mexico City: Planeta.

Paz, Octavio. 1961. *The Labyrinth of Solitude and the Other Mexico*, trans. Lysander Kemp. New York: Grove. Repr. with *Return to the Labyrinth of Solitude, Mexico and the United States*, and *The Philanthropic Ogre*, trans. Lysander Kemp, Yara Milos, and Rachel Phillips Belash. New York: Grove Weidenfeld, 1985.

Pernet, Henry. 1992. *Ritual Masks: Deceptions and Revelations*. Columbia: University of South Carolina Press.

Poniatowska, Elena. 1990. *Todo Mexico*, vol. 1. Mexico City: Diana.

Prieur, Annick. 1998. *Memas House, Mexico City: On Transvestites, Queens, and Machos*. Chicago: University of Chicago Press.

Rapport, Nigel. 1997. "The Morality of Locality." *The Ethnography of Moralities*, ed. Signe Howell, 158–76. New York: Routledge.

Romanucci-Ross, Lola. 1973. *Conflict, Violence and Morality in a Mexican Village*. Palo Alto, Calif.: National Press.

Roseberry, William. 1989. *Anthropologies and Histories*. New Brunswick: Rutgers University Press.

Rowland, Allison, and Peter Gordon. 2006. "Mexico City: No Longer a Leviathan?" *The Megacity in Latin America*, ed. Alan Gilbert. New York: United Nations Press.

Rubenstein, Anne. 1998. *Bad Language, Naked Ladies, and Other Threats to the Nation*. Durham: Duke University Press.

———. 2000. "Mass Media and Culture in the Post-Revolutionary Era." *The Oxford History of Mexico*, ed. Michael Meyer and William Beezley, 637–70. New York: Oxford University Press.

———. 2003. "El Santo: Many Versions of the Perfect Man." *The Mexico Reader*, ed. G. Joseph and T. Henderson, 570–78. Durham: Duke University Press.

Rugos, Ralph. 1994. "Q: What's the Difference between Superman and Superbarrio? A: Superbarrio Exists!" *LA Weekly*, January 14–20.

Sanchez Hernandez, Carlos Alfonso. 1997. *Mascaras y Danzas Tradicionales*. Toluca: Universidad Autonoma del Estado de Mexico.

Saunders, Neil. 1998. *Icons of Power: Feline Symbolism in the Americas*. New York: Routledge.

Serrato, Phillip. 2005. "Not Quite Heroes: Race, Masculinity, and Latino Professional Wrestlers." *Steel Chair to the Head*, ed. Nicholas Sammond, 242–59. Durham: Duke University Press.

Seyde, Manuel. 1953a. "La Lucha por la Vida I." *Revista de Revistas*, April 3, 73–75.

——. 1953b. "La Lucha por la Vida II." *Revista de Revistas*, April 12, 73–83.

——. 1953c. "La Lucha por la Vida III." *Revista de Revistas*, April 19, 72–75.

Smith, Peter H. 1979. *Labyrinths of Power: Political Recruitment in Twentieth Century Mexico*. Princeton: Princeton University Press.

Stein, Steve, Jose Deustua Carvallo, and Susan C. Stokes. 1986. "Soccer and Social Change in Early Twentieth Century Peru, Part 2." *Studies in Latin American Popular Culture* 5: 17–27.

Stern, Steve J. 1995. *The Secret History of Gender: Women, Men and Power in Late Colonial Mexico*. Chapel Hill: University of North Carolina Press.

Stevens, Evelyn. 1973. "Marianismo, the Other Face of Machismo." *Male and Female in Latin America*, ed. Ann Piscatello, 82–101. Pittsburgh: University of Pittsburgh Press.

Superluchas. 1997. "Hijo del Santo—La Tradicion Continua." June 17.

Suplemento de Lucha Libre. 1991. "La EMLL Coarta La Libre Expresion." October 31, 2.

Valentino, Hector. 1993. "La Máscara." *Mis Luchas por Limpios y Rudos*, April 1.

Vaughn, Mary Kay. 1994. "The Construction of the Patriotic Festival in Tecamachalco, Puebla, 1900–1946." *Rituals of Resistance, Rituals of Rule*, ed. William H. Beezley, Cheryl English Martin, and William E. French, 213–46. Wilmington, Del.: Scholarly Resources.

Vélez-Ibañez, Carlos G. 1983. *Rituals of Marginality*. Berkeley: University of California Press.

Viquiera-Albán, Juan Pedro. 1987. "Relajados o Reprimidos? Diversiones Publicas y Vida Social en la Ciudad de Mexico durante el Siglo de las Luces." Mexico City: Fondo de Cultura Economica.

Vogt, Evon Z. 1969. Zinacantan: A Maya Community in the Highlands of Chiapas. Cambridge, Mass.: Belknap.

Webley, Irene A. 1986. "Professional Wrestling: The World of Roland Barthes Revisited." *Semiotica* 58: 59–81.

Weiner, Annette. 1993. *Inalienable Possessions*. Berkeley: University of California Press.

Weismantel, Mary. 2001. *Cholas and Pishtacos: Stories of Race and Sex in the Andes*. Chicago: University of Chicago Press.

Wood, Andrew. 2001. *Revolution in the Streets: Women, Workers and Urban Protest in Veracruz, 1870–1927*. Wilmington, Del.: Scholarly Resources.

Wilson, Charles Morrow. 1959. *Those Magnificent Scufflers: Revealing the Great Days when America Wrestled the World*. Brattleboro, Vt.: Stephen Greene.

Zolov, Eric. 1999. *Refried Elvis: The Rise of the Mexican Counterculture*. Berkeley: University of California Press.

INDEX

Heather Levi is a lecturer at Temple University.

Library of Congress Cataloging-in-Publication Data
Levi, Heather, 1962–
The world of lucha libre : secrets, revelations, and Mexican national identity /
Heather Levi.
p. cm. — (American encounters/global interactions)
Includes bibliographical references and index.
ISBN 978-0-8223-4214-4 (cloth : alk. paper)
ISBN 978-0-8223-4232-8 (pbk. : alk. paper)
1. Wrestling—Social aspects—Mexico.
2. Mexico—Social life and customs. I. Title.
GV1196.4.S63L48 2008
796.812—dc22   2008023166